Western Life & Adventures in
THE GREAT SOUTHWEST

*To
my new friend,
Linda Craig.
for early-day information
and reading pleasure,
Cordially,
Dr. Elliott S. Barker.*

7/20/1977

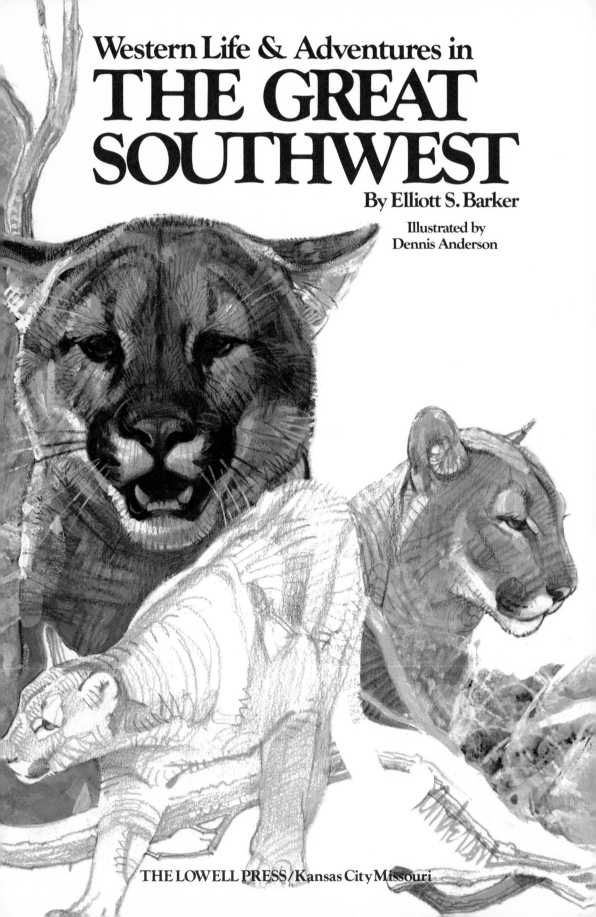

Western Life & Adventures in
THE GREAT SOUTHWEST

By Elliott S. Barker

Illustrated by
Dennis Anderson

THE LOWELL PRESS/Kansas City Missouri

Other books by Elliott S. Barker:

When Dogs Bark "Treed," 1946
Beatty's Cabin, 1953
A Medley of Wilderness and Other Poems, 1962
Outdoors, Faith, Fun and Other Poems, 1968

Originally published as Western Life and Adventures, 1889 to 1970

Western Life & Adventures in
THE GREAT
SOUTHWEST

DEDICATED TO:
The conservation of
Wilderness and Wildlife
which have been the dominant
interests and influences
of my life,
and the hub of my
vocation and avocation.

CONTENTS

PREFACE

M Y THREE CHILDREN, ten grandchildren and many readers of *Beatty's Cabin* and *When the Dogs Bark 'Treed,'* frequently have asked me, "When are you going to write another book?"

The usual answer is, "Whenever I can find time."

However, I realize how tragic it is for old-timers, who have a mass of information stored in their heads, to pass on without recording it. Some of my old-timer friends have had much valuable information buried with them.

I would not want to be in that category. So at eighty-three, I decided I'd better get busy. This volume of authentic stories is the result. It contains old-time, medieval and contemporary life and adventure stories covering an eighty-year period. Truly there is much more to tell, which I hope to get told before it is too late.

I humbly apologize for one thing — I have not given proper credit and attention to my mother, my sisters, my children and, especially, to my wonderful wife. They contributed more than I can tell in this volume to whatever success I have had.

Ethel married me when all I had was three saddle horses, a one-room place to live and a meager salary of $100.00 a month to live on. She, with our three children, Roy, Florence and Dorothy, as they came along, followed me to outlandish places wherever my work took me.

ix

Ethel ran our ranch and cowboyed when I was galavanting around trading cattle, cruising timber, chasing lions and doing other odd jobs to supplement the ranch income when times were hard.

Neither Ethel nor our offspring have ever complained. Instead they have loyally helped and encouraged me in all my undertakings. It would take another volume to pay proper tribute to my mother, my sisters, my daughters and my good wife. Perhaps I'll write it next and title it, WOMEN IN MY LIFE. No, Ethel would not like that.

ACKNOWLEDGMENT

ACKNOWLEDGEMENT, with appreciation, is hereby extended for the privilege of publishing the following listed chapters which were originally published in the magazines indicated.

"A Covered Wagon Journey," original title, "The Barkers Move West," *Old West* (1967.)

"My Favorite Fishing Holes," original title, "Magic Memories of Boyhood," *Empire Magazine* (The Denver Post, June 4, 1967.)

"My First Mule Deer Buck," *Empire Magazine,* (The Denver Post, October 5, 1969.)

"Pioneer Life on A Mountain Ranch, 1889-1908," *Frontier Times* (Western Publications, July, 1970.)

"Old Red or All Dog," *Outdoor Life* (Copyright Popular Science Publishing Company, Inc., 1947.)

"A Cougar the Hard Way," *Field and Stream* (Copyright Holt, Rinehart and Winston, Inc., May, 1969.)

"Three Rugged Days on A Lion's Trail," original title, "Saga of the West," *Colorado Magazine,* (September-October, 1969.)

"The Big One," *Outdoor Life* (Copyright Popular Science Publishing Company, 1968.)

"Battle of Bugling Bulls," *Empire Magazine* (The Denver Post, October 8, 1967.)

"This Happened to me — Believe it or Not," original title, "I say it was all True," *Empire Magazine* (The Denver Post, February 20, 1967.)

"Conducting Wilderness Trail Rides," in parts similar to "Pack Trip Through Wilderness," *Colorado Magazine* (May-June, 1970.)

A FAMILY'S COVERED WAGON JOURNEY

1

T HE SUDDEN BOUNCING on the spring seat of an ox-drawn covered wagon as it left the dim road and picked up speed on the prairie sod was fun for me, a three-old-nubbin, but not for the driver, my pretty fifteen-year-old sister. "Whoa, Spot! Whoa, Coalie!" she coaxed again and again. But it was no use, the stolid oxen, of all things, were running away.

Controlled only by voice command and a bullwhip there was no stopping them. Fortunately the terrain was smooth. Pa and Mother in two, horse-drawn, covered wagons with four little girls aboard, were far behind, and we were on our own.

Last night we'd made a dry camp and the stock had had no water since the day before. Now, in mid-afternoon, trudging along under a blazing sun, they desperately needed water. A shallow prairie lake lay a quarter mile ahead. When the thirsty oxen smelled and saw the water they took off in high down the gentle slope for it.

"Whoa, Coalie! Whoa, Spot! Whoa, now," the young bull-whacker commanded. Spot and Coalie paid no attention and ran hard for the shallow, mud-bottom lake. Nor did they stop at water's edge to drink but rushed as far out into the water as they could go until the wagon bogged down to the axles and they were belly deep in the sticky mud themselves.

"We'll get drowned," I cried. The fun of the fast, bouncy ride had all at once been replaced with fear the like of which I had never known.

"Shut up, cry baby," Ida said, "We'll get out." At fifteen my buxom sister Ida already knew how to speak with self-assured authority.

Benny, my tall, nineteen-year-old brother, who, with eleven-year-old Charlie, was driving some cattle and horses, had seen the fiasco and galloped up on his saddle mare, Nellie, to help us. "Stay in the wagon," he said, "we'll hitch on and pull it out backwards."

Once the oxen got their bellies full of water they began floundering in the muck but couldn't budge the mired wagon an inch. I was bawling and blubbering, scared stiff that the wagon would sink out of sight and we'd drown. "Hush up or you'll get throwed in the lake," Ida scolded.

By now Pa, driving one wagon and Mother the other, had caught up as had the loose cattle and horses. Benny and Charlie were busy trying to keep them from getting bogged down. Tugs were unhitched, neck yokes slipped off the wagon tongues and teams driven to the lake's edge to drink. Then the job of getting the ox-wagon out was begun.

First Pa waded in, crotch deep, and unhitched the still yoked oxen and drove them around and hitched their draw chain to one end of the rear axle. Next he hitched his team, Durgen and Old Yellow, to the other end beside the oxen. But good pullers as they were, the two teams couldn't budge the mired wagon. So Mother's team was hitched on ahead of them with another long chain.

2

"Now Spot! Coalie!" Pa yelled cracking the bullwhip over their backs as Mother and Benny handled the horses. "Now, all together." The three teams lurched against yokes and collars and the wagon began to move. Once started, the three teams easily rolled it up onto dry land.

I climbed down out of the wagon and went running to Mother to tell her about the runaway and my harrowing experience. The teams were rested a little while, then hitched to their respective wagons and the caravan rolled on over the Texas plains to make camp near another lake at sunset.

This was mid-September 1889. Squire Leander and Priscilla Jane Barker had sold out their small ranch-farm near Moran, Shackleford County, Texas, and were heading, with eight of their nine children, toward the Sangre de Cristo Mountains of New Mexico. The five hundred mile, overland journey had started on August 22, and now, just a few miles southwest of Amarillo, Texas, they had passed the halfway mark.

The children were Benny 18, Ida 15, Minnie 13, Charlie 11, Pearl 8, Mattie 6, Elliott (that was me, a three-year-old hellion), and Grace, a two month old breast-fed baby. My oldest sister Alice had married Troupe Turner and was living in Colorado.

The family's worldly possessions consisted of fifty-six head of breed-cattle, twelve head of mares and colts, a yoke of oxen, two teams of horses and three covered wagons loaded to the top of the sideboards with necessary travel and camp equipment, food, clothing and a few necessities for setting up housekeeping at trip's end.

The reason for pulling up stakes and heading for the New Mexico mountains was two-fold. The drouth and hard times of 1887 and '88 made a change in hope of finding a better situation seem desirable. Perhaps more important was my mother's health. She had long been severely afflicted with asthma and a change to a high altitude held hope of relief. Pa had corresponded with a Doctor Sparks, an asthmatic, who had settled some thirty miles northwest of Las Vegas at an altitude of 8,000 feet and who had been completely cured.

"We will try anything to get rid of that asthma," Pa had said. It may also be that under the surface there was a smoldering desire to get back into mountain country. Pa was raised in the Allegheny Mountains of Virginia, and Mother in the Blue Ridge country of North Carolina.

Squire L. Barker was a medium large, strong man with a heavy, reddish brown beard. He was an industrious, hard-working person of many skills — farmer, rancher, blacksmith, stonemason, millwright, and as a side issue, a Church of Christ preacher. He teased and joked a lot, had a rather violent temper, was kind to his family but firm and demanded strict obedience. He liked to hunt and fish. That, and his preaching (for free), were about the only things he would sometimes neglect his work for. He liked to have his own way, but Mother sometimes adroitly made him think her way was his.

Priscilla J. Barker, though plagued with ill health and burdened with raising eleven children (final count), was habitually cheerful. She sang a lot as she worked, some old folk songs but mostly religious hymns. She was always busy — keeping house, cooking, washing, ironing, sewing and making garden. Of course, the girls helped as they became big enough. Mother was of medium build, with brown hair and blue eyes. She fussed at us rather than punishing us and some way kept us in line.

They were both courageous and endowed with the

4

pioneer spirit. Otherwise they never would have started this five hundred mile, covered wagon trip with a six-weeks-old baby and seven other children.

Three days before the runaway episode the caravan was plodding along a little-used road across the broad plains when, to everyone's amazement, they suddenly came to what looked like the jumping off place. It was the south rim of Palo Duro Canyon, south of a little village known as Amarillo, Texas.

With trepidation the wagons were eased down the steep, rocky, winding road into the canyon. Pa with the oxen led to set the pace for Mother and Ida with the horse-drawn wagons. At one place the road was so steep that the hind wheels of the wagons had to be locked with chains to hold them back. We kids walked down the hill behind the wagons. Despite the precarious descent, the refreshing environment of the canyon was a novel and most welcome relief for the plains-weary family.

There was a small stream of crystal clear, running water and occasional deep pools with fish in them. My brother Charlie, at ninety-one, recalls that the rugged canyon with its verdure was one of the most beautiful sights he had ever seen — wildflowers, green trees and brush and wild grape vines with ripening fruit all over the place, and lush grass, stirrup high, in the meadow above the crossing. The crossing was somewhere near the old Goodnight Ranch.

Pa picked a nice camp site, carpeted with green grass, on a level spot overlooking the creek with plenty of firewood handy. It would be a two-night camp, and a more auspicious spot for the needs, comfort and enjoyment of the travellers and their livestock could not have been found anywhere along the five hundred mile trip.

Except for one team, the stock got the best of it for the lay over day was a mighty busy one for everybody. Supplies were running short, so one wagon was unloaded and Pa drove about eighteen miles to Amarillo to replenish them. Amarillo, just a village then, was founded in 1887 by H. B. Sandborn, a rancher and financier who was reported to have sold the first spool of barded wire in Texas. The location was about a mile from a little settlement called Ragtown. There Sandborn had just completed the original Amarillo Hotel which was to become famous throughout a wide area, particularly as a gathering and trading place for cattlemen.

At camp it was a clean-up and wash day. Benny and Charlie scoured the area for rattlesnakes and gathered wood for an all-day fire to heat water in big, iron kettles. It was nice to have wood instead of cow chips to burn. The accumulation of dirty clothes, towels and bedding of the family of ten was indeed quite a pile, and no washing machines to do the job. It was back-breaking, hand work in wash tubs with ribbed washboards and homemade lye soap.

Ida, 15, and Minnie, 13, helped Mother all day with the tremendous task. Ida was a leader. She was a strong, willing and competent girl who always cheerfully did her share of the work. Minnie was well developed for her age, too, but always was an unhappy child who looked on the dark side of every-day life. While she often complained she never shirked her assigned tasks.

Pearl and Mattie, 8 and 6, were a happy, congenial pair who never quarreled. Pearl was a skinny, red-headed, freckle-faced girl. She was very talkative and read everything available. Mattie was a happy, blond, plump, carefree youngster. She loved to romp and play, and life was just one big adventure. They did their share on this wash day by hanging clothes on bushes to dry, and taking care of Grace, their two-months old sister.

Benny and Carlie looked after the livestock which, with lush forage, was an easy task. Everybody took time out for a good bath in pools in the creek. Some of the kids got the bellyache from eating the sour, wild grapes.

At dusk Pa got back from Amarillo with a load of supplies and delighted us kids with some hard candy he bought at the country store. Both he and his team were tired and dusty. "I'll get a bath in the morning," he said. But Mother had hot water ready and insisted he take a tub bath in the tent. "Let's all be clean tonight," she said. Mother worked too hard that day and had a bad night with her ever-recurring asthma.

Things seemed to move slowly the next morning. Perhaps it was because everyone was loath to leave the verdant paradise in which they had revelled for two days. Pa said, "Get to work, we'll never get to New Mexico if we don't keep moving." But it was near noon when the teams were finally hitched up and laboriously hauled the heavily-laden wagons up out of the canyon to the flat plains on its north rim.

So far the caravan had been traveling northwest, but now it turned and headed almost due west, with Endee, New Mexico, seventy miles or five days away, the next settlement of any kind. The wagons rolled only a few miles that day and a dry camp had to be made on the wide-open plains. The stock had no water till afternoon the next day at the lake where the oxen ran away.

The trip to the halfway point had not been without

its day-to-day episodes inherent to early-day covered wagon travel. Readers would be bored if we attempted to record them all. But the happenings at the crossing of the Salt Fork of the Brazos River some twenty miles northwest of Haskell early in the trip and a couple of others are worthy of note.

It would be ridiculous to expect the reader to believe that I, then a kid of three, could recall the details of the trip as related here. The stories told by my parents and older brothers and sisters through the years make many of them seem so vivid that I do really remember them. For refreshing my memory of the stories told, about seven years ago I got a lot of information from my sister Ida, who has since passed away. I was dependent upon my brother Charlie, who was a practicing attorney and who died at the age of 92, to fill in the gaps and some details.

The Salt Fork was very alkaline or gyp, as it was called, unfit for humans, but stock could drink it. A spring coming out of the creek bank was cold and potable, so the water barrels were filled with the spring water.

Shortly after crossing the Salt Fork we pitched camp in the edge of a big prairie dog town. The spectacle of the little animals standing straight up on the rim of the rounded mounds around their burrows as they repeatedly gave their two-syllable, high-pitch, low-pitch, alarm bark was fascinating. With each bark there was a flick of the tail. When we kids approached the bark changed from a high-pitch low-pitch, to two high-pitch syllables, which is their danger warning signal.

After the twelve-by-fourteen foot wall tent, in which Pa, Mother, the girls and I slept, was set up and cow chips for fuel were being gathered at sunset, it was discovered that there were diamond-back rattlesnakes all over the place. Unable to endure the sun's heat, they were now emerging in the cool of the evening from burrows or other shelters. The oxen had been unyoked and the teams unharnessed and turned loose to graze. To round up the stock, hitch up and move camp seemed too big a task. So, since rattlers don't hunt folks up to bite them but strike only when approached too close, it was decided to stick it out. Usually it was Pearl's and Mattie's job to take an old tub and gather up the big, dried flakes of cow dung (cow chips) for fuel when wood was not available. But with snakes all around Pa and Benny took over that humble chore.

Mother recalled an old theory that snakes won't crawl over a rope on the ground and had Pa circle the tent area with ropes. Charlie and Benny, who were used to spreading down a sugan for their bed anywhere out under the stars, moved inside the ropes next to the tent. Whether or not the ropes kept the snakes out, none entered to disturb the sleeping family. Soon after sunup next morning most of the snakes disappeared to hide again from the sun's direct rays until evening.

Pup and Ring were two dogs with the outfit that we have neglected to mention, and who came very near being left behind. At noon the first day it was noticed that they had not followed, and Charlie and Benny rode all the way back to the old home to get them. They were just two good, mongrel dogs, although Ring was perhaps a quarter greyhound. At this camp they had opportunity to add to their novel skill in killing rattlesnakes.

Pup would tease a snake by circling it and barking viciously, while Ring stood by as close as he safely could, alert and ready for action. When the snake would strike, Pup saw to it that he missed, then instantly he would seize it just back of its head before it could strike again. Ring would grabe it farther back in his strong jaws. Then the dogs would sit back and have a tug-of-war until they pulled the snake in two. Before the long trip was over they had killed many a rattler that way and never were bitten.

The cattle and horses were rounded up and the teams hitched, but when the wagons started rolling on the day's journey the cattle, thirsty from having drunk the gyp water the evening before, tried to break back and run for the creek. Charlie, the eleven-year-old red-headed cowboy, was riding Nellie, a very skittish mare, that morning. As he galloped her fast to head off the cattle and turn them back, she ran smack into a clump of cactus. A big chunk stuck in the mare's flank and broke off. Instead of bucking, as even a gentle horse might, Nellie stopped dead still and stood there humped up and quivering until the young rider got off and jerked the chunk of cactus free.

And so, leaving prairie dogs, rattlesnakes, gyp water and cactus behind, the Texas emigrants were on their plodding way once more. The spring water in the barrels had been potable while cold, but when, as was inevitable, it became luke warm it developed an awful stench and became unusable. Fortunately in the afternoon we passed a well and windmill and the barrels were filled with good water. Such were the vagaries of covered wagon travel.

A few days later the emigrant family passed Matador which consisted mainly of the headquarters of the ranch of that name. The foreman, a picturesque cowboy with a deep blue birth mark covering one side of his face, rode for miles with the travelers subjecting them to all kinds of questioning as to who they were, where they were going, and the like. Perhaps he suspected they were nesters planning to settle on the huge ranch he claimed.

In our herd of cattle was a very large, heavy-horned Holstein bull who had yet to be defeated in a bull fight. The caravan came aross a herd of Matador cattle in which there was a big, red, long-horned bull. The bulls began bellowing and pawing the ground, challenging each other to battle. The ranch foreman said to Benny, "You better keep your stock moving and take care of that bull of yours."

Benny, always soft-spoken, replied, "Old Spot will take care of hisself."

"I'm a-warnin' you," the foreman said.

Charlie who had greatly enjoyed several bull fights along the way boastfully put in, "Spot will chase that bull of yours clear out of Texas."

Spot trotted out to meet his challenger, bellowing and eyes blazing. The two bulls circled each other, pawing the dry earth, each looking for an opening to charge in. Then they crashed head on and the desperate fight began. Wagons were stopped so that all could watch and root for Old Spot. The bulls viciously pushed each other this way and that. They backed off and came together again like a pair of locomotives.

It might seem that the challenger's long horns would give him the advantage but such was not the case. Spot got in between them constantly, manuevering for a thrust in the ribs. The struggle was a desperate one not quickly ended. But Spot was out-boxing his opponent, so to speak. The turf was dry, and they kicked up an awful dust.

11

At long last Spot got his chance and gored his antagonist a mighty blow in the ribs and knocked him flat. The Red bull bellowed in pain. He jumped up and took off as fast as he could run, but Spot was right after him ripping into flanks and hind quarters with sharp, heavy horns. After a hundred yards Spot turned back but the Red bull kept on going.

"I told you so," Charlie boasted.

The humiliated ranch foreman turned and rode away, and the wagons rolled on with something to talk and laugh about.

Three days later we were passing Plainview, a couple of miles to the west, when a mirage put on a spectacular show. The heat wave distortion of the atmosphere made the group of one-story houses look like tall watchtowers dancing on the plains — phantom prophecy, perhaps, of the oil derricks and grain elevators that dot those plains today. Many mirages, distortions of realities, were seen along the way but those at Plainview were by far the most spectacular.

Along here I was first introduced to big game which has been a vital part of my life. Pronghorn antelope were becoming common in the landscape view with a herd in sight almost constantly throughout the day. Often they would run parallel to the wagons for a little way, then cross only a short distance in front of them. Occasionally a coyote or two would be seen, but they were not relatively as plentiful as antelope.

We were camped on the high plains thirty miles southwest of Amarillo the night following the ox-runaway episode when we took the reader back to recount some of the experiences of the covered wagon emigrants during the early part of the trip. Now, back at that camp the next morning we find everyone anxious to push ahead for, with luck, in three days the New Mexico boundary would be reached.

The air was calm and warm when we broke camp. Then about ten o-clock a 'norther' struck like a flash. A brisk northwest wind, chilly as an iceberg, swept across the high plains. Fortunately there was no moisture with it, but the wind soon became so strong and cold that the livestock refused to face it and tried their best to turn back and drift with it. Teams threw their heads madly and had to be urged to keep going. Pa had to take over the ox team from Ida and use the bullwhip sharply to keep them in line.

The two young cowboys, wearing nothing but cotton shirts and trousers, as was customary for boys where we came from, almost froze to death. But despite the cold they had to ride hard for hours to keep the herd together and moving behind the wagons. Today Charlie says that in his ninety-one years he has never been as cold as he was then.

Such 'northers' are characteristic of the high plains and many lives have been lost and thousands of cattle have perished in 'norther' blizzards. Had there been rain, sleet or snow with this one it would have been disastrous.

There was no noon stop and everyone was worrying about the night camp and how the stock could possibly be held together. Then in midafternoon the cold wind died down. Bright sun soon took the chill out of the air with no real damage done. But the family had had a taste of unaccustomed things to come in New Mexico mountains.

Two days later the caravan came to the caprock, fringed with scrubby timber, and dropped off into the mesquite brush, yucca and red, sandy soil country of the broad Canadian River valley. The river itself wound its tortuous way through a rock-rimmed gorge some fifteen miles to the north. Camp was pitched a quarter mile from a water hole where the stock could drink. Dead brush and limbs from the scrubby trees provided plenty of fire-wood.

We suspected that we were now in New Mexico but could not be sure. The little settlement of Endee, two or three miles ahead, we knew was. Anyway, this was a pleasant camp in an environment wholly different from the broad, treeless prairie.

Next morning, as usual, Pa got everybody up early. He gazed down toward the water hole. Without saying anything to anybody, he got his heavy .45/75 Winchester rifle and set out toward the tank, keeping under cover as much as possible. Nobody paid much attention until the booming report of the big-black-powder rifle startled us all. "What's he shooting at?" was on everyone's tongue.

Then he ran around the water tank and disappeared. Impatiently we watched and waited. After a time he came back with an antelope on his shoulder. "Goody, goody, now we can have meat and gravy," Pearl cried. Indeed, fresh meat would be a welcome change.

Pa threw the antelope down beside a wagon, and we all gathered around to inspect the first big game animal we had ever seen. Mother even left her breakfast chores to look it over. Pa unloaded his rifle and put it away in the wagon. Then he said to Benny and Ida. "You grease the wagons while I dress this critter and take care of the meat."

Greasing the wagons was a tedious, but necessary, every-day chore. The big greasy nut that holds the wheel

14

on the spindle had to be unscrewed and taken off. Then the top of the wheel was cautiously pulled outward until the end of the spindle rested about midway of the hub of the wheel. Thus the inside segment of the spindle was exposed. Then, holding the wheel steady, the hard boughten axle grease was liberally smeared along the top of the spindle with a wooden blade. This done, the wheel was pushed back in place and the black, greasy nut screwed on tightly. It was quite a chore by the time all twelve wheels had been greased.

Mother, with Minnie's and Pearl's help, had breakfast ready by the time the wagons were greased and the antelope was skinned and quartered. Breakfast consisted of oatmeal, sorghum molasses, sow-belly (fat bacon), gravy, biscuits and coffee. Milk for the children was provided by two part-Holstein cows in the herd that had calved shortly before the trip was started. We'd brought along a whole barrel of homemade sorghum molasses.

Grace, a two-month old infant when the trip started, was faring as well as any child in the finest home or nursery. She rode in a well-padded, homemade cradle, suspended to the back of the spring seat of Mother's wagon thus avoiding the jolts. Pearl and Minnie looked after her most of the time, then Minnie would drive the team and keep the wagon rolling while Mother breast-fed the child and changed her diapers. At night the cradle would be unhooked and moved into the tent by Mother's bed.

After breakfast Pa caught up the horse teams, harnessed and hitched them to the wagons, while 15-year-old Ida brought in the oxen, yoked them and hitched them up. Charlie was busy rounding up the cattle and loose horses. Mother and Benny, with the help of

15

the little girls, took down the tent, rolled up the bedding, packed the kitchen equipment and supplies and loaded the wagons. There was a job for everybody every morning.

The oxen were very gentle and tractable. When driven in they would respond to voice command and take their places by the wagon tongue. Ida would then lift one end of the heavy yoke and put it on top of Coalie's neck. She'd slip the wooden bow around his neck from below and push its ends up through the holes in the yoke, and insert the key pins to hold it there. Next she would put the other end of the yoke on Spot's neck and put the bow on in like manner.

The back end of the draw chain was anchored by the double-tree pin through a link. Near the front end it was attached to the wagon tongue. When the oxen were yoked, Ida would lift the wagon tongue and hook the chain to the draw ring and they were ready to go. Benny or Pa would often help her with this heavy chore, but she was proud to be able to do it alone.

At the tiny settlement of Endee, a little way southwest of present-day Glenrio, road information was procured, and now the family was happy that it had safely reached New Mexico. "Where will we build the house?" Mattie wanted to know. But it would still be many days travel before that spot was reached. The next objective was abandoned Fort Bascom, about seven miles north of present-day Tucumcari.

It was a hard two-and-a-half day trip to the old fort for the road was crooked and a part of it sandy. The ground cover in this area was quite different from the short grass country of the plains. While there was some grama and buffalo grass, there was also the tall blue-stem grass and lots of the short mesquite and yucca. All this provided cover and food for the blue quail which were abundant. There were more jackrabbits and cottontails than we had ever seen before. Once we kids were delighted when a coyote loped across the road carrying a jackrabbit in his mouth.

Passing the stark walls of old Fort Bascom our route more or less paralleled the Canadian River past the present Conchas Dam and, I believe, a village called San Hilario, the first Spanish-American settlement we had come to. From there on that's what they all were.

Some twenty miles ahead was a high, rim-rocked *mesa* rising steep and rugged over a thousand feet above its base. That lay between us and Watrous to which we were headed. At the village Pa was told there was no way around but that there was a steep, rocky road to the top. The rest of that day and the next the wagons rolled up grade toward that awful *mesa*. Camp was made near its base. To plains folks not used to mountains the prospect of getting wagons up that terrible climb seemed mighty dim.

Next morning Pa scouted the road by horseback and found it as bad or worse than he had expected. "We can get the wagons up to that first bench," he reported. "But from there on up we'll have to pull the wagons up one at a time with two teams." Even at the bench there was no place to turn out of the road, so brakes were set tight and the hind wheels chocked up with football-size rocks.

Mother's team was hitched on in front of Pa's and the grueling haul began. Pa walked alongside and drove the lead team, while Ida rode in the wagon to drive the other. Benny walked along behind to chock up a hind wheel with a big rock whenever the teams stopped to rest, which was every little way. Mother, Pa and the older children never forgot how steep and rocky the Olguin Hill was and the ordeal of getting the wagons up it.

The double team portion of the climb was nearly a mile long and, despite dozens of rest stops, the teams were in a lather when they reached the top of the awful hill. Leaving the wagon there, they walked and drove the teams back down the hill for Mother's wagon. As before, Pa walked and drove the lead team while Mother rode in the wagon and drove her team. I rode with her, and Grace was in her crib as usual. This time Ida and Minnie followed to chock up the wagon whenever the teams were stopped to rest. Pearl and Mattie walked behind, while Benny and Charlie hazed the cattle and horses up the hill.

Pa, Ida and Benny went back for the ox-drawn wagon with Pa's team, while Mother and her helpers got a late dinner. Dinner was the mid-day meal in those days. Pa hitched his team on ahead of the oxen and walked beside it. Ida drove the oxen who needed prodding more than driving, while again Benny was the chock up man. This trip was the most difficult one because the horses pulled faster than the oxen, so that meant holding them back and prodding the oxen constantly to keep their efforts synchronized.

What a relief when all the wagons and stock were atop the *mesa* and that terrible hill behind them. It had consumed the better part of the day getting up there, but after an hour's rest they pushed on a few miles before making camp. Again we were on high, open plains some thirty-two miles from Las Vegas and twenty-five from Watrous. Las Vegas was the larger, a real lively trading point, but Pa decided to head for Watrous because it was on Sapello Creek and his friend Dr. Sparks had said there might be a good chance to homestead there. Both places were on the main line of the A.T.&S.F. Railway which had been built into New Mexico only ten years before.

Food supplies were replenished at the general store in Watrous when they reached that point two days later. Then the caravan headed upstream a couple of miles to make camp in the lush valley. At dusk a man by the name of Kroenig rode up to complain that the camp was on his land. He wanted it moved. Pa didn't take kindly to that idea and thought the land owner was being unreasonable because grass was plentiful. But Kroenig kept fussing about it and Pa, finally, gave him a dollar and a half, or about two cents a head for the stock, in payment for the privilege of staying the night there. He said it wasn't enough but Pa balked at raising the ante and the land owner rode off still grumbling.

The Spanish-American village of Sapello was reached the next afternoon just six weeks after leaving Moran, Shackleford County, Texas. There Henry Goeke, an old German with a Spanish-American wife, was the king-pin of the area and claimed the land there-about. He gave permission to camp in a little valley a mile south of the village. There we stayed several days while Pa scouted for a place to homestead. By then Mother's asthma had almost left her. "If we go a little higher," they reasoned, "maybe it will all go away."

Pa's horseback trip took him some twelve miles up Sapello Creek before he found a place that suited him. But a man by the name of Jones had already filed a homestead entry on it. For some reason Pa wanted that particular place badly and made a tentative deal to pay Jones a hundred fifty dollars to relinquish his claim.

19

That would leave it open to the next applicant to homestead. Pa wanted to talk to the family before closing the deal and came back the second day. The way he described it made it sound like paradise.

We then moved camp about six miles to an off-stream ranch owned by a Mr. Romero. The first day there a Mr. Johnson, who owned a place just below the one Pa wanted, came by with a wagon load of vegetables he was taking to Las Vegas to market. They were fine vegetables and he showed us a head of cabbage that weighed forty pounds. Right then Mother said, "That's where I want to go."

The die was cast. The upper Sapello Canyon, later named Beulah, would be the Barker family's new home. Pa rode back up there and closed the deal with Jones paying him a hundred fifty dollars for his relinquishment. Then he came back and made a quick trip to Las Vegas and from there to Santa Fe by train and filed his homestead entry on a hundred-and-sixty-acre tract.

Back at camp on the Romero ranch, arrangements were made to have all but thirty head of cattle taken care of there. Then on October 12, 1889, the emigrant family of ten broke camp for the last time and moved up to the new homestead. It was an eight-mile trip over a pretty rough, mountain road with lots of steep up-and-down grades, but nobody minded bad roads now that the long, tedious journey's end was in sight.

The narrow canyon in fall color was a beautiful sight. A small trout stream lined with willows and alders wound along the bottom. There were some open meadows, but open land available for planting of crops was very limited. The aspen and oak-brush-covered slopes would have to be cleared up.

There were groves of huge, tall pine trees, and some blue spruce in the bottoms, while the higher and steeper slopes were covered with forests of pine, Douglas fir and white fir intermingled with aspen and Gambel oak. Five miles west towered the majestic Sangre de Cristo range.

The house was just a crude log cabin about twelve by-twenty feet with a loft, reached by a ladder, where at first the kids had to sleep. Adjacent was a small, half-completed aspen log room which was finished as soon as possible. Such was the new home, and the prime objective of moving to it had been accomplished — Mother's asthma was completely gone.

It was most remarkable that no rain at all had fallen on the travelers from the day we left Moran, Texas, until we arrived at the new home in Sapello Canyon, a period of fifty-two days.

The fall continued to be warm and dry until November seven, then it began to snow and really made up for lost time. The first day Pa thought it would be a good time to go deer hunting and it proved to be, for he bagged a nice fat buck and two doe mule deer with his .45/75 rifle — enough to provide meat and gravy for quite a spell. There was no closed season or bag limit at all on game then.

The unforeseen snow continued to fall for three days and nights. When it finally quit there was a full three feet of the cold, white stuff on the ground. The family was caught wholly unprepared. Getting in enough dry wood was a chore, but attempting to keep the horses and cattle up on the south-exposed hillsides where they could get some food, browsing on oak brush, mountain mahogany and other brush plants was a frustrating, never-ending job. There was no hay to feed them. So Pa and

Benny cut pine and fir trees for them to eat the green needles. That caused the cows to slink their calves. Later some straw at ten dollars a ton was purchased from a neighbor. By spring half the cattle and horses had succumbed to the rigors of the New Mexico winter.

More land was needed to be cleared to plant a crop the next spring and in that regard the heavy snow was a blessing. The fall had been warm and the ground was not frozen when the snow fell, and of course it did not freeze under it. So with feet wrapped in gunny sacks as improvised overshoes the men folks began shoveling snow off and grubbing out aspens and oak brush on a fertile hillside. Even the older girls helped pile the brush for burning.

By spring several acres had been cleared and, at the proper time, was planted to potatoes. The productivity of the cleared land was marvelous, and that fall a thousand dollars' worth of potatoes were marketed in Las Vegas. Except for chewing gum, which was a nickel a package then as now, that would have bought as much as five thousand dollars will now!

There was hay for the stock also when winter set in again. The house had been improved, a stable and a potato cellar built, pole fences put up and other improvements made. Benny, perhaps longing for his sweetheart Beulah Wagner, had been dissatisfied with the country and had gone back to Texas, where he passed away a year later. But he left a memorial. Benny stood on a pole fence, reached up and cut the top out of a six-inch pine sapling he'd used for a post. Pa thought it would kill the tree and scolded him. But a branch took over for the trunk, grew out, up and around the cut top and made a

12-inch tree with an arc in the middle. Marks on the pitchy stub made by Benny's ax eighty years ago are plainly visible, and the tree is still growing.

Deer meat was available for the taking and sometimes wild turkeys also. One day that first summer while Pa was working on the stable, Ring and Pup suddenly began barking fiercely a little way up the canyon. He went to see what all the ruckus was about and found that they had a huge, strange, tawny animal treed. He ran back toward the house and yelled to Mother, who was working in the garden, to "bring the gun quick." Mother ran in and got the big rifle and some cartridges and hurried to meet him with us kids tagging along.

"The dogs have got a big, long-tailed varmint up a tree," Pa said. "You all better go back to the house."

We didn't go back, but just waited there. Pretty soon came the big boom of the rifle. We waited anxiously. After a little while here came Pa dragging a real big, male mountain lion, the first of many that he and his sons were to take through the years in the vicinity of the ranch.

There were yet two boys, David Marion and Squire Omar, to be born there to bring to eleven the children of Squire L. and Priscilla J. Barker, of which five survive—all but one past eighty.

The fine potato crop had relieved the family's precarious financial situation. Good, free summer grazing for the stock was found on the open range in the Lone Tree Mesa area. Garden vegetables of unexcelled quality had been produced in great quantity. Wild game was plentiful. Cutthroat trout were fun to catch and regularly supplemented the menu. The wolf had not had pups on the doorstep after all.

The environment was peaceful. The attractiveness and beauty of the canyon inevitably had its effect. Everybody was busy, healthy and happy.

The Barker family, with members and multiple descendents now prominent in life, had taken deep, enduring roots in the majestic environs of the upper Sapello Canyon — truly a Beulah Land!

2 MY FAVORITE FISHING HOLES

L YING FLAT on my belly on the big rock
I dropped a baited hook into the swirl-
ing water at the head of the pool. Like a flash, a whopping, fine cutthroat trout struck hard and the hook set
solid. From the way my limber willow pole bent and
quivered, I knew he was the biggest trout I had ever
hung onto. He darted about the pool, flopped at the top
of the water then rushed this way and that.

He was too heavy to flip out and, with no reel to pay
out line and take up slack, I was scared to death he'd get
away. Quickly I squirmed up closer to the edge of the
rock to get better arm action. Of course, I could do still
better if I stood up, but I knew it would scare the fish in
the lower end of the pool, and I needed some of them, too.
A nice string of trout might mitigate my punishment for
swapping a hoe for a fishing pole.

For a twelve-year old boy the tedium of weeding the
garden in mid-afternoon when trout were striking in his
favorite fishing hole sometimes made the temptation to
slip away to wet a line irresistible. That is exactly what
happened to me that afternoon seventy years ago. Time
has not dimmed the memory of that thrilling experience.

Never before had a trout so challenged my imma-
ture angling skill. This one provided all the action that

any kid could want. But thrills were mingled with fear that I'd lose him, for the lunker tried everything in the book to get away. Fortunately the pool where the small stream rushed in against the big rock was not large and I could follow his gyrations without a showdown as would happen should he head down stream beyond my reach.

Once he went to the bottom and sulked and I thought the line was hung up on drift wood or a rock. Suddenly he came alive again, made a wild rush then broke water, wriggling violently, and I gaped at the size and beauty of him.

After what seemed an hour, but perhaps was less than ten minutes, the game old fellow began to tire and strained against the line less and less, and finally gave up. When, for the second time, I was able to bring him to the top of the water without his flopping, I slowly lifted him with bent pole up the necessary three feet to clear the edge of the rock and backed the pole to bring him to me. With trembling hands I held him tight, removed the hook, popped the back of his head on the rock to stop his wiggling, held him up and stared with zest.

He was not over fourteen inches long but to a twelve-year-old kid he was a whale. With olive green back, red belly and black-spotted sides and tail he made a mighty pretty picture. So thrilled was I that the other fish in the pool and what might happen to me for quitting the garden were forgotten. I ran back to the house as fast as I could to show Mother and the other kids my fine catch.

No doubt about it, every boy should have a favorite fishing hole! He surely is missing something worthwhile, inspiring and a source of great joy if he doesn't. Not only

does a boy's fishing hole provide him with healthy outdoor recreation for mind and body, entertainment and a
peck of thrills, but it also provides him, as a man, with a
memory keepsake which, as the years pass, becomes a
source of thrilling reminiscenses.

When I was a Scout-age kid, a dozen or fifteen years
before Scouting was born, I was doubly fortunate in having two favorite fishing holes — one, the big-rock hole,
up stream from our mountain home and another, the
dipper's-nest hole, quite a bit farther downstream. The
pictures of them and the fun and thrills they gave me re-
main today unfaded and in sharp focus — a satisfying
memory keepsake.

The stream that ran through our mountain ranch
on the east side of New Mexico's Sangre de Cristo Mountains was small, and for the most part, brushy. But there
were many pools and riffles where the gamy, cutthroat
trout lurked. Those beautiful trout and the enchanted
waters in which they lived were a constant temptation to
abandon whatever a boy might be doing to float a fly or
drown a grasshopper. In summer, spring and fall it was
angling, but sometimes in winter a horse-hair snare was
used successfully to provide an off-season repast.

My big rock fishing hole was open water and very
hard to get to from three sides without being seen by the
wily trout. If they saw me they would dart with wriggling tails for cover in deep water at the head of the
pool or under the big rock forming its east side. The big
rock was a sandstone slab about twelve feet long and
eight feet wide slightly tilted toward the stream with the
top edge two feet above the water line.

The stream flowed swiftly against the upper corner
of the rock and made a swirling pool as it turned at right

angles along the side of it. The water soon quieted, the stream widened and became shallow over an apron of rubble and gravel. There trout loved to swim high and feed actively on insects and larvae that floated by.

An expert fly caster might well have taken trout from below, but we country boys with home-cut willow or stiff boughten cane poles were not skilled enough to do it that way. It was great fun, though, to crawl up back of the big rock, lie flat of belly on it out of sight of the fish and cautiously drop a gray hackle or a grasshopper in the water, let it drift down stream and hope for action.

One thing that made it a favorite fishing hole was that I, and others who fished it that way were seldom disappointed. When small trout were caught they would be carefully released and tossed back into the turbulent water so as not to frighten the other fish. Our mountain streams carried several times as many trout then as today's fisheries biologists consider top capacity. They were fat, active and well-proportioned trout, too.

Saving the whirlpool at the corner of the big rock till the last, as we often did, provided much pleasure in anticipation of what would happen there. What a thrill it always was when a ten or eleven-inch trout struck hard, darted about the pool and broke water until, with quivering willow pole, I'd flip him wriggling and flopping out onto the big, flat rock. Then I'd kill him and put him on my green willow stringer.

Just one such experience would make a confirmed angler out of any boy worth his salt. How much juvenile delinquency would be overcome if every boy could have such a wonderful, God-given privilege!

In June we watched the trout busily engaged in

their spawning activities in the gravel beds in the riffles. They were not so wild then but they would not take bait of any kind, nor would it have been sporting to take them at that time even if one could have. I think we kids instinctively realized that.

At spawning time the males were more highly colored than ever, and it was a thrill to see their flashing red bellies as they fanned out a nest in the gravel or chased an intruding male away. Spawning was completed in a short period and we were delighted when they became fair game again.

Although not as productive, my downstream favorite fishing hole was the more charming. It was a bit over a mile from home — too far to reach when I was supposed to be weeding the garden. It was shady and brushy and required much more skill to fish it successfully. I am at a loss to find words to describe my youthful sentiments about that pool and the thrills I used to get every time I fished there.

For some thirty feet above, the water came rushing noisily down over a slick, uneven bed of granite into a deep, surging pool, then flattened around boulders and finally spread out over a wide, mud-bottom area. This was caused by silt deposits behind a cribbed-up diversion dam about six feet high, built to feed water into a ditch to a mill pond. From there it was flumed to a twenty-foot water wheel which provided minimum power to operate my dad's little sawmill.

Half way down the rapids there was a recess in the rock bottom that formed a little pool about as big as a bath tub, but we didn't have bath tubs in those days to compare it to. The pool was turbulent and frothy but the water at one end of it was quiet enough to be a favorite place for a nice cutthroat trout to live. Rarely would there be more than one trout in it.

My fishing hole proper at the base of the rapids was gouged out deep by the rushing water which churned and bubbled there, then quickly spread out, flowing slow and smooth over the mud bottom. There were spruce trees along the bank and willows and alders enough to make landing trout quite a problem. The tub-sized pool in the rapids was hard to get a hook into because of a huge pine log whose jagged, broken end jutted out over and a foot above it.

This place was a paradise for water ouzels, or dippers as we called them. As one approached the spot of a morning the dippers long, trilling songs were beautiful and thrilling as they were repeated over and over again. Every year they built a bulky nest of moss in a recess in the jagged end of the log, which, itself, was moss covered. The spray from the rapids kept the moss green.

While I'd be fishing just a few feet in front of the nest the dippers would continue to feed their young. It was intriguing to watch them go up under an overhanging lip of moss that hid the nest. It was as if they just vanished in a bank of moss.

When the young were ready to leave the nest they simply dropped out into the swirling little pool to be washed on down the swift water into the big hole. They would be doused under several times but each time popped up again and finally swam about for a few minutes in the quiet water. Then they would climb up on a rock or the bank and begin their characteristic bobbing movement.

Another pair of dippers would build their nest in the

31

cribbing of the dam where a thin sheet of water poured over and they would have to fly through it to get to the nest. Despite this and the frequent diving, it was amazing to note that their feathers were always completely dry. I was amazed to see how well and fast they swam since their feet are not webbed like waterfowl.

Occasionally a chattering kingfisher would fly in and perch on the dead limb of a spruce tree. He would seem to be paying no attention to anything in particular, then suddenly he'd dive into the shallow part of the pool and come up with a six- or seven-inch trout crosswise in his big beak. While the competition did not exactly please me, I did admire him for being able to take a trout from the broad stretch of open water where I was unable to cast a lure without scaring the fish away.

Once I saw an osprey — I didn't know then what it was — make a high dive into the mill pond and come up with a ten-inch trout in his talons. He flew right over me with the trout held head first in his talons instead of crosswise as I had been accustomed to seeing kingfishers carry their prey in their beaks. When I told the family about seeing "some kind of a big ol' hawk dive in the pond and catch a fish," they accused me of daydreaming.

It was in the mud bottom lower end of my favorite fishing hole that I used to see a lot of marks that looked like bird tracks and wondered what could have made them. Then one day I was amazed when the mystery was solved. A dipper was, as usual, bobbing up and down on a rock, then he suddenly dived under the water and began walking around on the mud bottom feeding on such aquatic insects as he could find. If it hadn't been for the tracks the family wouldn't have believed that one either. But ornithologists would have believed both stories.

But I am neglecting my fishing, just as I did then with the many side attractions. I had to crawl under brush to the very edge of the pool to be able to get a hook in the water. That meant I must stay crouched low to keep from being seen. If I was successful in keeping out of sight, the surging, bubbling water at the head of the pool might yield one or more nice trout, and two or three small ones that had to be thrown back. I'd land them by swinging the pole around sidewise to the bank. We had no reels and had never heard of a landing net, and with our poles it would have been useless anyway.

While some nice trout could always be seen in the open shallow water below, it was a rare thing that I could get a grasshopper or fly out there without scaring them. When scared they would dart, wriggling unbelievably fast into the deep frothy water to hide. Those were sure enough wild trout, remember, not hatchery stocked. In fact, I doubt if I had ever so much as heard of a fish hatchery.

Whatever my luck below there was always joy in saving the bath-tub pool under the dipper's nest until last. There would be a nice trout there and he would strike, too. Could I hook him and get him out of that tricky spot without losing him? I couldn't lift him out but would have to let him flop out into the rapids and follow down to the big pool. Then if he was still on I would swing him around to the bank — maybe! However it turned out it was always an exciting thrill.

The best fun I ever had there was the time I got a fly into the bath-tub pool and an eleven-inch cutthroat struck viciously, flashing red sides at the top of the water. He missed, but some way the hook caught him in the back just behind the dorsal fin. Well, sir, he felt like a real three-pound lunker. I was afraid he'd get loose in the rapids, but I had no choice; he went into them anyway and, as I started to follow, I stubbed my toe, fell down and turned my pole loose.

I scrambled to my feet and caught up with the pole as it reached the water's edge. Then I had a barrel of fun trying to bring him under control without breaking my leader. He led me up and down the bank and once even out into the water. If you have ever hooked a fish in the back you will know what I mean when I say even a small fish is not easy to handle without a reel. But this one finally tired out and I was able to ease him over to the bank and sort of horse him out.

Perhaps only a boy can enjoy to the hilt a favorite fishing hole like that, but to a boy it can be supreme joy. By the time I was sixteen I had found the Pecos high country affording bigger and exciting waters and these favorite fishing holes were beginning to lose their former charm.

Then in 1904 when I was seventeen past, along came the worst flood in New Mexico's recorded history — nine inches of rain in two days. That undercut the big rock, tilting it steeply into the stream. Then drift wood lodged against it causing the stream to shift its channel some thirty feet away. Recently my wife and I picnicked there, with a daughter and two grand daughters and one would never know that there had ever been a big rock fishing hole there.

The other one was ruined too. The dipper-nest log was washed away, and a part of the rapids including the bath-tub pool is gone.

But I have a memory keepsake which I have cherished for three score and ten years, and it will last till I am a hundred if I should live that long. That convinces me that every boy should be able to have and enjoy a favorite fishing hole even as it was my great privilege.

3

MY FIRST BUCK

I N THE very early 1900s New Mexico folk didn't pay much attention to what game laws there were. Mountain ranchers and farmers had wild meat to supplement the larder about whenever they chose. My Dad and older brother were both hunters and kept the large family supplied with venison throughout the winter months.

At thirteen — that's sixty-nine years ago — I was an over-grown, husky kid. I had trapped and shot coyotes, and shot squirrels, blue grouse and one bear. Also I had killed a couple of doe deer. Now, home from school in Las Vegas, twenty-five miles away, for Thanksgiving vacation, I got it into my head that I wanted a big ol' mule deer buck. Despite the talk about the abundance of game in the good old days, deer were not at all plentiful in our area on the east side of the Sangre de Cristo Range. There were lots of mountain lions, and a year later I took four in one day, but that's another story.

Sapello Canyon in which our ranch was located, was in rugged country. North of the canyon the ridge was steep and covered with oak brush in open pine timber. The higher ridge on the opposite side was more densely wooded with pine, Douglas and white fir and aspen. Up stream about two miles where a neighbor, F. A. Blake, lived, the canyon forked with a high, timbered, flat-topped ridge between. The north fork was called John's Canyon.

The snow now lay one to two feet deep on the north slopes and from four to eight inches on the southern exposures. That made for fine trailing if I could just find a buck's track. Dad had work he wanted me to do, but at the early morning breakfast table I talked him into letting me take his .45/75 Winchester rifle and go hunting.

"Work the south hillside up to John's Canyon," he said, "and you might find a buck's track. Then," he cautioned, "take it easy and try to see him first."

I loaded the magazine of the long, heavy rifle with ten cartridges and put a dozen more in my pockets. I wasn't going to be caught short. (Later I preferred a three-shot magazine.) I was a good shot with my Stevens .22 single shot rifle, but the old .45/75 was too heavy for me to hold steady unless I could get a rest on the side of a tree or something.

With two pairs of woolen socks in my heavy, high-topped shoes and toting that heavy rifle I climbed half way up the south-facing ridge. My dog, Towser, that I had tied up, some way got loose and came to me and wanted to go along. I had quite a time making him go back, but I knew that if I shot at a deer and missed he'd chase it for a mile or more. He felt greatly insulted.

I took it slowly as Dad had told me to, and watched carefully for a buck. Before long I flushed a doe and two six-months old fawns from behind a recently fallen white fir tree on the needles of which they'd been feeding, and they bounded off up the hill. They'd seen me first so I determined to be more careful and watchful.

I'd gone about a mile along the brushy hillside

when, in the six-inch snow, I came upon the fresh tracks of a bobcat which I followed for a few yards. Suddenly he had taken off in great leaps and I thought I had jumped him. But no, at the end of the three eight-foot leaps were the features of a blue grouse he had caught and eaten right there. Now I wished for Towser; he'd have treed the cat for me.

I plodded along cautiously watching for a buck, or at least for a fresh track to follow. At last I topped out on the ridge and started down the other side, which was good deer country, but the snow was deeper and the walking harder so I followed the ridge-top westward hoping to hit the track of a buck that had crossed over one way or the other. On and on I went until I was even with the canyon forks where F. A. Blake lived.

There the ridge turned to the northwest to form the north wall of John's Canyon, and I continued laboriously on. Soon to my delight, in a little saddle or gap, I came upon the tracks of a real big buck that had very recently crossed over from the north to the south slope which, at this point, was covered with Gambel oak brush in scattering pine timber.

I slowed to a snail's pace and followed the tracks which showed that my buck was browsing — in my mind he was sure mine. It was now about ten o'clock and I thought he would be bedded down somewhere not far ahead. The sun, through a hazy sky, had warmed up and my heavy corduroy coat was bunglesome and hot. I started to take it off and leave it there and pick it up after I'd killed my buck, then decided I'd better not.

I had gone about a quarter mile, ever so cautious and watchful, when I stopped to scan the opposite side of a little draw that lay ahead. I stepped to one side for a better view through the trees and, shame on me, I broke a little dead limb. Instantly a buck with a fine set of antlers sprang from his bed above a big pine tree and bounded away around the hillside.

I got off two shots at about two hundred yards, the last just as he went out of sight. I well realized that, with the wobbly rifle and the buck bounding away in characteristic mule deer style, there was very, very little chance that I'd made a kill. I scrambled through the brush as fast as I could to check for blood, hoping that I would find the buck dead or mortally wounded. I found no buck, and the tracks showed that he had run on at top speed.

I was sorely vexed that I had fouled up that opportunity. I'd about decided to give up on this buck and go hunt for another one when suddenly blood spots on the snow began to show. There wasn't much, just a few spots beside the tracks at each bound. He didn't have a broken leg for he was using all four feet normally. With blood, even though he was just nicked, I would have to follow on and try to get him. I'd been taught never to leave a wounded animal in the woods.

The buck ran steadily along the hillside for a half mile and then topped out on the ridge and slowed down to a trot, then a walk. Blood spots continued to show on the snow, perhaps a cut finger might bleed that much, but he was hit. I waited there for a while for him to get over his scare and quiet down. It was about noon and I ate a sandwich and apple I had in my coat pocket, and ate snow to quench my thirst.

In half an hour I took to the tracks again, traveling slowly and cautiously. He meandered along the ridge for another half mile, then turned down hill and headed for the canyon. I was fearful that he would cross John's

Canyon and take refuge on the timbered ridge beyond. And that's just what he did, but I followed him anyway.

The steep hillside south of John's Canyon was densely timbered with aspen, young spruce and fir, reducing visibility to a few yards. The foot-deep snow made the climb awfully hard and tiring. I knew I'd never see the buck here, but maybe on top or the other side I might. I realized with some misgivings that I was a kid a long way from home, but on this course we were not getting any farther away.

Sweating and panting I finally topped out on the high flat ridge. For some distance the buck had been walking and stopping now and then, so I knew I had not spooked him again. Blood spots continued. When he had stopped I could see that they had come from his right hip. It seemed that the wound was not at all serious. Because of his frequent stops I thought I should soon catch up.

Ahead lay rather open aspen woods for a half mile across the flat-topped ridge. I could see for a hundred fifty yards or more, but shooting through the trees would be difficult, particularly if it were a running shot. The snow was now quite wet from the hazy sun, and I could travel without making any crunching noise. Step by careful step I eased along, intently peering through the aspens ahead and to right and left. I was determined to see him first.

And I did. Suddenly there he was, tail to me, about a hundred yards away nibbling on the twigs of a snowberry bush. My heart began pounding my ribs. I cocked the rifle and raised it slowly to take aim. I reckon I had buck ague pretty bad for I just could not hold the barrel steady enough for a sure shot. So I eased sideways a couple of steps to steady the barrel against a tree. That was my mistake, for the buck caught the movement and bounded away.

This time I got off six shots before he went out of sight. But through the trees it would have been difficult shooting for an expert, and much more so for a kid with buck ague and a heavy rifle.

As before I rushed ahead to see if, perchance, I had hit him. To my surprise I had, for now there was a little blood showing on the left side of his tracks also. It wasn't much, and I noted that he was still coming down on all four feet in his hasty get-away. I berated myself in unduly obscene language for not taking the off-hand standing shot.

Now I had to decide whether to follow on or give up and head for home. Pondering that question I followed the tracks to the rim of the *mesa*-like ridge where it broke off steeply toward the south fork of Sapello Canyon. The buck had headed straight down the hillside and, since I'd have to go that way to hit a trail for home anyway, I decided to wait an hour to let him quiet down and then make a desperate last try.

When I set out on the tracks again the sun was dropping fast toward the high Sangre de Cristo Range a few miles to the west. I surely would not have much time. I followed the tracks down the brushy slope to the creek in the canyon bottom. By then the sun had just gone down behind the Range. The buck, perhaps concluding that the young hunter posed no real danger, had not run far. His tracks in the snow showed that he had been stopping now and then, shielded by a bush or fir sapling, to look back for his tormentor.

The canyon bottom and the slope beyond for a

couple of hundred yards were heavily timbered. Above the timber was a loggy burned-over area where visibility would be good and there were browse plants, where the buck, if he was as hungry as I was from the long chase, might stop for his supper. So I determined to climb up the hillside through the timber and have a look in the burned area before giving up.

I clambered up through the foot-deep snow as fast as my weary legs would take me for dusk would soon be upon me. At the timber's edge I paused to look ahead, but no buck was in sight. Ahead some fifty yards was a clump of spruce saplings which hid a part of the open area beyond. He might possibly be there.

As I eased forward I noticed that the buck had been feeding, so I knew he must be nearby. I was tense and my heart was pounding but tired legs were forgotten. Cautiously I eased around the young trees, my eyes searching the new area as it came into view. This, I well knew, was my last chance to redeem myself.

The light was getting bad, so I didn't see him until, a hundred fifty yards ahead, the buck snorted and bounded away angling from me. I jerked the heavy rifle up and it boomed twice before he went out of sight. He showed no sign that he was hit, yet I must go see. If I had wounded him badly I'd have to come back tomorrow and try to get him. Never leave a wounded animal to suffer!

I was just about played out and thought my tired legs would never get me around the hill through the logs to where he went out of sight. Finally I got there and found no sign that my bullets had connected. I was about to turn back and head for home, but something impelled me to follow on a few yards farther. Lucky it was that I did.

My eyes bugged and my weary legs came alive when I saw the big, fine buck lying stone dead with his back down-hill against a log. My, oh my, was I ever a proud, jubilant kid! I jumped up and down, I patted and stroked him and examined his fine, ten-point antlers and kissed that old rifle. Then I looked to see where I had hit him and found the bullet had gone in his left flank. I later found that the heavy slug had ranged forward across the body cavity and passed through his heart. An accidental perfect shot! The other shots had just creased his right hip and his left leg above the hock.

It was getting dark when I suddenly realized that I had a job to do before I could start the long trip home. My hunting knife was a broken off butcher knife that I had crudely shaped on a grindstone. When at last I came to my senses I stuck him but got little blood for his heart was pierced. Then I turned him up a little more on his back and field dressed the buck after a fashion. At least I finally got the viscera out so he wouldn't spoil. He was too heavy to move so I had to leave him as he had fallen.

Now to get home in the dark was a real problem. It would be two miles on a very dim trail to F. A. Blake's place. That rifle got heavier and heavier and my legs more wobbly as I gropped my way through foot-deep snow in the moonless night. At long last I saw a light ahead. It had to be in Blake's window. I knew Mr. Blake, who was living alone there at the time, had a saddle mare that he thought a lot of. Maybe he would loan her to me. I didn't see how I could go another two miles on foot.

Instead of lending me the mare, Mr. Blake insisted that I spend the night with him, but I knew my Dad would be out hunting for me if I didn't show up mighty soon — he might be out now. At last Mr. Blake consented and we took a coal oil lantern and went to the barn and saddled her and I was on my way. In all my life no saddle has ever felt better.

When I got home Dad was already at the stable saddling a horse to go hunt for me, and he gave me heck for staying out so late. But at last, when he let me tell my story, he was pacified and agreed to go help me pack the buck in next morning.

I had learned that perserverance is often necessary in successful hunting. I also learned that it is the part of wisdom and good sportsmanship not to shoot at game unless there is a reasonable chance of making a clean kill, a rule I've been following for seventy years.

PIONEER LIFE ON A MOUNTAIN RANCH 1889-1908

HUNTING AND FISHING were a part of life on the ranch in the Sangre de Cristo Mountains where my father homesteaded in 1889 when I was a three-year old nubbin. However, those pleasure-able activities were secondary to the long hours of hard work every member of the family had to put in to eke out a living. Our farm-ranch combination was small with limited revenue capacity, and outside range was available for only about a hundred head of cattle.

With a small, water-powered sawmill to supplement the meagre farm and livestock income we lived com-fortably, and the seven younger of eleven children got a fair to good education. That, however, involved some sacrifices and hardships on our parents.

When I was thirteen the annual three-month school term for the Barker and neighbor children was aban-doned and mother took us youngsters to Las Vegas, twenty-five miles away, where we attended school. That, of course, was hard on Pa to keep things going at the ranch. We all loved the ranch and went back for holidays and weekends whenever possible. It was on such holidays that I bagged my first buck deer and mountain lions.

During the summers there was abundant work for all — farming, range riding after cattle, cutting and hauling saw logs and helping at the sawmill. Naturally, I liked the cowpuncher job the best. Someway we managed to get in a bit of fishing now and then. There was no hunting in summer except for bear, and that calls for explanation.

During that era both black and grizzly bears were classed as predators, and the state paid a $20.00 bounty. That would be near $200.00 now, for a saddle slicker cost $2.50 then compared to $25.00 now.

As time permitted we hunted bear for sport and for needed extra cash. We still-hunted them, used dogs and trapped them. How times have changed. Now bear are classed as game and a license is required to hunt them, despite the fact that they do considerable damage to livestock. Trapping is rightfully prohibited.

A ludicrous bear-hunt incident happened when I was about seventeen years old. It was a chilly, dark afternoon with a drizzling rain. Going to camp to hunt bear I was leading a pack burro on a narrow trail along the hillside a few yards from the brushy creek bottom. My rifle was in the scabbard, the burro's lead rope was looped over the saddle horn, and my saddle slicker covered everything.

I was drowsing along, carelessly astride a rather snorty mare. Suddenly, some fifty feet below in the creek bottom, a big brown bear reared up out of the tall vegetation and woof-woofed a couple of times. It startled me, and the mare more so. Instantly she whirled around, got the lead rope under her tail and bucked me off on my head. Then she took off on a lope down the canyon, pulling the burro after her until he went around a tree and broke the rope.

I quickly got my forked end down again, and that

beautiful bear, after running a few yards up the opposite slope, stopped and sat down to look me over. For minutes we gazed at each other. I had found what I was hunting for, but my rifle was in the saddle scabbard no telling how far down the canyon.

I finally caught the mare and burro and came back to the site of the wreck, but the bear was gone. It would be unsportsman-like to trap bear today, but sixty and seventy years ago things were different.

In addition to his 160-acre homestead Pa bought an adjoining 160 acres down stream. That helped, but agricultural resources were still limited. The canyon was narrow and the tillable land was in patches along the winding creek bottom and lower slopes, most of which had been cleared of oak brush and aspens with grubbing hoes to make it arable. In the early years all hands had worked at this. My older sisters piled and burned the grubbed out brush, and I got in their way.

A grubbing hoe is a double-bitted tool with one stout bit turned crossways and the other longer and narrower than an ax bit. Thus one digs and pries out rocks with one blade and cuts off roots in a hole with the other. Using it all day can give one a double-bitted back ache, too.

Although money was scarce there were some hired hands — Spanish-Americans, who worked for fifty to seventy-five cents a day and board or a dollar a day and board themselves. We Anglos, so called, were the minority group of whom we hear about the other way around today. In that general area there were five times as many Spanish-Americans, then called Mexicans, as there were Anglos, or Gringos as the Mexicans called us. But we got along well despite the language and ancestral nationality barrier.

Our best-paying crop was potatoes, but we raised lots of vegetables, too, such as cabbage, turnips, carrots, beets and parsnips which we marketed in Las Vegas, a two-day round trip with wagon and team. When today we pay twenty cents a pound for vegetables I recall how we were lucky to get a cent a pound then.

For winter forage for livestock we raised timothy and clover and oats, cut green, for hay. The mountain land was very fertile and produced fine, heavy crops. My father's oats took first prize at the Chicago World's Fair in 1893. His bundle of oats was seven feet three inches tall with heads eighteen inches long.

My mother was an expert gardener. She always had an acre or so vegetable garden patch adjacent to the house. Despite cooking, washing, ironing and keeping house for a big family — of course the girls helped — she always found time to work in her garden. She loved it and it responded bountifully to her green-thumb touch.

The sawmill was a small one, mostly home-made, with a capacity of only 1,500 to 2,000 board feet of lumber a day. It was powered by a 22-foot diameter, overshot water wheel. Since the creek did not supply enough water to operate it efficiently, Pa built a small reservoir which, when brim full, would supply power for a two-hour run. Then we would have to stop and wait a couple of hours for it to fill again. While waiting we would go into the woods and cut a few saw logs or haul in a load to the mill. Water ouzels would build nests in niches under the leaky flume from pond to mill.

From the time I was fourteen on I made a hand at the sawmill, in the woods with an ax, and on one end of a crosscut saw. I liked that better than farming. By the time I was eighteen, in my own estimation, I was an ex-

49

pert lumberjack and teamster. Pa and my older brother, Charlie, didn't agree but encouraged me to keep on working at it.

My ego got a jolt when I was driving a four-horse team with saw logs on the heavy wagon down the road on a steep hillside above the mill pond. The brake rope broke and the wheel team couldn't hold the heavily loaded wagon back and I couldn't keep it in the road. A wheel went over the bank and the wagon turned up side down. I jumped just in time and landed in a pile of rocks, but held onto the lines and kept the teams under control. The toggle chain broke and the logs rolled into the mill pond.

I finally got the horses untangled and loose from the wagon, with no harm done except that one of the horses and I had lost some skin off our legs. That wreck put a kink in my teamster ego, but I said, "Everybody turns his wagon over sometime." Figuratively how true that is.

I am sure we handled our seventy-five to a hundred head of cattle differently from most ranchers. Ours wasn't a bona fide cattle ranch according to western standards. There weren't any real cowboys, and didn't need to be, for the cattle were all gentle. They could easily be driven anywhere they wanted to go! They would come when called. When Pa gave his stentorian soo-ook, sooky call at feed yard in winter or on the range in summer the cattle would come a running. We all used the cattle call after a fashion, but not like Pa.

At branding time we corralled the cattle. A fire was built to heat the SLB branding iron. Then on foot we'd rope a calf and pull it up to a snubbing post. We'd get a noose on his hind feet and stretch him out while someone grabbed his tail and yanked him over on his side and held him there for the ordeal. After the SLB was burned on his right hip, both ears would be tip-cropped and the right one spilt, earmarked, for easy identification on the range. Lastly, Pa would use his sharp pocket knife to make steers out of bull calves. We boys learned to perform that operation, too.

Sometimes even a gentle old cow would get fighting mad when her calf bawled under the hot iron, and would be liable to come up behind and hook someone in the seat. Once my younger brother, Omar, about twelve, turned and saw a sharphorned old brindle cow charging straight at him. He gave a terrific yell and took off like a scared jack rabbit for the five-foot pole gate with Brindle bellering right at his heels. There was no time to open nor climb over the gate. Fantastic as the chance to hurdle it might seem, he tried to. He almost made it, but stubbed his toe on the top pole and landed ten feet beyond rolling away.

Moving the cattle in spring from the ranch to summer range on Lone Tree Mesa and Beaver Creek was a real chore for they would be poor and weak, and it was a 2,500-foot climb in a mile and a half. Pa and three or four of the boys and girls were required. Those gentle cows were stubborn and took advantage of every switchback in the steep, rocky trail to sneak off in the brush and hide. But with a lot of whoops, hurrahs and whistling we'd finally get them there.

The summer range was lush and once there the cattle loved it and were about as hard to drive down rolypoly fat in the fall as they were to drive up in the spring. Hopeful profits from the cattle operations were always reduced by losses.

51

Once when a ditch from the creek to irrigate the meadows was cleaned, some water hemlock roots were left exposed. Three cows found and ate them and died within minutes. Larkspur, water hemlock and other poisonous plants on the range caused losses. Sometimes lightning killed one or more, and both grizzly and black bears took their toll. The worst bear loss we ever had was in 1913 after I had left the ranch. A big, lone grizzly, killed fifteen head of our cattle, including a Hereford bull, on Beaver Creek in a period of two weeks.

Mountain lions rarely killed cattle — once in a while a calf or yearling — but they considered sheep, horses and especially colts, fair game. A neighbor, Frank Blake, attempted to summer a hundred head of sheep on Beaver Creek, and a lioness with two kittens got in the sheep corral one night and killed twenty head.

When I was fourteen, a country merchant, J. Y. Lujan, six miles down Sapello Canyon from the ranch, paid me $5.00 to take two mules to Lone Tree Mesa to pasture for the summer. They were huge Army mules he had bought when Ft. Union was abandoned. A week later while riding after our cattle, I found that a lion had killed one of the mules and had been eating on it. The carcass was too heavy to drag to cover but the lion had made a show of covering it by raking grass and dirt up against it.

Ten days later he killed the other mule nearby out in the open and followed the same procedure as with the first one. After finding it I rode to the edge of the *mesa* overlooking an open cove in the middle of which, a hundred yards below, was a truck-size rock. There on the rock the big lion was lying sunning himself. I had only my .22 single shot rifle, but I got off to take a shot at him

ssed for church, the S. L. Barker family poses near its New Mexico mountain ranch. Young Elliott
ker stands behind his father in this portrait taken about 1900.

Elliott S. Barker, wife Ethel and children, Florence and Roy, when Barker was Supervisor of Car
National Forest, a position he held from 1916 to 1919.

Barker ranch house where the author lived and worked from 1919 to 1930.

A. W. Sypher, above, a fellow forest ranger and a man upon whom Barker leaned heavily during the rough and tumble early 1900s. Barker, left, an expert hunter and guide, poses in 1926 with a 220-pound, 8-foot lion and a mule deer buck taken the same day.

Barker, standing above, readies deer hunters for their trek into the wilderness in 1908. While a long-time guide and renowned hunter, Barker has dedicated his years to wilderness conservation and the orderly preservation of such wildlife species as the mountain lion.

Bighorn sheep obtained by Barker from Banff, Alberta, Canada, to stock New Mexico's Sandia Mount̄a between 1939 and 1941. (Photo by New Mexico Department of Game and Fish.)

During Barker's administration as New Mexico State Game Warden, a pitiful 5-pound bear cub with singed hair and burned feet was rescued by one of Barker's rangers from a raging fire. After the cub was nursed back to health, Barker arranged for its donation to the U. S. Forest Service, specifying that its life be devoted to conservation. It was this cub, known as SMOKEY BEAR, that became a legendary national symbol for fire prevention and wildlife preservation.

While Barker was State Game Warden, the New Mexico Department of Game and Fish trapped transplanted more than 3,000 antelope and started 70 new herds.

Elk obtained by Barker from Wyoming during his tenure as New Mexico State Game Warden be released for restocking of the Jemez Mountains.

anyway. The lion saw me and bounded for cover like a scared house cat, his long, black-tipped tail carried high and waving.

My brother Charlie had a good stout saddle horse named John. He was smart, and to avoid work he would wander off and hide out so we would miss him when we wrangled the other horses. One day after that happened we heard him whinnying as he came bolting down the brushy hillside to the corral like the devil was after him.

We went to see what was wrong and found that a lion had left his four claw marks on each side of his back from whithers to hips, and a piece of flesh the size of one's hand was hanging loose from his ham where the lion had bit him. John had been lucky and bucked the lion off. He had learned his lesson and never again strayed from the other horses.

While I was growing up we didn't have many English-speaking neighbors and social activities for the family were limited. We had an organ which mother and the girls could play. Often after supper the family would gather around the organ and sing religious and other songs. For a time there was a sort of literary society consisting of the Barker, Blake and Ground families, and there were interesting discussions and debates. On Sundays there would be church services, for my father, in addition to being a rancher, farmer, blacksmith, stone mason and sawmill operator, was a minister of the Church of Christ.

During the summer we would have two or three neighborhood picnics in some remote nook in the canyon. A big Fourth of July picnic and patriotic celebration was a must, and was attended annually by friends from as far away as Las Vegas. Every family brought food and there would be home-made ice cream and gallons of lemonade. Stronger beverages were taboo. Flags would fly, someone would make a patriotic speech and the youngsters play games. It was a social gathering and celebration that we all looked forward to.

After finishing high school in Las Vegas in 1905, I spent a year at the ranch working at whatever there was to do which was always plenty. I hunted and trapped and got started guiding and packing parties on hunting and fishing trips into the high country which is now known as the Pecos Wilderness Area.

Then a brother-in-law talked me into going into the photographic business with him. To prepare for it, in the spring of 1906 I went to Effingham, Illinois, where I attended the Bissell College of Photography for six months. After that I went into business with my brother-in-law, John Phillips, at Texico, New Mexico, on the broad treeless, Staked Plains. I soon found that living on the plains and working in the photographic dark room a lot didn't suit me at all. After a year of it I became so homesick that I gave up the deal and went back to my beloved mountains, horses and dogs.

During that year my dear mother had passed away and I was needed at the ranch more than ever. During the winter of 1907-08 Pa and I batched, and I worked at the sawmill, logging and looking after the cattle. But I found time to do some hunting for deer, mountain lions and trapping for coyotes and bobcats.

I had a humiliating experience with three novice lion hunters from out of state. When we mounted our horses at sunup to start out, my three mongrel lion dogs were excited, romping around, barking and making a lot of fuss for they loved to hunt. One hunter said, "Barker, we'll never find a lion with those dogs making all that racket, leave them home."

I said, "We just can't hunt lions without dogs. They strike a track, follow it and eventually tree the lion for us."

"No, they'll just scare them away," he insisted, and refused to go with us.

"You tell me where there is a good place to hunt," he said. "I'll go there and you folks go somewhere else."

"All right," I said, "but you will never get a lion that way." I directed him to a ridge leading to rugged Hermit Peak where I had often found lion sign. He went there and we went our way. We rode far and wide and hunted hard all day without even finding a track. Shortly after we got back at dusk, here came the dogless hunter with a lion skin draped across the back of his saddle.

"Where in hell did you get that?" I asked, astounded.

"I went where you told me," he said, "and at noon climbed up on a house-size boulder in a patch of scrubby aspens and ate my lunch. Then I stretched out in the sun and went to sleep. When I woke up half an hour later I stood up and looked around trying to decide where to go next. On another boulder like mine a hundred yards away I saw a lion lying there asleep. So I just up and shot him. It's easy without dogs."

What could I say? Now sixty-two years later, having hunted lions off and on all my life and having taken a hundred twenty-five of them, I have seen only two without use of dogs. His was a one-in-ten-thousand chance.

I had been unable to see any way to get a college education, so at twenty-one it was high time I decided what I wanted to do and get with it. The U.S. Forest Service was in its infancy and after careful consideration and conferences with some Forest Rangers, I decided that would be a good field of endeavor for which I might qualify. A college degree was not required then, though it is now.

When a Civil Service examination for the position of Forest Ranger was held in Santa Fe on April 23 and 24, 1908, I rode the two-day trip across the mountains and, along with about twenty others, took the test. It was a one-day written exam in a variety of questions and a one-day field test on compass surveying, timber cruising, log scaling, riding, packing a horse with camp outfit and fire-fighting tools and like activities. I'd have to wait till November to learn whether or not I had passed. In the meantime I stayed at the ranch and continued my activities as a professional guide and hunter.

When bear come out of hibernation in the spring their fur is prime, and stays so for a while and that is a good time to hunt them successfully. Then again in the fall when they have fattened up preparatory for hibernation the fur gets good and they may be successfully still-hunted in areas where they are feeding on berries, acorns or pinon nuts. When they are real fat in the fall is the best time to hunt them with dogs for they can't run far, as they do when thin. Mid summer is a bad time to hunt bear from every angle and we left them alone then except when they got to killing livestock.

In the summer of 1907 bear had killed a number of both cattle and sheep in the upper Pecos country across the Main Range from our ranch. Pa had also lost one cow. In the spring of 1908 some of the grazing permittees on the National Forest who lived north of our place asked me to go over there and try to take the stock killers. So, the first June as soon as the winter's snow drifts

would permit I set up my bear hunting camp at 11,500-foot Spring Mountain on the edge of that area.

My brother Charlie went with me for two or three days. We soon found tracks of a real big grizzly with two cubs right near camp. There were still lots of big snow drifts in the timber and on the east side of the range's escarpment. The ground was soft enough to make trailing them possible, and we followed their hot-fresh tracks all one day but could never catch up with our quarry. Our dogs would run black bear but they just had not lost any big grizzly.

The tracks showed that while the sow was foraging for anything she could find to eat—turning rocks and tearing up rotten logs for insects or a mouse nest—the cubs would climb a snow drift, wallow around a while and then slide down the steep side of it on their fannies. Then they would run and catch up with mamma, who kept right on traveling as she foraged. Pickings were slim for no livestock had yet been brought up to summer range. We had to be very careful not to run onto them suddenly and find ourselves between mamma grizzly and her cubs.

After Charlie left, a cub stepped into one of my traps and I shot the mother when she charged me. The dogs bayed the other cub. Then a few days later my dogs succeeded in stopping a fair sized boar grizzly and I eased up and shot him. These bears evidently were the stock killers for there were no more reports of killing that season.

I sold the four skins for $75.00 and got $80.00 bounty. Besides helping the stockmen it was pretty good money for two weeks work.

That summer I packed several parties into what

is now the Pecos Wilderness Area to camp, fish and take scenic side trips. One party of eight men, mostly M. D.'s from St. Louis, Missouri, I well remember. They were nice guys with plenty of money but hard to control. It was early August and grouse were just not big enough yet to be fair game, but they insisted on killing them anyway. They caught and kept a lot more fish than we could eat and that was against the rules my mother had instilled in me.

One man wanted to kill a doe deer in summer red coat, probably suckling fawns, and I almost had to use force to prevent him from doing so. I laid the law down to them that evening that no deer were to be killed in summer, and they agreed to lay off. Imagine my amazement and chagrin the next evening when that same fellow came into camp toting the hind quarters and loins of a two-month old calf he had killed for camp meat! I made him take me back the next morning to where he had killed it to find the mother cow. She was there, and by her brand I found out who she belonged to. I made him give me forty dollars, which was four times what the calf was worth then, which I later paid to the owner. Right or wrong we couldn't waste that fine veal.

The day to go home came but they had had such a good time they decided to stay one more day. That was O.K. by me for it meant more money in my pocket. Then about one o'clock they changed their minds again and wanted to go in. They took down the tents while I wrangled the horses. It was twelve miles on a steep, rugged trail over the high range to the ranch. To keep them from being caught on that bad trail after dark I decided to send them on ahead and I'd bring the camp stuff later.

Horses were quickly saddled, and I got them started. They were doubtful about finding the trail, but I assured them that the horses would follow it straight home, and they made it by sundown.

It was two o'clock when I got started collecting the duffel, bedrolls and elaborate camp equipment they had insisted upon bringing. Then I was delayed by a hard rain, and it was dark before I got the five horses and two burros packed. I led one horse and strung the others out with lead ropes tied to the tail of the horse ahead, making a string of five to lead. The burros would follow. I had fun getting over the range in the pitch dark, but by midnight I made it.

That was by far the best-paying party I ever took care of, and they had more duffel and equipment and fancy food than I had ever seen. Also they were undoubtedly the most reckless and hard to keep in bounds. When they got out in the wild they seemed to discard all restraint and thought the world was theirs to do with as they pleased. We still have folks like that today.

Early November 1908, a Dr. Graham, Jay Hilliard and Walter Walker all of Indiana, employed me to pack them in on a deer hunt. We went horseback with three pack burros to the head of Bear Creek, eight miles from the ranch. There was snow on the ground and it was very cold at the elevation there of 11,500 feet, but the big bucks ranged high.

We pitched camp by a spring in a sunny park, and then discovered a sorry camp in the timber nearby. It turned out to be an old, gray bearded, hermit-like prospector named Coleman. He was not dressed for winter—overalls, cotton shirt and jacket and a ragged overcoat—but he did have good overshoes.

68

His shelter was a spruce brush lean-to, his bed an old tarp and three sheep skins. Kitchen equipment was a water can, skillet, coffeepot, cup, tin plate, big spoon, fork and butcherknife—a pitiful outfit.

When he came in from his "diggins" he came straight to our fire where I was getting supper. He looked hungry and we asked him to eat with us even though he was as grimy as a human can get. I'd brought along a pot of chili and beans and prepared plenty of other food, too, and fortunately I did for he ate ravenously. He said that for a week he had been living on venison and coffee.

"I stayed on," he said, "because I'm just about to hit it rich in my 'diggins' down there." He pointed into the head of Bear Creek. He became a regular boarder and our food supply dwindled.

I offered him a blanket from my bedroll but he refused. How he kept from freezing is a mystery, and why any human would choose such a life is imponderable, yet he was voluble and happy.

That night Walter became worried that the elevation was too much for him, and so decided to give up hunting. "I'll tend camp," he said, "and enjoy looking over these wonderful mountains as much as I would getting a buck."

Their sleeping bags were the lace-up type—before zippers. Hilliard ate more chili and beans than was good for him. Suddenly in the middle of the night he had to get up and go right quick. His sleeping bag was laced up tight and the laces tied. He pulled the strings wrong and got a hard knot that he couldn't get loose in the dark. He called for help and Doc Graham and I crawled out of bed and tried to help him get out, but we were not in time. If you have ever had a case of chili diarrhea you can well imagine the mess he was in. Oh my, Oh my!

Come morning Doc and I were the only ones fit to go hunting. We very soon found the tracks of a very large mule deer buck leading into the alpine forest. We followed it carefully. It was the most accommodating buck I ever saw. He soon stopped and we could see his antlers but he presented only his rear end, as a target. I told Doc he could break the pelvis bone and get him down, but he wouldn't shoot, and the buck went on out of sight.

To my surprise in a hundred yards we caught up again, and again only his white rump could be seen. Despite my urging Doc wouldn't shoot. The buck trotted on and I was sure we'd lose him. As a guide I liked to get my hunter a shot, but I didn't like to have him pass up a sure shot at an exceptional trophy buck. We'd been within forty yards and to break the pelvis bone was a cinch, and the coup de grace would be administered instantly. I warned Doc that he'd never get another chance like that. But he did. Entirely out of character the huge buck stopped again headed away and let us get within forty yards of him. Again I said shoot. Doc reluctantly broke him down with his .30-06 Winchester and I rushed up and finished him off with my six shooter.

I congratulated the Doctor for taking as fine a trophy as anyone could ask for. He said, "The only thing wrong is that it was too damned easy."

Hilliard was feeling all right when we got back to camp and had his pajamas and blankets washed and hanging on limbs to dry. Walter had lunch ready and after we ate, I took Hilliard out hunting. Right away we found an eight-point buck, and Hilliard downed him with one shot. That being his very first hunting trip he was delighted. The hunt was over with the least effort and fewest shots of any hunt where game was bagged that I had ever been on. We packed the bucks to camp the next day, skinned and quartered them and packed out the next.

We agreed to leave all the left-over grub for Coleman. When we gave it to him he said, "No I won't take it unless you let me pay you for it."

"Pay with what?" I asked.

"I'm about to strike it rich and when I do I'll pay you double," he said. With that understanding we left the groceries and took off.

When we arrived at the ranch there was a letter from the U.S. Civil Service Commission telling me that I had passed the Ranger examination with a grade of 86.4, putting me well up on the list.

In a couple of weeks I had offers of an Assistant Forest Ranger job, the starting classification, from three different Supervisors. I chose the Jemez National Forest. Thus ended my ranch work and guiding for a while, but a bit of hunting and fishing continued to be a part of my life.

5 RANGERS TO MATCH THE ERA

Cuba, Territory of New Mexico, an isolated Spanish-American settlement sixty-five miles from the nearest railroad, was my first assignment as an Assistant Forest Ranger. I reached my destination on January 2, 1909, after an eight-day trip from our ranch west of Las Vegas. The trek was made horseback, leading a pack horse carrying my bedroll and camp equipment.

As previously arranged, I met A. W. Sypher, the Assistant Ranger I was to work with, who had arrived the day before and rented a two-room adobe house, with stable and corral, for our headquarters. There was no Ranger Station, and we had to provide our own living quarters and horse feed out of our seventy-five dollars a month salaries.

I had stopped a day in Santa Fe to receive our instructions from Forest Supervisor Ross McMillan. He told me that two men sent to Cuba eight months before had been unable to cope with the rough situation and had left the country. He warned me that it truly was a difficult assignment and especially for a young man of my age, but he went on to say that my partner, A. W. Sypher, was much older and experienced and a war veteran of the Philippine Islands campaign.

The Supervisor advised us to live and work together and always be home by dark. Of course we would always go armed. We were to avoid situations that might get us into trouble and to stay away from saloons and a bawdy house a mile out of town, a notorious trouble spot.

He told me that the Cuba area was dominated by a shrewd, unprincipaled politician—we'll refer to him as Epifanio Ortega for convenience—who was causing the Forest Service all the trouble he could. We found that to be an understatement. There were only ten Anglos, or Gringos as they called us, in the area. The Spanish-Americans, for the most part, were poor and illiterate and few of them spoke English. The majority of them were good citizens and would have cooperated with the Forest Service except for the dictates of the local *mayordomo* as local leaders and bosses were called.

Such was the situation we faced. Fortunately, Sypher was nearly twice my age, mature and experienced in dealing with rough situations and tough people. My strong point was that I could speak Spanish like a native, and it was to stand us in good stead.

Ranger Sypher thought that it would be to our advantage to not let anybody know that I could understand the native Spanish language. We agreed to play it that way in hopes of finding out a lot of things that we were not supposed to know about. Sypher warned me not to speak a word of Spanish. "Remember that God had reasons for giving you two ears and only one tongue," Sypher said.

The Jemez National Forest, created on October 12, 1905, had been under administration long enough for the situation to be under control. However, an addition on the west, including the Cuba country, was created

73

April 24, 1908, and there the present trouble was centered. Epifanio Ortega was a rancher, stockman, merchant, postmaster and an influential Territorial politician. He, like certain other leaders, resented any curb on his free use of the public lands and its resources as he saw fit for personal gain.

Our job was to see that the land and its resources were used in accordance with the Forest Service regulations and multiple-use policies, and to convince the people that it would be to their advantage in the long run. It certainly would be. Now, for the first time, the common people would get a fair break with the big owners of cattle and sheep, who had long been in the habit of over running the ranges with excess numbers of stock. It was common practice to cut timber on public lands in any quantity desired for domestic or commercial use. There was one sawmill operator cutting timber on some private lands and also on the new addition.

Naturally we had to put a stop to that and require that any timber desired for commercial purposes be purchased, with living trees to be cut marked in advance. Building material, posts, firewood etc. required by residents on or near the Forest were free, but the regulations provided that free use permits be issued to authorize such timber removal. There were many such permits and it took a lot of time getting the people, most of whom could not read or write, to understand what it was all about.

Most of the free use permits were issued in the field on notebook-size forms, with a carbon copy for the Forest Supervisor. Our writing, using a saddle or knees for a desk, was not too legible. Once the Forest Supervisor returned some permit copies with a hand-written four word note attached. We studied the note all evening before we finally made out what it said. It was initialed by the Supervisor and said, "illegible, rewrite and return." I plainly printed a note saying "can't decipher your note," and sent it back with the illegible permit copies. I received no more comments on my writing.

The regulations required anyone grazing stock on the National Forest to obtain a grazing permit by the first of April. Ten head in the aggregate of work, saddle and milk stock would be under free permits, but grazing fees had to be paid on the remainder. The fees were very low compared to those charged for grazing on private lands.

We had trouble getting stock owners to apply for either free or paid permits mainly because Epifanio Ortega encouraged them to defy the Forest Service regulations. It was a long, hard job getting compliance with the grazing regulations, but finally, just short of going to Federal Court, the *mayordomo* agreed to comply and others followed.

Our plan for me listening and not letting on that I understood Spanish worked well for a while, but I slipped and got into a hell of a fight. Then we decided that my Spanish would be more valuable in explaining matters to the natives in their own language and help get their cooperation. That really proved to be correct, and we realized that we should have followed that course in the beginning. Throughout my career in the Forest Service my knowledge of Spanish proved to be my greatest asset in dealing with the Spanish-Americans, who were by far the heaviest users of the National Forests of northern New Mexico.

We had a few brushes with the sawmill operator

but finally got him straightened out when we made a
sale of saw timber to him. There was very little other
commercial timber demand. Free timber permits, though
a petty business, were important and required a lot of
time and patience. It served to keep us in constant contact with the people and proved to them that the Forest
Service was not their enemy, and that they would always be treated fairly.

Dealing with both big and little livestock owners
was the troublesome problem. Many settlers had stock
on shares from the big owners, which, contrary to regulations, they would claim as their own. Many would
not apply for a permit for all their stock.

One fellow who had two hundred goats applied for
only one hundred. Before they found out that I could
understand Spanish, I heard him boasting about putting
one over on us. He was much surprised one morning
to find us at his night corral at daybreak waiting to
count his goats as he turned them out to graze. He
wanted to know how we found out, and Sypher said
una urraca (a magpie) told us. After he found out about
my Spanish he said to me, *"Tu era la urraca."* (you were
the magpie), and after that he called me *La Urraca,*
and we became friends.

We received cloth notices in both languages advising the public of the Forest Service regulations which
we were told to post in conscpicuous places. Ortega's
store was the best place, but he refused permission.
"That's our first real set back," I thought. The window
to the post office was in a board partition between it
and the store. Sypher said nothing, but went right ahead
and tacked up an English notice on one side of the window and a Spanish notice on the other.

Ortega always carried a snub-nosed pistol in his coat pocket. Now he was aghast at Sypher's defiance of his orders and said, "Mr. Sypher, I told you not to put up posters on my property."

Ortega, who spoke impeccable English, thrust his hand in his coat pocket and shouted, "I demand you remove them at once!"

Twirling the hammer he'd used in his fingers, Sypher looked Ortega in the eye and said slow and softly, as was his manner of speaking, "That's a United States post office, and those are Government posters. I am a United States officer and I have orders to put them up. The bastard that tears them down will wind up in Federal Court so quick he'll think lightning struck him."

That was a long speech for Sypher, and its firmness dazed Ortega. Before he could recover we walked out. The notices stayed up and thereby the great *mayordomo* lost face with the people he was accustomed to dominate.

One big job we had to do was to run and post the boundary of the new addition. It was a difficult undertaking for some of the area was unsurveyed, and even in surveyed country the section corners and lines were hard to find. Despite the difficulties, by the first of May we had run out and posted three sides of our district, the fourth being adjacent to the original Forest. However, we were not as lucky with the boundary posters as we were with the notices put up in the post office. A great many of them were torn down.

We found a sheepherder using the cloth posters he'd torn down for dishrags. Another was using one for a handkerchief. Then one day a twelve-year old girl ran across the road ahead of us wearing a dress skirt made

out of the 10 by 14 inch boundary signs. We gave her
dad such a going over that there were no more sign
dresses. Her mother took the stitches out, washed and
ironed the signs and returned them to us. Then she volunteered to do our washing for a month free.

An incident worth relating happened while we
were on the boundary job. To save long rides back and
forth we camped out some. We'd picket one horse near
camp and hobble the other three. One morning the
hobbled horses were gone. I saddled the one picketed
and set out on their tracks. I soon discovered that they
were no longer hobbled and that puzzled me. I followed
on as fast as I could and finally overtook them.

When I didn't come back right away Sypher went
out and checked the tracks to see what the score was.
He found man and mule tracks where our horses had
been unhobbled. The mule tracks had left the same way
they'd come in, and Sypher followed them afoot. I got
back to camp at two P.M., but Sypher was not there. In
a couple of hours I saw him coming, riding a sorrel mule
with a sheepherder walking fast ahead of him. I got
busy starting supper, and when I looked up Sypher was
walking toward camp and the herder was high-tailing
it the other way on the mule.

My partner had a bruised fist, but all he ever said
about it was, "That bastard won't turn our horses loose
no more." Obviously he had followed the mule tracks
about ten miles to the sheep camp, beat hell out of the
herder and rode the mule to our camp and made the
herder come along to take it back. Sometimes we simply
had to play games with them. There were many other
incidents for which there was justification for retaliation.

When we found permittees with more stock than permits called for we did not bring trespass proceedings against them, provided they would apply for and obtain a permit for the excess stock. By the first of June we had most of those situations cleared up, except Ortega's.

Ortega owned several hundred cattle and several thousand sheep ranging on and off the National Forest. His cattle were looked after by several Spanish-American cowboys and a big, black man called Andy. We continually ran onto him at most unexpected times and places. He was always friendly and respectful, but we were sure his job was to keep Ortega right up to date on our activities.

Ortega simply refused to make application for any of his stock that grazed on the new addition. The matter was in the hands of the Forest Supervisor and Ortega was defying him to do anything about it. He claimed that creation of the addition to the Forest was unconstitutional.

In the latter part of May, Ranger W. B. Bletcher came over from the Senorito District to visit us. He had just returned from the Supervisor's office and told us that Ortega had appealed to New Mexico's lone Delegate in Congress, to the Governor and Senators and Representatives from other western States to get the addition nullified. He said Ortega had openly defied Supervisor McMillan to do anything about his livestock grazing without permit.

"What's old Mack going to do about it?" Sypher asked.

"That's Ortega's worry," Bletcher said. "He has the political pull here in New Mexico, but with James Wilson as Secretary of Agriculture and Gifford Pinchot as

Chief Forester backing him, McMillan will make him back down."

"Meanwhile what do we do about it?" I asked.

"The U.S. District Attorney is starting action," Bletcher said, "But he must have accurate figures on the number of stock in trespass, so we'll have to count his sheep, herd by herd, and round up his cattle."

"That could mean serious trouble for us," I said.

"Sure could. Are you scared?" Bletcher asked.

My temper flared. I jumped up with a vitriolic retort on my tongue, but Sypher stopped me. "Sit down!" he commanded.

When I had quieted down, Sypher said, "Bletch, take back that question. The kid ain't got sense enough to be scared of nothin'."

Bletcher apologized, and we shook hands. Right there a friendship started which lasted as long as he lived.

Then Bletcher told us that Ortega had filed all kinds of charges against us — misconduct, disturbing the peace, intimidation, shooting dogs, (we'd shot prairie dogs) insulting women, selling permits and keeping the money and such rot. Now Sypher jumped up and exclaimed, "That old bastard! Why I'll . . ."

"No you won't, Pardner." It was my time to interrupt. Turning to Bletcher I asked, "What does Supervisor McMillan think of all this?"

"Oh, charges have been filed against him, too. He thinks the Washington office will send an inspector to investigate," Bletcher said.

"What does that fool, Epifany, hope to accomplish?" Sypher asked.

"Get you two fired. He sure don't like the way you

are tearing down his playhouse," Bletcher said laughing.

"Let's go to bed," Sypher said. "I ain't a gonna lose no sleep over it."

Next weekend we visited Bletcher at Blue Bird Ranger Station. He had a good house, barn and horse pasture provided him. Quite a contrast to our rented adobe hut, stable and no pasture. We also visited with the Couloudons and Freeloves who operated a sawmill, and with the Stubbs family, caretaker at the old Senorito mines which had ceased operations. We had the first meals not of our own cooking in six months.

About two weeks later we got word to count Ortega's sheep. This was fairly easy. We'd locate a band and select a place where we could set up an improvised brush chute to run the sheep through. Invariably the herders would ask if we had Ortega's permission. We answered by saying, "He knows about it." They assumed that if he knew about it and didn't stop it that it was all right. Sometimes black Andy was on hand and checked our count but did not interfere. As I recall we counted four thousand seven hundred sheep, excluding the lambs.

A short while after that Bletcher and another Ranger, Frank Blake from Coyote District, came to assist us in rounding up and counting the cattle. That's where we expected trouble. It had been rumored that John Clark, Ortega's bodyguard on outside trips, an ex-heavy weight prize fighter and operator of a saloon and bawdy house just outside the village of Cuba, would lead the cowboys in stopping us. Clark was a gunman and a bad character. It was at his place where our predecessors got into trouble and were beat unmercifully. We had stayed away from his place for, as McMillan had told me, we would have enough trouble without looking for it.

When we began the roundup we had a little trouble with Black Andy and three cowboys, but when reminded that we were Government Officers they backed down. The next day we got word by a messenger to call off the cattle roundup. That really stumped us. Sypher expressed our feelings when he said, "Well I'll be damned!"

"What can this mean?" I asked.

Blake said, "It means Old Mack ain't got guts enough to buck Ortega."

"No, Frank, I'm sure that's not it," Bletcher said. "I'll back Mack all the way."

Sypher and I agreed. We had utmost confidence in our Supervisor. We'd just have to wait and see. We returned to our place and waited impatiently for a letter from the Supervisor. Meanwhile we had a couple of small forest fires to put out. During the spring and summer we had perhaps a half dozen, but none serious.

One evening we had visitors. Charlie Watrous, Ranger on the Bland District, and an inspector from the District (now Regional) Office, whose name I can't recall, rode in. An inspector from Washington had started with them, but he had become very saddle sore and had been fed so many tales of the Cuba situation that he decided to turn back and make a report exonerating us.

Impatiently we waited another day for the Supervisor's letter. When it finally came I was designated to read it to the group. Omitting details in substance it said; "Ortega and his attorney spent days wrangling over the situation. I stood firm. When convinced the U. S. District Attorney was actually filing trespass proceedings, and that his cattle and sheep were being counted to back it up, Ortega caved in. His political pull had not paid off.

He agreed to make application for all his livestock if I would stop the trespass proceedings. I agreed provided he'd withdraw his charges against my rangers and me, and stop his monkey business. He raved and ranted and threatened, but finally agreed to it all in writing. Our big troubles are over. Thanks, and good luck."

When I finished Bletcher let out an ear-splitting war whoop. Sypher and Blake drew their revolvers and riddled the opposite adobe wall with six shots each. The room was so filled with black powder smoke from their .45 colts that we rushed outside half strangled.

Blake wanted to go to Clark's place and celebrate, but we said no. Now we wouldn't have to ride together and could get twice as much work done. We felt sure that the people generally now would cooperate with us, and they did for the most part. The Inspector, Watrous, Blake and Bletcher left next morning. Sypher and I, with tensions relaxed, began planning for the future.

The twenty-fifth of July, *El Dia Santiago*, was approaching, and a big celebration was being planned. This was a great feast day among the Spanish-Americans throughout New Mexico, and in many communities featured *La Corrida del Gallo*, the rooster pull, and often horse races also. Roosters were buried alive with head and neck sticking out. Contestants rode past in a gallop, leaned down to grasp the rooster's neck and pull him out. If successful, other contestants gave chase and tried to take it away from him before he or his partner reached the deadline two hundred yards away. The rooster could be used to bash a pursuer over the head when one closed in before the deadline was reached. It was a rugged sport with thrills, spills and usually some fights.

Bletcher, Sypher and I decided to participate. Horses

were a part of our lives and we had some good ones. Sypher rode his pride and joy, a big, dun gelding he called Bronco. Bletcher rode his very fine, big, fast saddle mare Queen, and I rode Fanny, a small but fast little mare.

Horse races were first and we were humiliated when a cowboy on a scrawny looking little gray gelding beat Sypher's Bronco on a $25-matched race bet. Then to offset that, Bletcher's Queen beat an imported race horse brought in by Ortega and raced by John Clark with a professional jockey riding it. To beat Ortega and Clark really put us ahead.

Bletcher and I teamed up for the rooster pull. Fanny was fast and small, and I was long armed. I'd gallop by, lean down and pull the rooster and try to get it to Bletcher on Queen for the getaway.

On my first pass, I luckily got the rooster and passed it to Bletcher as he rode alongside, and he made it to the finish line before our opponents realized what was happening. I was lucky in getting the rooster again on my second pass, and my opponents gave us a lot of trouble but we finally got away.

After that I missed a couple of tries to the delight of the contestants, some of whom had been successful. When I finally got my third rooster a fellow recklessly plunged his horse into me, trying to knock Fanny over, but she kept her feet. Then another one rushed at me and, holding the rooster by the legs, I bashed him in the face with it with all my might. That rooster simply disintegrated and I rode Fanny to the finish line, but all I had was a pair of drumsticks. It was not a humane game, I'll admit, but participants were often treated as rough as the roosters and horses.

The next time they ganged up on us and blocked the way with their horses. Bletcher saw what was happening and put spurs to Queen and recklessly dashed into their midst, knocking horses every which way, and sprawling riders all over the place. Queen went down to her knees, but instantly was up and off again. Fanny and I quickly followed through the gap which 'Bletch' and Queen had opened and reached the finish line unscathed.

Now Sypher sensed real trouble brewing and suggested that we quit while we were winning. He didn't want to start a fight that might very well jeopardize the gains we had made. He said the Stubbs family had just left for home. Bletcher said, "They have asked us to have supper with them." That suited all of us.

Perhaps rooster pulling was not in the line of duty, but by participating in their games and holding our own we were thereafter more or less accepted as members of the community and, as such, we were able to get along much better with them.

To say that there was no more trouble on this district would be ridiculous, for there was plenty; but we had overcome the worst. Ortega's influence was waning, and the people began to throw off the yoke with which they had been oppressed. They had had few educational, social or economic opportunities, and it was time their status was improved.

Much more could be told of adventurous activities, but I'll end this narrative of the Cuba District when it was wild and wooly by saying that in August I was assigned to batch with Bletcher at Blue Bird station, and work the south end of the District from there. Sypher was sent a few miles north of Cuba where the Forest

Service rented him quarters and a pasture. From there he would handle the north end.

In October I was transferred to the Pecos National Forest which had been under administration for many years. It was a welcome change.

6 OLD RED WAS ALL DOG

OLD RED was one of a litter of ten. I picked him out and took him home when he was only three weeks old. We called the sad-eyed, long-eared, wrinkled-faced, red pup Old Red right from the start. The name just naturally seemed to fit him. The pup's facial expression was one of sadness and premature wisdom and understanding. He was very homely, and yet quite handsome, depending upon one's point of view.

Old Red's sire was a big, aggressive, grizzly, red blood-hound. His mother was a small, bright-eyed, red-bone bitch. Both were well-trained, cold-trailing hunting dogs.

My time was fully taken up with my job as a U. S. Forest Service ranger—stationed in what is now the Pecos division of the Santa Fe National Forest, and in looking after my young wife and infant son. Actually, I had no more need for a hound pup than I had for a wooden leg. But I loved a good bobcat and mountain-lion dog, and this pup looked to me as if he had what it takes to make one.

So when Andy Jackson offered to give me one of a litter of well-bred pups, I picked out Old Red. My young wife and I had not been married long enough for her to object. Instead, she started right in to help train him, despite having her hands full caring for our baby boy, only a few months older than the pup.

Yes, we really did start to train that pup—train him to trail—by the time he was a month old. We would offer him a piece of raw meat, then take it away. Then, while one of us held him with his eyes covered, the other one would drag the piece of raw meat around the kitchen floor and leave it out of sight behind a table leg or something.

When Old Red was turned loose he would pick up the meat scent on the floor and waddle around following it at a snail's pace, with his nose to the floor and his long ears dragging it on either side. At last he would work out the trail and find the piece of meat, and we would let him have it as his reward. At first the meat was pressed firmly against the linoleum and dragged only a few feet so it would leave a good scent. Gradually, as Old Red's training ability developed, we made longer and lighter drags. By the time he was two months old he would follow a meat drag all around the yard, and from then on he learned to work out complicated, criss-crossed trails.

The next step was to teach him to chase Inky, our big black cat. Inky wasn't afraid of any little old long-eared pup, and we would have to say "Scat!" to get him to run so the pup could chase him from one room to another. When Old Red was three months old we would take him and Inky out on the hill a couple of hundred yards from the house and turn Inky loose and let him get out of sight in the brush. Then Old Red would be released and encouraged to follow the cat's trail wherever it might lead.

He quickly learned to pick up the scent and follow on until he found his quarry. Sometimes Inky would go straight to the house and Old Red would bring him to bay under the porch. Other times Inky would stop in the brush and defy the pup to do anything about it. In that event, Old Red would bark and jump at the cat, and duck back quickly to avoid Inky's sharp claws.

It wasn't long, though, until Old Red got a little too aggressive. One day he forced Inky to climb a tree and perch on a low branch just out of reach. Boy, did that long-eared pup make a fuss about that! From a little distance one would have thought a whole pack of hounds had a lion up a tree, as the pup frantically barked and bayed, with the changeable tones of his adolescent voice, for all he was worth. It surely looked then as if he had the makings of a good lion and bobcat dog. And naturally we were proud of him.

Not long after that I was transferred to a remote station on the Carson National Forest in the high, cold country of northern New Mexico. The late Dr. Aldo Leopold, nationally known conservationist, was my new forest supervisor. That was in December, 1912, when Old Red was about five months old.

The pup followed me everywhere I went and soon learned to help me find my saddle horses in the brushy horse pasture. After a little encouragement he would pick up the scent of the horse tracks and follow them up, baying regularly as he slowly followed the route taken by the ponies during the night's grazing.

By the time Old Red was seven months old he was a big handsome fellow with exceptionally long ears and sad, intelligent eyes. His color was solid red with just a slight yellowish tinge, except that in the center of his breast there was a little diamond-shaped patch of white, and two toes on the right front foot were white also. He was a good-looking, and as good a prospect for a sure, cold-nosed hunting dog, as one could ask for. Then we had an accident that came very near ending his career.

I had ridden a few miles from the ranger station to run out some survey lines, and Old Red had followed me as usual. I left Nig, my saddle horse, tied to a tree while I worked afoot for several hours. When I got back I cinched up the saddle, maybe a bit too tight, and got on as Old Red frolicked playfully around the horse. As I touched spurs to Nig's sides to turn him toward home, he suddenly tried to buck me off, and it was all I could do to keep my seat in the saddle. Old Red got in the way —and Nig's shod hoofs came down on top of him.

When I finally got Nig straightened out, Old Red was lying there howling feebly and unable to get up. Examination showed that his back, just above the loins, was broken. He also had a couple of broken ribs. I feared the dog was ruined, and I came near shooting him right there to put him out of his misery. Someway, though, I couldn't quite bring myself to do it. Instead, I decided to carry the pup home and see what we could do for him.

I laid Old Red on top of a boulder where I could reach him from the saddle, got on again, gathered him up in my arms, and rode slowly home.

We cared for Old Red in every way we knew how, but for weeks he lay on a blanket behind the kitchen stove unable to raise his hindquarters off the floor. Finally when I came home one evening my wife ran out to the barn where I was unsaddling my horse and joyfully exclaimed, "Old Red's been walking today! He can get up all by himself."

That was good news for sure. Old Red continued to improve and in another two months he could get around pretty well and follow me on short trips. But he never regained full control of his hindquarters. They would sway first to one side and then the other as he walked or ran. His hind feet simply wouldn't follow his front feet. To see him travel reminded one of a wagon with a broken coupling pole going down the road. But someway or another, his hindquarters always managed to keep up, even though following a meandering route. He was comical and pitiful, too, but all the same I was glad I had not shot him.

My first chance to try Old Red on a bobcat came one September day when he was fourteen months old. I was riding by some beaver dams in Cleveland Gulch, three miles from the Cow Creek Ranger Station, late in the afternoon, with Old Red following a few yards behind. Suddenly, I saw a large bobcat coming down the canyon toward us. The cat had not spotted us, and when I dismounted from Nig I found the beaver dam was high enough to hide us from the cat.

Sneaking up to the dam so I could look over it without being seen, I let the cat come on until he was right across the beaver pond not more than 100 feet from me. Then I shot him with my .32/20 Colt six-shooter, partly breaking him down in the loins. He plunged up the hill, half dragging his hind parts off into the brush.

I let him alone for about ten minutes; then I led Old Red over and put him on the bloody trail. When he smelled the blood and the scent of the cat, he took to the trail in full cry with a high-tuned, excited voice like an experienced trail hound. A hundred yards or so up the hill Old Red got the surprise of his life when he ran

92

smack into the wounded bobcat crouching against a big log. The first that Old Red knew he had caught up to the bobcat was when he got a stinging swipe across the nose with four powerful, sharp claws that left their deep and bloody marks.

Old Red, howling as if he had been half killed, ducked back down the hill with his tail between his legs. But before he got to me he turned, went back, and began barking at the cat from a safe distance.

I have found that in training a young hunting dog the best way to stimulate interest is to enter personally, (or at least pretend to) into the dog's chase or fight with a cat, bear, or lion. So I went on up and got a club and beat the ground and bushes all around the bobcat, acting as if I were fighting it at close quarters and urging the pup to get into the fight. Thus encouraged, in only a few moments Old Red was in the thick of things. He would go in and grab the bobcat's hindquarters, then dodge back to avoid having his face clawed again.

When I thought Old Red had had a good lesson I shot the bobcat in the head. The pup went in at once and wooled the big cat around with great satisfaction, despite his bloody nose.

Old Red's wobbly hindquarters, with resultant moderate and uncertain gait, didn't keep him from chasing lots of prairie dogs. I let him do so to his heart's content, for I thought perhaps the exercise would strengthen and stabilize his injured back, but he never got much better.

One day Old Red had the misfortune to grab the hind end of a big fat prairie dog just as it was about to duck into its hole. No sooner had Old Red caught it and given it one good shake than the prairie dog clamped its long, razor-sharp incisors into Old Red's left ear two

inches from the end. Old Red made the mistake of turning the prairie dog loose, but the prairie dog didn't
reciprocate. Instead, it held on as Old Red tried to shake
it off, swinging it in a big circle around his head. All
the while howling as if he were being beaten to death.
The prairie dog held on until its hold tore out, splitting
the end of the ear into two strips which never did grow
back together. After that Old Red continued to chase
prairie dogs but was careful not to catch another one.
He learned his lessons fast.

My daily horseback trips (we had no cars and
mighty few roads in the national forests in those days)
frequently took me through areas where there were
deer and wild turkey, although they were less plentiful
then than now. A hound naturally likes to run deer; and
breaking lion, bear, and cat dogs from trailing deer is a
major problem. Some dogs never can be broken. Old
Red was different. He never did run a deer. The first
few times he put his nose to a deer track, I scolded him
and called to him to come and leave it alone. He very
soon got so he paid no attention whatever to a deer or
a deer track.

Occasionally he would find a porcupine, but once
he learned that the quills were unpleasant he would
simply hold the porky at bay until I came up to shoot
it. Porcupines were plentiful and quite destructive to
timber; and we rangers, as well as the ranchers, killed
them on sight.

In November, 1913, when Old Red was sixteen
months old, there was a sudden heavy snowfall which
reached a depth of about fourteen inches. It quit snowing about noon, and Charlie Gilbert, a young man employed by the Forest Service to trap wolves which were

then doing a lot of damage to livestock in the region, came by the ranger station and suggested that we take Old Red and go bobcat hunting.

That was fine with me, so we rode three or four miles over to some rough hilly country on the Onofre Valdez sheep range, where we knew some bobcats had been ranging. The snow was deep and heavy, making traveling difficult for the horses—and harder still for Old Red with his wobbly hindquarters, even though he followed in the trail broken by the horses. The snow hung wet and heavy on bushes and branches of trees, but our leather chaps and heavy coats kept us dry, except that snow got into the front and back of the saddles as we leaned over first to one side and then the other to miss snow-laden branches.

A wet seat is not too pleasant a sensation, but we forgot all about that when we suddenly came to where several bobcats had plowed through the snow in single file sometime after it had stopped snowing. Old Red got the hot scent of the bobcat tracks about the same time that we saw them, and needed no encouragement to take up the chase. He at once gave tongue and bounded off on the trail at a surprising speed, his hind feet as usual landing several inches first to one side and then the other of the tracks made by his front feet.

"To hear that hound bellow and see all those tracks he makes," Charlie remarked as we followed on, "it appears like we have a whole pack of dogs!" And that is just what it did seem like, but actually Old Red was all alone doing his stuff like a veteran.

Treeing a bobcat isn't hard in that kind of snow, and it wasn't long before we recognized the different tone of voice as Old Red's bellowing changed to sharp staccato barking. He was barking treed at his first bobcat. He was only a quarter of a mile ahead of us; but someway, when dogs bark treed one always has to put spurs and hurry on up to see what, where, and how it is.

We loped our ponies through the brush and over snow-covered rocks to where Old Red was talking enthusiastically up a little brushy pine tree not more than thirty feet tall. At first we could see nothing up in the snow-laden branches, but Old Red said he was sure, and there was the track of but one cat going on past the tree.

We got off and looked more carefully. Then, one after another, we discovered three half-grown bobcats crouching well out on limbs where they were almost completely hidden by the heavy snow that clung to the branches. The first bobcat that Old Red treed was triplets! We were proud of his performance — and he seemed to feel the same. One after the other Charlie shot the half-grown cats out with his .25/35 rifle. Old Red jumped right in the middle of each one as it hit the ground and had fun wooling them around there in the deep snow.

But we didn't delay long. Tying the cats on the backs of our saddles, we sicked Old Red on the mother cat's trail, and after a brief moment of indecision he took out after her as fast as he could make it through the heavy snow. Failing to realize that there was a fourth cat in addition to the three he had put up the tree was Old Red's only mistake on this hunt. He never made that kind of error again.

The chase after the mother cat was a bit more difficult than treeing the three kittens had been. She got into some cliffs where the going for Old Red was pretty tough. But he stayed with it, despite difficulties and his physical handicap, and at last, just at dusk, forced the old lady to take a tree. Charlie shot her, tied her on the back of his saddle, and we started home well satisfied with our afternoon's work and mighty proud of Old Red's performance.

Before we reached home Old Red lagged farther and farther behind. He was just about played out. We waited for him to catch up and I took him up on the horse in front of me and carried him on in. He had earned a ride.

After that chase Old Red took bobcats in his stride, but occasionally he'd lose one because he couldn't negotiate very rough or brushy country fast enough. In cat hunting he developed a remarkable technique which he figured out all by himself. Frequently, while on the track of one bobcat, he would encounter the track of another one crossing it. Old Red never missed the second track, but would stop and test it out carefully. If it wasn't made by the cat he'd been following he would pass it up, even though it might be much more recent, and continue on the original trail. But if it was the same cat crossing its own track he would follow the fresher scent without hesitation. I had the opportunity to check him many times in snow trails, and he always stayed with the cat he started after.

How extremely sensitive must be the nose of a dog to be able to distinguish between the track scent of two different cats! Perhaps more remarkable is the dog's ability to reason out the situation and decide which track to follow. My admiration for a good cold-nosed dog is unbounded, and I never ceased to marvel at Old Red's unusual abilities.

Fifty-odd years ago there were lots of lobo wolves, coyotes, and bobcats in the Amarilla Division of the Carson National Forest, but mountain lions were rather scarce. Hence, when Old Red's chance to stage a solo lion hunt came unexpectedly in January, 1914, when he was but eighteen months old, I welcomed the opportunity for Old Red.

One cold clear morning—with my .32 Winchester Special rifle in the scabbard and Old Red following along behind, wobbly as usual — I set out on Nig around the hill to where a rancher had just reported seeing the tracks of four lobo wolves. Surprise! Surprise! Just imagine my elation when, upon arriving at the spot, I saw that the tracks weren't made by wolves but by a whole family of mountain lions! Such luck was better by far than I could have hoped for.

Despite the fact that the lion family had passed by three days before, I was dead sure we were due for some excitement that day or the next. The snow lay twelve or fifteen inches deep in the timber on the north exposure, while the southerly slopes were barren. Under those conditions, Old Red surely could work out the three-day-old tracks without too much difficulty.

When Old Red, who had lagged behind, caught up with me, I said not a word to him, for I wanted to see what his independent reaction to his first lion track would be. He put his nose into the round, four-toed prints in the snow and smelled them deliberately. His tail began to wag with pleasure, slowly at first, then gradually faster and with more emphasis, like a bandmaster's baton as the music quickens pace.

Old Red took a few steps on the trail and sniffed the lion tracks carefully again. Then, with body tense, and tail, beating time to the hound song he was about to voice, he looked back over his shoulder at me and slightly raised the base of his long red ears as if to ask, "Shall I go on?"

I made neither sign nor sound, just left it to Old Red to make his own decision. He deliberately took a few steps forward and sniffed the tracks again and again. Next he looked back at me once more with an expression that said, "You didn't say no." Then he turned to the tracks, let go with a long-drawn-out bawl — and set off with determined enthusiasm in pursuit of the four lions.

To come upon the trail of a female lion with three young ones is not unusual. But a trail such as this — consisting of papa lion, mamma lion, and their two half-grown kittens — is a rather rare occurrence. On this occasion no group composition could have suited me better unless it had included even more specimens of the species *Felis concolor*.

Off through the timber Old Red went, giving tongue freely and with such vigor that the canyons echoed with the legato music. Ducking and dodging the saplings and low spruce limbs, Nig and I followed on, trying to keep up. In spite of our efforts, Old Red steadily increased his lead until he came to a stretch of barren, frozen ground where he had a little difficulty with the three-day-old tracks. He worked them out without help, though, and speeded up again when he hit the snow over the top of the next ridge.

For several hours we followed the meandering trail over ridges and across canyons without any noticeable freshening of the tracks until finally, in a little glade on a flat ridge top, we found where the lions had killed and eaten a porcupine. They had spent at least one whole day right there. There were several beds under trees at the edge of the glade, and the whole area was tramped down where the youngsters had been playing.

A large aspen out in the opening had been broken

off by the wind, leaving a stump about ten feet high with the rest of the tree trunk still attached and sloping off to the ground for twenty-five or thirty feet. Those playful little longtails had climbed up this fallen tree trunk to the top of the stump and jumped off dozens of times. The tracks in the soft, wet snow recorded their antics as plainly as a written record would have.

From this spot on, the trail was noticeably fresher and much easier for Old Red to follow across the next barren slope. For half an hour we made good time; then things began to happen fast. Crossing a ridge into dense spruce and fir timber, all of a sudden we came to where the lions had killed a big buck deer, probably two days before, but they had stayed there feasting on fresh venison until practically nothing but the head and the heavier bones of the carcass were left.

Old Red jumped the female lion right there, and to judge from the prints in the snow of the long leaps she made, she ran off down the hill at a tremendous speed. The dog was hard at her heels, but she ran downhill nearly a mile before she took to a big fir tree for safety. Old Red was fonder of bellowing and barking on a trail than any other hound I have ever seen, and the music he made on that hot chase down through the timber was something to hear. When he treed the lioness, he cut loose more vigorously than ever as he shifted from an excited legato to frantic staccato barking. When I came up, Old Red acted beside himself with joy, partly because of what he had done, and partly in anticipation of a chance to wool the lion.

Because of the density of the forest, I had to get right under the fir tree to see her. But there she was, thirty feet up, her full, white belly resting across a couple of stout limbs and her front feet draped over a third one, while her long, black-tipped tail and one hind leg hung down clumsily. The other hind foot was braced against the tree trunk to keep her from sliding off the branches. She was panting hard from the long run, and although her tawny sides were scarcely visible, her round gray head made an excellent target as she nervously looked straight down at us.

Old Red jumped all over me in his excitement when I drew the rifle from its scabbard and started to aim, for he knew very well what that meant. Then he resumed his barking up the tree. At the crack of the rifle the lioness stiffened and quivered for a moment, then relaxed and slid slowly backward off the limbs on which she was resting. She came tumbling down through the branches to land at the base of the tree only a few feet from us.

Old Red instantly pounced upon the lifeless body and, with deep-throated growls, wooled it off down the steep slope until it lodged against a log. At first he bit at her flanks, then went to her neck and chewed and chewed as if he thought that was necessary to finish the job. At any rate, he was having fun.

Leaving the lioness right there, we climbed back up the long steep slope to where we had first jumped her. Old Red went on ahead, for this time he knew there were more lions and he was eager to pick up their tracks. That didn't take long; he was giving out steadily with his resonant voice before I got there.

The three lions, I found, had gone leisurely around the hillside before we jumped the female at the deer carcass. I hoped Old Red would single out papa lion's track and tree him next, for otherwise he might travel a long way while we were messing with the younger ones.

101

But this was Old Red's field trial, so to speak. I was just tagging along to do the shooting. So I made no effort to control the situation or to interfere with him in any way.

They must have heard us jump the mother, for the three lions were already about half a mile around the hill. There they had separated. Papa lion had quickened his pace and gone up the hill, while the young ones had turned back down. Old Red chose the tracks of the two cubs and put in after them as fast as he could go, making noise enough for a whole pack of hounds. I touched spurs to Nig's sides and hurried on. Soon, away off down in the canyon, Old Red barked treed for the second time that day; and, recklessly smashing through the aspen and spruce thickets, I rode to him.

Old Red was talking straight up at a yellowish-red, half-grown lion clinging precariously, just a few feet above his reach, to the trunk of a small spruce tree. We made quick work of the little sixty-pound lion, and when Old Red had wooled the carcass around a moment and saw that it was really lifeless, he voluntarily left off and started back uphill to find the other cub.

It wasn't long until the woods again began to ring with Old Red's jubilant baying on the trail. This young lion made a little circle, then doubled back toward the place where we had killed the mother. It made quite a run but finally treed over in the next canyon at the edge of an open park where an old road comes up from Tusas Creek. The cub proved to be a female, a little smaller but more contrasting in color than its brother. Both were very fat and their fur was much longer than the mother's.

Old Red was getting mighty tired and Nig was lathered with sweat and badly winded from more than an hour of hard riding over steep, rough, snow-covered country in the time since we had jumped the first lion. So I unsaddled to let Nig cool off and rest for an hour before setting out on what I anticipated would be our hardest chase; for with all the fuss we had made it was certain that the old male lion was putting distance between us.

Old Red, though obviously tired, was still very much excited — and hugely pleased with himself. He would curl up on the saddle blankets for a moment, then get up, trot over to inspect the little lion where it lay near by, and come back to where I was sitting on some dry pine needles with my back to a big tree, and whine and try to lick my face as much as to say, "Just look what I did!"

When Nig had got his wind and dried off, I saddled him up and rode toward the spot where papa lion had abandoned the youngsters to seek his own safety. As before, Old Red took the lead and was 100 yards or more ahead of me when I heard him bellow long and loud, with a rising inflection to his resonant voice — signifying that he had found sign, and was off on Big Tom's trail.

It led up the hill into deeper snow, making the going tougher for Old Red and slowing him down so that I could almost keep up with him. Just before topping out on the main divide, Big Tom turned to the right through the spruce and aspen thickets at the heads of side draws that led to the main canyon. The going was plenty difficult for dog, horse, and man alike, but we kept on and on until at last we crossed over into the head of Deer Trail Canyon. From there an old rutted road leads over the divide to the ghost town of Hopewell, which once was thronged with miners.

The snow was belly-deep to my horse, and Big Tom was evidently having a hard time breaking trail. Old Red, taking advantage of the path the lion had made in wallowing through the snow, was crowding him ever closer and closer, and talking to him at every jump. Big Tom suddenly gave up his attempt to get over the divide and doubled back sharply down the hill in a desperate effort to get away. Happily, as the cat came back near his own track Old Red picked up the body scent and cut across toward him, thus gaining so much distance so suddenly that the longtail gave up the flight and took refuge in a big fir tree.

I imagine Big Tom was greatly surprised to see only one dog come up to the tree, for as usual Old Red had sounded like half a dozen hounds on the trail. In any case, there Big Tom was, standing straight and defiant on a limb about twenty feet up, waving his tail slowly from side to side, and panting with open mouth as he looked down upon his lone tormentor.

Truly, the lion with his big, round gray head, his brownish-red back, tawny sides, white belly, stout grayish legs, and long black-tasseled tail made a wonderful picture as he stood there balanced precariously on a limb. But the sun was setting and there was no time to waste in admiration of the predator, however fine a specimen he might be. One thing was very certain—he would kill no more stock or deer.

When I had shot him and Old Red had finished chewing on his fourth and biggest lion for the day, I packed the lion on my saddle horse and set out afoot across the ridges to where we had killed the last cub, as that was directly on the route home. It was dark when we reached the little carcass and put Big Tom's beside it, so that we could return later with a sled to pick up the whole family.

As we went on to the ranger station, Old Red was so tired that once more I carried him on the horse in front of me. That was pretty hard on Nig, for I had ridden him unmercifully hard in bad country and deep snow that day. But I recalled that it had been his hoofs, while he had been foolishly exhibiting his surplus energy a year before that had crippled Old Red for life.

It was very late when we got to the ranger station. My wife was even more pleased than I when I told her how wonderful Old Red had been on his first lion hunt. We were mighty proud of Old Red, for treeing a family of mountain lions in one day was a fine record for an eighteen-month-old hound pup to hang up alone.

Next morning Charlie Gilbert came by and went with me after the lions. We left Old Red at home, for he was so stiff and sore in his back and hindquarters that he could hardly walk, but upon our return Old Red claimed the lions as his own, and when some of the neighbors came over to see our trophies he wouldn't let them come near.

All that January it snowed quite a lot and the whole country was white. Then on the last day of the month we had another ten-inch snow, followed by two nights and a day of very high wind which drifted the snow badly and covered up all wilderness tracks except those in the most sheltered spots. Riding across to the native village of Petaca after the blow died down, we came upon a male lion's track in a deep canyon where the wind had not struck. The track had been made two nights before, so most of it had been subjected to at least a night and a day of drifting snow.

Old Red took out at once on the 36-hour-old track and followed it without difficulty for some distance. Then the track led out up a ridge toward a high, rock-rimmed *mesa*. The going got pretty hard along the wind-swept ridge, but in some way Old Red finally worked things out as far as the rimrock. There he had quite a time finding where the lion had gone.

After a while he found where the lion had come up through a break in the cliff and out onto the snow-covered plateau. That is, the cat had come out there some thirty-six hours before, when the snow was fresh and untouched by the wind.

Not a track was visible now anywhere. I hadn't much idea whether the lion had followed the rim of the *mesa* —and if so, whether he'd gone to the right or left—or had proceeded straight across to another canyon a mile beyond. While I pondered which way to go to cut for sign in less windy spots, Old Red began working the scent right out across the snow-covered *mesa*. I sat on my horse and watched him in amazement, then followed on, keeping thirty or forty paces behind, while he deliberately and laboriously followed the track, though it had been completely filled in and every vestige of it obliterated by the drifting snow.

That long-eared hound dog would smell every twig of brush, weed, and protruding rock along the route. Once in a while he would thus pick up the scent of the lion where its side or tail had touched some object above snow level. To verify the faint scent on the brush or rocks, Old Red would at once stick his nose way down into the snow at that point and shift it to one side or the other, or forward or back, until he finally found a buried footprint and got the sure lion scent from it. Then he would raise his wet snowy head and bawl long and loud, to let the world know he was on the track for sure.

After that he would go straight ahead a few paces and again begin testing brush, low-hanging tree limbs, and jutting volcanic rocks. He would keep this up until he picked up the dim scent again. Again he would prove he was right by finding the track buried deep under the wind-packed snow.

Thus slowly, patiently, but surely, Old Red worked that deeply snowed-in track clear across the mile-wide *mesa*—worked it at a turtle's speed of about a quarter of a mile an hour. I marveled at his superlative sense of smell and his superior faculties for making full use of it.

At last, dropping off the *mesa* into a timbered slope, we found where the lion had killed a deer about a day and a half before. But the tracks leading away from the hill down the slope were hot fresh, as if the lion had just moved on at our approach. Old Red took out down-hill at top speed, baying steadily, head high, and paying no attention whatever to the track, as I sat on my horse and watched the opposite hillside.

Soon I saw the tawny beast running up out of the canyon toward the rimrock above. Old Red, in hot pursuit, lost distance at first; but as the longtail, his belly packed with venison, became winded from his first burst of speed, the dog gradually closed the distance between them. The lion succeeded in reaching the base of the rimrock and started around it, but Old Red was gaining and talking so loud and steadily that the longtail couldn't take it and quickly sought out a pinon tree for safety. I rode around there, shot him and took him to the station.

It was indeed a thrilling race that I had had the rare opportunity of witnessing. But the race itself was a routine affair compared with the superb job Old Red did in following a cold, completely snowed-in lion track. Never before, nor since, have I seen trailing to equal it.

When spring came and forest-ranger work piled up so that all thought of hunting predators had to be dismissed, Old Red's score stood at nineteen bobcats and five mountain lions—treed all by himself. Not bad, we thought, for a long-eared, crippled-back pup not yet two years old!

That fall I was promoted to Deputy Supervisor with headquarters at Taos and thereafter had little opportunity to hunt, but did take another lion and several bobcats. After being stolen for two years we got Old Red back in poor condition. He soon got distemper and despite all we could do, we lost the best hunting hound that anyone ever had.

ASSISTANT RANGER TO FOREST SUPERVISOR

7

AFTER ten months on the Cuba District my fellow Ranger, A. W. Sypher, and I had the situation under control so that it seemed that one man would be able to handle it. Sypher was left in charge and I was transferred to the Pecos, now a division of the Santa Fe National Forest. I was delighted because that country had been my stomping ground, and I would work under my old friend, Tom Stewart, who had just been made Forest Supervisor.

I was assigned to the Pecos District and batched alone that winter. I rode a lot getting acquainted with my district and the people, and checking for trespassing livestock and illegal cutting of timber. In the early days there was much of that sort of thing going on. I also had charge of a timber sale—marking trees to be cut, scaling logs, counting ties, measuring pilings, and overseeing brush disposal. In February, all Rangers began taking applications for grazing permits from stockmen and settlers living on private lands within and near the Forest.

H. S. Arnold was a large grazing permittee whose ranch was a big block of land in the Chaparrito-Cow Creek area. I had never met Mr. Arnold and knew nothing of his family. In mid February I rode to his home on Chaparrito to get his grazing application for the ensuing season. Mrs. Arnold told me he was on Cow Creek bailing hay, so I rode on over there. At the bottom of the hill I saw activity down the canyon by the haystacks.

When I headed my horse that way, a movement behind a clump of willows on the creek bank caught my eye. Why I was impelled to ride over to see what it was, I don't know. To my surprise and embarrassment there was the doggon', prettiest, sixteen-year old girl I have ever seen! She was embarrassed too, because she was fishing out of season, without a license, through the ice and using a horse-hair snare, all of which was against the law. She had a nice string of cutthroat trout, too. I, as a Forest Ranger, was a Deputy Game Warden. Oh, my!

The age of chivalry was not dead, and neither was that of honor. I had taken an oath of office to enforce the game laws without fear or favor. But now I couldn't enforce the law without fear—fear I'd wreck my chances —for the instant I saw her my mind was made up. I had a talk with her dad and he, good naturedly, contended that she was too young to be put in jail and he was too poor to pay a fine. The up-shot was that she was sort of remanded to my custody, and she's been fishing with me ever since. But, Ethel says, "I never violated the law again, just see what happened to me the first time!"

I am reputed to be a fair public speaker, and when one of my grandsons asked me how I learned to talk in public I said, "When I was courting your grandmother she lived on a ranch fifteen miles from the Ranger Station. Her dad was one of a dozen subscribers on a Forest Service telephone line, each of which had a special ring. The Arnold ring was a short, a long and a short. I called

my girl up often, and it got so when I'd ring a short, a
a long and a short a dozen receivers would come down
click, clickity, click, and there I was learning to talk in
public."

In April, 1910, I'd been assigned to build a telephone
line from Glorieta to Panchuela Ranger Station, a distance of twenty-eight miles. I'd seen a few telephone lines
but had never had any experience building one. I studied
the manual to learn how to splice the heavy No. 9 wire,
how to tie it to the insulators and how to climb the poles.
It said, "set climbers spurs firmly in the pole, keep body
at arms length from pole, lean back on safety belt and
keep knees away from the pole." I climbed my first
twenty-four foot pole all right. But when I got to the
top and looked down I felt insecure and instinctively
hugged the pole with my knees. That of course, caused
the hooks to come out and I burned that pole all the way
to the ground. Oh, how I wished for my chaps. I did all
right after that; my knees were too sore to hug a pole.

I had a crew of five Spanish-Americans, and a black
cowboy called Nigger Jim cooking for us as we camped
along the line route. Jim was smart, a good cook and a
good worker. He was also a professional bronco rider.

A curious old man visited camp and we explained
to him that the line would enable us to talk from Panchuela Station to Pecos. He picked up a piece of the wire
and carefully examined the end of it and said, *"No puede
hablar porque no tiene abujero.* You can't talk through
it because there is no hole in it." After the line was in
operation I took him to a wall phone in Pecos and had
him talk to Mr. Stewart at Panchuela. He went away
shaking his head and muttering, *"Pero como, como.* But
how, how."

Five miles from Panchuela Station there was a mile-long strip of land owned by a huge, six-foot-four miner named Alexander who refused to grant a right-of-way across his land. We completed the line to his property, skipped it and finished to the Ranger Station.

We were camped adjacent to his property. Poles, wire and other equipment were there ready to close the hiatus. Supervisor Stewart went to Las Vegas to get the County Commissioners to grant an easement along the road right-of-way, and Alexander went along to protest it. Stewart gave me explicit instructions not to start the job until he got back, which he said would be the next day. But he didn't show up next day, nor the next nor the next, and we were getting pretty tired sitting around waiting.

The evening of the third day Nigger Jim said, "Mr. Barker, what you 'spose old Alex would do if'n he comes back and finds the line done built?"

I said, "I reckon we'd be in a peck of trouble, you heard what Stewart said."

'I know Mr. Stewart, don't you fret none 'bout what he gonna do," Jim said, "I betcha old Alex won't darst tear down no Govamint propity. Let's do it, I'll dig post holes."

With Jim's needling, next morning by daybreak we'd had breakfast and all hands were working hard to complete the line before Stewart and Alexander got back. And we finished just in time. I thought sure that Stewart would have an easement, but he didn't.

Alexander started raising hell with us and making dire threats. Jim said, "No use you talk that way, Mr. Alex, you can't whip seven of us."

112

Stewart took me to task severly for disobeying his orders. I felt real bad and thought from the rough way that he talked I'd be fired. But as soon as Alexander rode out of hearing, Tom got off his horse, put his arm around my shoulder and said, "Elliott, that's the smartest thing you ever did. I failed to get a right-of-way but let's see that big S B tear down Government property."

Jim had it figured right. Within a month Alexander had me to dinner with him and applied for a phone connection on the line.

During that summer and the next we maintained the Supervisor's headquarters at Panchuela Ranger Station. Work on my district was normal, nothing exciting. We laid out a number of trails and built them and strung a telephone line to Grass Mountain fire lookout station. That, and the grazing and timber sale work kept us humping. Actually Tom Stewart liked field work so much better than he did the office that, for a great deal of the time, he did my field work and had me do his office work. We had a Deputy Supervisor but he was on special timber work assignments most of the time.

I had started as Assistant Forest Ranger at $75.00 a month with no quarters nor horse feed allowance. In 1910 I was promoted to $91.66 and by the spring of 1911 I had the title of Forest Ranger at a salary of $100.00 per month and quarters furnished. That wasn't much but I persuaded Ethel Arnold to share it with me, and on May 17, 1911, we were married. What happened for a while after that is kind of hazy. But I suppose I kept on building trails, riding the livestock ranges, looking after timber sales, and surveying Forest homesteads.

We lived in Santa Fe the winter of 1911-1912, and

I recall two special assignments. One was a thirty-day job with two helpers tracing out old section lines on about fifty miles of hitherto unmarked Forest boundary and posting it. The other was two weeks with a lion hunter, S. L. Fisher, to stop some severe horse killing that was going on. We succeeded in taking four large male lions in the two weeks. That stopped the killing for a year or two. We had some rugged chases with good hounds which I enjoyed very much.

In June 1912, our son Roy was born, and that fall I was transferred to the Carson National Forest. Our first station was at Servilleta ten miles from the nearest settlement at Tres Piedras, where the Supervisor's office was located. All there was at Servilleta was the Ranger Station and the Denver and Rio Grande narrow gauge railway station. I made the four-day trip horseback with pack horse carrying bedroll and camp outfit, and shipped our meager household goods by railway freight.

Ethel, with our six-months old son, was to come a few days later on the little train. It happened that the very afternoon she was to arrive, a lady Hippie—only we called people who looked like that tramps in those days—came to the Ranger Station asking for food and a place to spend the night. I fixed her something to eat, then I met the train.

As we approached the Ranger Station there was that disreputable looking character standing in the door. Now Ethel does not swear, but as I remember it she said something like, "What the hell goes on here?" Anyway they got acquainted and, it being too far to get to Tres Piedras that night, she slept in my camp bed. The pedestrian turned out to be intelligent and well-educated and was walking across the country to prove something or an-

114

other. We were harrassed by tramps there as it was far between stops.

That was a bleak, cold country, but pinon and juniper firewood for stoves and fireplaces was plentiful. The only domestic and horse water was brought in each week in a wooden railway tank car. Jack rabbits and cottontails were in great abundance. I could stand on the front porch any morning and shoot a half dozen with my .22 rifle if I chose. Coyotes were exceedingly plentiful, also, but had no reducing effect on the rabbit population. However, in the winter of 1915-16 a disease killed off practically all jacks and cottontails, and coyotes killed a lot of deer and raised more hell with sheep than ever. There were a considerable number of lobo wolves in the general area.

Aldo Leopold, who was a great conservationist and later became the nation's greatest authority on wildlife management, was the Forest Supervisor. That was fortunate because my hobby had always been wildlife, and I was glad I had been transferred. Looking back, I feel that it was a great privilege to work under that great man. Our relations at once became most cordial, and I am sure that our close association had a lasting influence on my life. Our friendship lasted right up to his death.

That winter I traced out and posted a lot of Forest boundary, and rode a lot to prevent trespass by sheep wintering on adjacent public lands. They'd edge over every chance they got. In the spring I had to visit a half dozen villages on my district to take grazing applications. There were lots of cattle and even more sheep on my district.

Supervisor Leopold rode with me quite often help-

115

ing me to get acquainted with my district. We discussed game and predators a lot, and made field observations. One day on an open pine *mesa* with a foot of snow on the ground we came across the track of a big dog wolf. He had been traveling in the characteristic jog trot and Leopold was impressed by the even spacing of the tracks and the perfectly straight line they followed. Checking with a stick we found that there was not a half inch variation in the length of his steps. I had noted that ofen.

Ninety per cent of the residents of my district were Spanish-Americans, most of whom spoke little or no English. For me that was no handicap, for I spoke their language fluently and they were more cordial and cooperative with me than they were with those who did not speak Spanish. This contributed to better public relations.

One day I was crossing Petaca Mesa and met a young man afoot and carrying a rope. When I spoke to him in Spanish he began talking excitedly as tears ran down his cheeks. He said he had come up there to get his saddle horse only to find that a pack of wolves had killed him the night before and had feasted on him. He was really shook up. I sympathized with him for my saddle horses had always been an intimate part of my life.

I back tracked him in the six-inch snow to his dead horse and found that a pack of five wolves had done the job. Their tracks were an open book to read how they caught and killed the nice, fat, young saddle horse. I had only my .44 Colt six-shooter, but I took up their tracks and followed for several miles. Finally I caught up with them bedded down in pinon timber below a *malpais* rim. I emptied the pistol at them and wounded two, but they got away. From then on I carried my .32 Winchester Special rifle.

Not long after that I came across a cow that three wolves had killed the night before. I followed the tracks leading away in about a foot of snow. Soon I found where they had been bedded and had left only moments before. It was now snowing and getting late, but I followed on hoping to overtake them before dark. That I did, and got a standing shot and knocked one flat. I glimpsed the others running for the *mesa* rim and I loped to it and urgently rode along it until dusk trying to get a shot.

When I came back I discovered that the one I'd shot had got up and headed for the rim, too, leaving a very bloody trail. It was now quite dark and snowing fast, so I headed for home intending to come back in the morning and follow up the mortally wounded bugger.

It snowed and blew for two days and nights. Finally when I forced my horse to flounder through the drifts to the spot no vestige of the bloody trail could be found. These incidents are typical of many experiences I had with lobo wolves on my district.

In the spring of 1913 we moved from Servilleta to Cow Creek Ranger Station, nine miles west of Tres Piedras and nearer the center of the district. It was a pleasant site at the base of Tusas Mountain. The house was built of logs, poorly chinked and with rough, twelve inch boards for a floor. Water had to be drawn from a well and there was no plumbing, just drafty outside toilet — not much of a place to bring a young woman with a year-old baby. But then, as it always has been, wherever my work has taken me Ethel has loyally gone along and put up with it and me.

There was a timber sale for which I had to mark timber, sometimes on snowshoes, scale logs and check

117

brush disposal. I had many Forest homestead applications to examine and report on (Act of June 11, 1906), supervise the fire lookout, and occasionally extinguish a small forest fire. But the big job was connected with grazing of cattle and sheep. We had far too many sheep on the Forest and were trying to reduce them to the carrying capacity of the range.

To my regret Aldo Leopold had become ill and had taken a year's leave. I missed him because our interests coincided. But Raymond Marsh, his successor, was a fine man and a good Supervisor to work for.

The big grazing job that I did was to work out a system of individual allotments for herds of 800 to 2,000 sheep, describe each and translate the boundary descriptions into Spanish. This way we could hold each permittee responsible for proper use of his allotted range. Until then several herds were assigned to big community allotments, and when things went wrong each one blamed another. There were protests, but the new system worked and was adopted on other districts.

At that time all travel was done on horseback or by horse drawn rigs of one kind and another. The Carson Forest did not own a motor vehicle of any kind. I had three or four saddle horses and a spring rig similar to a buckboard — less sturdy but more comfortable. I removed the back seat and moved the front one back a foot. That gave more room in front and still plenty behind for camp outfit, saddle and horse feed.

For winter I built a sleigh, using two-by-twelve boards for runners half-soled with one-by-six-inch boards to scoot over the snow like skis. I used the rig seat and tongue and draw shafts on it, and it really did the job in that very snowy country.

My horses served both under saddle and in harness. I would carry my saddle wherever I went in rig or sleigh, and if I had need to go beyond the end of the road I'd leave the outfit, saddle a horse and go on. It worked like a car or truck with horse trailer today. I frequently had to be away over night and leave Ethel alone. The nearest neighbor was about two miles away. At such times, summer or winter, she had to feed the other horses and milk the cow. But I would leave her plenty of firewood and a barrel of water on the back porch.

At Cow Creek station we would often hear wolves howling at night, and it was a thrilling sound, but we well knew we'd soon hear of another cow or horse killed by them. One evening wolves were howling right near the Station pasture. I had an Airedale, an eight-month old bloodhound pup and Old Red, a fine hound, told of in another chapter. The dogs took out after the wolves and I soon heard an awful rumpus and was afraid my dogs would be killed. I blew my cow's horn frantically to call them back. When they came the pup was bloody all over. I took him in the kitchen and found that he had been badly slashed through the throat. We sewed up the big cuts and he got well but lost his voice. His trail baying after that was just a hoarse whisper.

Next morning at the corner of my horse pasture I found where five wolves had killed a colt and eaten most of it. I helped an old trapper set well-concealed traps around it. That night the wolves came back and howled again several times. We hoped they'd get caught. But no such luck. They decided the area around the colt carcass was unsafe, and killed the colt's mother nearby.

Once I was riding north of Tres Piedras and met a sheepherder, horseback and greatly perturbed. He said that the evening before he had lost about two hundred sheep from his herd, a cut we called it, and was unable to find them. It had snowed about four inches during the night and covered the tracks. I joined in the search.

In the side of Bald Wind Mountain we found where they had been while it was snowing. We followed the tracks and soon came upon the worst bloody mess I have ever seen. An old bitch wolf and two nearly grown ones had found the sheep and killed, or mortally wounded, eighty-seven of them. A number were left alive, their flanks ripped open and entrails dragging. At the end of the killing spree, they had eaten from three carcasses, while the others had been killed for fun.

About the first of February I had to send Ethel to Santa Fe to give birth to our second child. It was twenty-five degrees below zero when we left at daybreak in the sleigh on the nine-mile trip to catch the ten o'clock train, and it was twenty below when we got there. I heated a twenty-pound rock, wrapped it in gunny sacks and put it in the front of the sleigh under our lap robes and it helped keep us warm.

A month later I met the afternoon train with the same outfit to take Ethel, Roy and his fifteen-day old sister, Florence, home. The snow near Cow Creek was still awfully deep, but was packed hard where horses and sleigh had traveled often. A mile from the Station one of the horses got off of the beaten path, bogged down, floundered around and fell and couldn't get up. I had to unhitch him to get him up on his feet and onto the hard track. Then I backed him to his place beside his team-mate, and hitched him up again. Through it all Ethel sat there complacently with the two babies; obviously she had utmost faith in our horses.

We had an old heavy carpet on the living room floor to seal off the cracks. When the wind blew the carpet would hump up like an elephant was under it. Twenty degrees below zero was common, and often it was thirty. I've ridden all day and when I returned told that the thermometer had not been up to zero.

Two miners spent the winter at Hopewell in the high country and got snowed in. In the spring, as soon as snow would permit, a cowboy and I floundered through deep drifts to see if they had survived. Finally when we got there, to our amazement, the clothes line was hanging full of women's underwear, nighties etc. I exclaimed, "Well, I'll be damned, there must be women here!"

The cowboy said, "Yep, unless those lonesome miners are kidding themselves to beat hell." We had not known they'd brought their wives.

That summer's work was much like the previous one — counting in thirty thousand sheep, seeing that they stayed on their allotments, eating *chili con carne* at sheep camps, fire prevention and suppression and timber sales.

But Sundays we often fished religiously. I'd carry little Florence in a blanket sling and Roy would toddle along. He'd be good if I gave him a fish to play with. Fishing a small stream with bait, Ethel called to me to set the can of worms down as she needed one. I did and went on ahead. But Roy got to the can before she did and when she got there he was eating angle worms. She washed out his mouth, but some had gone down. I wanted to give him some of my dog-worming medicine, but Ethel didn't think that was appropriate. Anway we had fun fishing, and Roy is now Chief of the Division of Fisheries of the New Mexico Department of Game and

121

Fish, with thirty years tenure in fisheries work not counting that early experience.

There were homesteaders in sagebrush country outside the Forest where only a super optimist could hope to make a living. One of them from the East showed me two dozen Belgian hares he had bought. "The way they breed, they'll make me rich," he said. "I'll start shipping in October."

I stopped by again in October and found only the original two dozen hares. When pressed to explain, he sheepishly said, "I've just discovered that they are all bucks."

That fall I was transferred to the Supervisor's office, which had been moved to Taos. We found comfortable quarters, and I was glad for the family, though I liked field work better than office work. My experience on the Pecos helped me now. That winter I worked mainly on grazing trying to find where and how stock numbers could be reduced to prevent further over-grazing.

We had a number of very large sheep permitees, one with 23,000 head. It seemed to me the logical place to start reductions was with the big permittees. But they bucked like Brahma bulls and brought political and other pressures to prevent it. Gradually, however, until World War I, we made considerable progress without hurting the small owners.

Raymond E. Marsh was a good Supervisor and a very fine man. He had a degree in Forestry and was tops in timber work, but his experience in the field of grazing was limited. In that area he leaned on me and my knowlege of Spanish, which helped there in the office as much as it did in the field. I'll have to tell this authentic story on my old friend:

While in charge of a timber reconnaissance party a stranger came to his camp riding bareback with only a rope noose around the horse's nose. The stranger said he and his partner were camped down the canyon a little way and that their horses had got away and they couldn't catch them, nor could they corral them riding bareback with no bridle. He begged Ray to loan him his new saddle and bridle, assuring him he'd be back within the hour. Kind hearted Ray loaned him saddle and bridle. But the stranger, saddle and bridle never showed up again.

In the spring of 1915 I was put on a land classification job under Frank E. Andrews, long-time Supervisor of the Jemez and Santa Fe Forests, who was given this assignment. The object was to classify all National Forest land to ascertain and show on maps the uses to which the various areas were best adapted — timber, grazing, agriculture, waste lands, etc. I worked the Amarilla and Jicarilla Divisions of the Carson, covering every square mile, partly horseback and partly afoot. It was a grueling, tedious job which kept me away from home most of the time all summer.

I believe it was late in 1915 that Supervisor Marsh's father passed away and he took a year's leave to settle up the business. I had been promoted to Deputy Supervisor and was now named acting Supervisor. I was familiar with the duties, but always had someone over me to make the final decisions. Now it was my responsibility, and that makes one act a bit more cautiously. But we had a good staff and the administration went forward without a hitch. Regional Forester Paul G. Reddington was sympathetic and backed me all the way.

In addition to several sawmills on the Forest, about

that time a huge timber sale was made to a Denver operator, Hallack and Howard, in a fine stand of mature ponderosa pine. While that sale was administered by the Regional Office it still demanded our attention in many respects.

Grazing problems continued, for much of the range was still overstocked, and attempts to remedy it always met resistance. Instead of reducing, it seemed everybody wanted to increase their herds.

Emmett Wirt, influential Indian Reservation trader, had three allotments for a thousand sheep each. He pressured me to issue to his friends a permit for twenty-five hundred head. I couldn't. He insisted, "There's plenty of grass, you don't know the area like I do."

To test him I said, "All right I'll put a third of those sheep, 833 head, on each of your allotments; you just said there's plenty of grass."

He squirmed, then said, "Here son, have a cigar, you're smarter than I thought you were. Forget it."

In a year Supervisor Marsh returned and resumed his old duties. But he remained only a short while and was transferred to the Coconino Forest in Arizona. I was then promoted to Supervisor. The Regional Forester congratulated me and said, "With only a high school education you have made it from Assistant Forest Ranger to Supervisor in seven years. I think that's some kind of a record." Ethel and I were proud.

Space will not permit giving a resume of the Carson personnel, but I had a good staff in field and office whose hard work and loyalty contributed mightily to whatever success I had.

The basic operation routine was administration of timber sales and grazing, issuance of free-use permits for firewood, posts and building timber required by settlers in and near the Forest, trail building, prevention, detection and suppression of forest fires and examining, surveying and reporting on Forest homestead applications. With one exception we were fortunate in being able to control forest fires before they became serious. Timber and grazing trespass was diminishing.

The lobo wolf menace to livestock on the Amarilla Division became so serious that permittees offered an eighty-five dollar bounty on each wolf killed. Wolves are smart and only a few were taken. Once I found where eight wolves had killed a cow in Valle Gavilan and had been joined at the carcass by seven more. The evidence in the foot-deep snow was unmistakable. I followed the fifteen-wolf pack until dark hoping to catch up but they out-traveled me.

In the fall of 1916 the Forest Service hired Pete Gimson, an old-time wolfer, at a retainer salary of forty dollars a month, arranged a guaranty of the $85.00 bounty and got the County to guarantee to pay its $20.00 bounty. Many idealists maintain that the bounty system never works, but it did in this instance. In September and October Gimson and his sixteen-year old boy took sixteen lobo wolves, ten of which were adults and the others almost grown.

That fall J. Stokley Ligon, U.S. Biological Survey predator control agent, spent a week with me inspecting the area and obtaining evidence of the damage being done. He was astounded, and agreed to take over the control job the following year, which was done and the wolf menace eventually was eliminated.

Supervisors Leopold, Marsh and I made considerable progress in stopping overgrazing through gradual reduction of permitted sheep. Then on April 6, 1917, came the declaration of war (World War I). I was flabbergasted when I received orders through channels from the Secretary of Agriculture to grant temporary permits for many additional sheep and cattle in a program designed to met the war-caused increased demand for food.

I argued with the Regional Forester that it would do serious damage to the ranges, cause loss of gains we'd made, result in stockpiling of livestock, reduce available food supply and inflate prices. He said, "You may be right, but orders are from the summit and we must comply."

So some new permits were issued. Permittees bought additional stock and saved all ewe lambs to increase herds 25 to 50 percent. When the war was over immediate reductions back to former numbers could not be made without financial injury to permittees. So the range continued to be over-stocked and damaged. Livestock had been stockpiled and prices had soared beyond reason, then in 1920 the big balloon burst, and most stockmen went broke, especially those who had gone in debt. One of the Carson's largest permittees, I prefer not to give his name, could see no way out and blew his brains out with a Colt .45.. The policy from the summit proved to be all wrong.

The fall of 1917 was exceedingly dry and the fire hazard became great. Late in November I spent the night at Gold Hill Lookout Station in the Taos Mountains to make sure fire detection vigilance was at maximum efficiency. Leaving there next morning I rode south along the timberline divide, and in mid-afternoon dropped off into the Rio Pueblo de Taos drainage.

At once I saw wind-driven smoke in a side canyon.

I rode to it, and found the fire had already covered about two acres and was burning briskly. It was impossible for me to do any good trying to put it out. There had been no lightning, so I rode around the windward side to try to determine how it got started. At the edge of the green timber in a tiny opening by a spring I found an Indian hunter's abandoned camp. There had been a camp fire, spruce boughs cut for a bed, moccasin tracks all around and nearby a deer had been dressed. It was out of season for deer hunting. The fire had started there and burned eastward with the wind.

I hurried for Taos to organize a crew to put the fire out, but dark overtook me and I got into some terribly rough, trailless country. It was ten o'clock when I got to the Taos Indian Pueblo, which is three miles from Taos. I aroused an Indian friend and had him notify the Governor while I rode to Taos. I told him I'd be back very soon. At Taos I got my staff out of bed and had them start recruiting fire fighters and getting tools and supplies ready. Then I rode back to the Pueblo to get a big crew of Indians, for with the high wind it would be difficult to control the fire.

After talking to the Governor, through an interpreter, he asked the War Chief to assemble the Council for a powwow. I was impatient, but I just could not hurry the Indians. Meanwhile the Governor asked where I'd come off the mountain. When I told him where, he said, "No, you can't come down there with a horse."

I said, "It's rough, but I did come down there."

Then he asked, "When did you come down?"

I said, "Tonight, just a little while ago."

He said, "Well, in the dark maybe you can come down there, but in daylight it's too steep and rough."

127

The council took its time, and the delay was maddening when immediate action was in order. Despite their dependence on the watershed, they would agree to send twenty-five men only if I'd guarantee they'd be well paid, well fed and some bedding furnished. The Forest Service always paid and fed well. The Spanish-Americans required no such guaranty.

The crew from Taos started at daybreak and the Indians a while later. The fire was crowning out here and there and burning fiercely. We exerted all our strength and endurance for two days and nights before we brought it under control. After seventy-two hours without a wink of sleep, at sunrise the third day I curled up in a blanket and instantly was dead to the world. Without having moved a muscle I awoke when sun was setting. I ate a big supper and, when assured the fire lines were being properly patrolled, I slept for twelve hours more. The fire had burned over six hundred acres and was perhaps the worst we have ever had on the Carson.

During the war there were many extra activities that Forest Service personnel had to engage in, despite the fact that several of our men volunteered for military service. I was exempted from service because of defective hearing and of the key position I held. With other citizens I traveled all over the County to attend meetings and make patriotic speeches to keep up public morale and sell war bonds. While others spoke through interpreters I would speak first in Spanish, then in English or vice versa.

Many Forest officers were deputized by the U.S. Marshal to be available for help if or when needed. I held such a commission. In September 1917, I was at the San Antonio Ranger Station early one evening when I received a phone call advising me that a man named Naggel, an Austrian I believe, was wanted for suspected sabotage of grain elevators in Kansas. He was supposed to be at the Maupin Ranch, and they wanted me to arrest him and bring him to Taos. The Marshal said he might be dangerous.

I saddled Spike, a fine, coal-black saddle horse and set out on the thirty-five mile night ride. Arriving a little before daylight, I concealed myself and Spike in a draw a couple of hundred yards from the house to wait for daylight and Naggel to come out. I carried my .44 Colt revolver on the belt of my leather chaps. At sunrise Maupin and a man I took to be Naggel came out into a field of shocked oat hay across the road from me. They were checking to see if the oat hay was dry enough to stack.

They were in shirt sleeves and unarmed. I got on Spike and rode to a pole fence between the road and the field and called them over. The suspect admitted he was Naggel. I showed my badge and told him he was under arrest and would have to go with me. After some heated arguments with Maupin, who objected to me taking his harvest hand, Naggel agreed to go, but asked to go to the house and get his coat and some other things. I put him in front, rode to the house, got off and went into the kitchen with him. A steep stairway led up from the kitchen to the bedroom which opened directly in front of the landing. I hesitated a second or two to speak to Mrs. Maupin, when I heard Naggel hurrying up the stairs. I hurried after him as fast as my spurs and chaps would permit. At the landing I saw him throw his coat off the bed with his left hand and reach for something with his right. I closed in and jabbed my pistol in his back and said, "Drop it or I'll kill you!" He had turned half way around when his cocked .45 Colt clattered to the floor.

A split second delay and I would have had to shoot or be shot. It was close. As a Forest Officer and Game Warden I have made many arrests, and several times felt the need of having a side-arm ready, but that is the only time I have ever had to draw my gun.

At Tres Piedras I turned Naggel over to the U.S. Commissioner from Taos, but he let him escape enroute. He was recaptured and there is more to his story, but I was not involved so I'll skip it. However, several years after he was released from custody he wrote and asked me to return the gun with which he had tried to kill me. I answered and said, "If you think you are man enough come get it." He didn't.

The most trying experience of my Forest Service tenure, or in my life, was the influenza epidemic in the fall of 1918. At the time I was Chairman of the Taos County Red Cross, and the brunt of organizing and supervising relief work fell to me. It soon became evident that so little could be done as a preventative or to save lives, it was heartbreaking.

One would talk to a strong, healthy man today and two days later he'd be dead. It hit whole families, particularly of the poorer class, of which there were many, and, thankfully, skipped others. We had but one doctor there at the time, but obtained six more and nine nurses from St. Louis, Missouri. But there was little information about the disease or how to treat it. We converted a church and a school into makeshift hospitals, but it did little good except to give some poor folks a comfortable place to die.

Father Giraud, the Catholic priest, Fred Mueller, a dentist, and I constituted a sort of volunteer committee to seek out desperate situations and supervise relief work. We ran into some unbelievable situations. One night we had word that a large family in the outskirts of town was in dire need of help. About midnight Father Giraud and I went to the house. A twelve-year old girl met us at the door; she was the only one able to wait on the sick. There was no fire and the lamp provided a dim light.

I went to the bed where the father and mother lay. I laid my hand on the man's forehead, it was cold and clammy. The young girl said, *"Mi Papa murio ayer.* Papa died yesterday."* then the priest kneeling beside a pallet where three children lay, cried out, *"Dio mio, este esta muerta tambien!* My God, one of these is dead also." Another child died before we got them to the hospital. A six-months old baby and the grandmother were all of the family of nine that survived. In sixty days we buried twelve hundred and fifty people out of a population of twelve thousand.

With pathos I relate this incident: Onofre Valdez, a sheep permittee, loved his sheep, took good care of them and was one of my best permittees. He had a nice wife and three fine children. He became very ill and the Forest Ranger near his ranch got a doctor from Antonito, Colorado. Upon examination the doctor told Onofre that if he had any business that needed attention he should give instructions right then because he could not live till morning. Onofre said, "No, doctor, no."

The Doctor said, "I'm sorry, Onofre, but God has called you."

Onofre said, "No, I can't die. Why what would become of my sheep."

131

Working in the midst of flu victims, living and dead, for six weeks I escaped it as, thank God, did my wife and two young children. By then it had subsided and the epidemic was about over. I came home on November 9, about midnight. I'd been helping Giraud and Mueller with some mopping up jobs. I was not sick but was very tired and went right too bed and to sleep. In two hours I awoke as sick as I have ever been. The next day I became unconscious and remained that way for a week. It was two weeks before I knew the war was over and the Armistice signed. The out-of-town doctors and nurses had little else to do now and gave me every possible attention and pulled me through, or else I was just too ornery to die.

The flu experience had left me somewhat depressed, and the grazing job ahead foreboded trouble, and besides I had never been able to shake off the desire to be a rancher in the mountains where I was raised, so I resigned my position as Forest Supervisor effective April 1, 1919. My ten years experience in the Forest Service had been a wonderful educational experience which was to stand me in good stead when, twelve years later, I was appointed State Game Warden of the State of New Mexico.

I am proud of the letter I received from the Acting Chief Forester, A. F. Potter, upon my determination to leave the Service, It says:

"Dear Mr. Barker:
"I have learned with considerable regret of your decision to leave the Service. You have made an enviable record as Forest Supervisor of the Carson and I want to take this opportunity

of extending my best thanks and congratulations on behalf of the Service for your noteworthy accomplishments during your period of service, and also extend my best wishes for your success in your new undertaking. If the Service cannot retain you as one of its employees, you may be sure that we shall welcome you as one of its permittees."

QUALIFYING AS A NEW MEXICO RANCHER

8

I N NEW MEXICO, they say, to qualify as a bona fide rancher one must go broke twice. On that basis, within eighteen months after I left the U. S. Forest Service to ranch I was half qualified, I had acquired a part of the original S. L. Barker lands and some adjoining it, and bought a hundred head of cattle at war-inflated prices. When the bottom dropped out in 1920 my investment wasn't worth thirty cents on the dollar. Like many other ranchers, I was broke! But we decided to stay with it, realizing that our cattle operation income would have to be supplemented from other sources.

On sixty acres of plow land we raised heavy crops of oat and pea hay, and on forty acres timothy and clover. It required most of the hay to feed the livestock in winter, but we sold a little. A blight that had invaded the area prevented raising potatoes, which had saved the Barker family thirty years before. But we raised the finest vegetables imaginable — carrots, beets, turnips, parsnips, cabbage and lettuce — which we sold for a cent to a cent and a half a pound. For several years our 350 to 400 pound calves brought only $12 or $14 a head.

We worked hard and did anything honest to try to

make a living. In winter I hunted bobcats with my dogs and trapped coyotes. Unlike other things fur prices held up, bobcats brought $5 to $12 and coyotes $8 to $15. I also took paying guests on mountain lion hunts whenever I could get customers. One such hunt is told in chapter nine.

Occasionally I took a timber cruising job that brought in a little money. But that meant being away from home and placed a heavy additional burden on my wife, Ethel, to take care of the ranch and stock, even though we had a hired man. On a few occasions I was away as much as thirty days at a time. But we needed the money.

In 1921 another baby, Dorothy, came along. She was a beautiful child, wanted and most welcome. But that kept Ethel tied down even more than before, and for a time prevented her from riding after cattle in the mountains with me as she loved to do.

An unusual circumstance made me a little extra money on one timber cruising job. The State Land Office had sold several million board feet of timber to be paid for on the basis of its cruiser's estimate. When the purchaser thought the estimate too high, as in this case, the procedure was to have the estimate checked on the ground by a timber cruiser selected by the State and one by the purchaser and one agreed upon by those two.

The purchaser asked me to come to Santa Fe to arrange to do a job for him. About the same time the State Land Commissioner made a similar request, but neither one explained what the job was. Arriving at Santa Fe I found that both purchaser and Land Commissioner, unbeknown to each other, had selected me as their man. Under the circumstances they agreed to dispense with the other two cruisers and accept my individual estimate of the timber. It helped when they paid me half again as much as they otherwise would have.

Once a forest fire got out of control on a big block of community land (an old Spanish Land Grant) in which Gross Kelly Co. of Las Vegas held timber interests. It was the responsibility of the County Commissioners to put it out, but after a week they were getting nowhere — you can't fight forest fires with politics. Employed on a partisan political basis, the would-be fire fighters were more interested in prolonging their jobs than in putting out the fire.

The Gross Kelly Co. manager asked me to take charge. I agreed, provided I could fire any and all men who refused to cooperate and work hard.

The County Commissioners would not agree, so I got in my Model T Ford and started back to the ranch. Enroute the Manager overtook me and said they had concluded to agree to my terms and would pay me $25 a day to put the fire out. My Forest Service fire-fighting experience and training well qualified me to do the job.

They had a big fire camp set up and about a hundred men fiddling around on the job. I got my cowboy-rancher friends, Dee Bibb and Jim Whitmore for foremen, and by three P.M. we were at camp. Fortunately there was no wind to speak of, and the fire was burning slowly in second growth pine timber. I had all the men brought to camp and organized them in squads of seven men with a straw boss in charge of each. I made clear what was expected of them and outlined clearly my plan of action. They were fed a hearty meal, and told that they would have to work all night. I would do overall supervision horseback.

The fire was out on the windward side. I split the squads into two groups, sent one to the north side under Jim and the other to the south side under Dee. They were to begin at the back side where the fire was out and build a firebreak along the live fire line toward the front to pinch it out. The squads were distributed at hundred yard intervals and would leapfrog each other as they successively caught up, and a patrolman would be dropped off every quarter mile to see that the fire didn't break over the line. They were supplied with canteens of water and some sandwiches throughout the entire night.

I had to fire only two men. By sunrise we had completed three miles of firebreak on each side and lacked only two miles having the fire pinched out. I appealed to the men to stay on the job and finish it before the heat of the day. Most of them stayed and by ten A.M. we had the fire surrounded and under control. I let half the men go and spelled the others patrolling the line to catch any break-overs.

By noon the next day it was all over, except that Dee Bibb and a couple of patrolmen would stay on a few days for insurance. They paid me a hundred dollars for forty-eight hours work. These extra earnings were all that made it possible for us to ride out the five-year depression following World War One.

We all worked. When Roy was ten he would milk cows and ride with me helping with the range cattle. He did all kinds of chores. One day when he and his eight-year-old sister, Florence, had been asked to weed a few rows in the garden, their mother caught them playing instead of weeding and accused them of being lazy. As she walked away she heard Florence ask Roy,

137

"Do you know why God makes weeds grow in the garden?" Roy didn't know, and Florence said, "It's so little kids won't get lazy."

We always kept three or four milk cows and sold butter and cream. We also raised a few hogs which we butchered in late fall and made our own smoked bacon and hams. Of course we butchered our own beef in winter only, for we had no refrigerator. But Ethel canned beef, fruit and vegetables. With all that and butter, cream, cottage cheese and eggs our grocery bill was kept to a minimum.

As her special project Ethel took up turkey raising. Her objective was to produce a hundred turkeys for Thanksgiving and Christmas market each year. But to do that she had to start with double that number of poults. Some natural loss was to be expected, but the loss to predators was excessive.

After they were able to fly, the poults were healthier roosting outside in the nearby pine trees than in a building. But great horned owls often would come in, one after another, and catch the young turks until we killed the raiders. Bobcats also, would sneak in, climb a tree and grab off a turkey now and then. But my good Airedale hunting dogs would hear the commotion and would usually be able to tree the cat before he got away so I could shoot him.

Coyotes, however, did the most damage. As the poults became old enough the flocks would range in the fields across the creek from the house up to a half mile away foraging for grasshoppers and other natural foods. Often when they would get close to the woods that rimmed the fields, a coyote would dart out from cover and grab off a turkey. The others would pert, pert, pert fran-

tically and fly back to the house. The dogs would rush over there yelping and chase the coyotes away, sometimes making him drop his prize, but the damage had been done.

I kept traps out most of the time, but no matter how many I caught there would soon be another one or two come along. Coyotes are smart and hard to trap, some extremely so. There was one big dog coyote that taxed my patience and ingenuity. I thought I was a pretty good trapper but, for a period of two weeks, this old fellow went around my traps no matter how skillfully I concealed them, and disdained my usually effective scent lures.

About every second day Old Smarty, as Roy named him, would catch and carry off another turkey. It was nearing Thanksgiving, and each one he took meant one less for market. I hid in the field one day with rifle but he didn't show up, and I had no more time to spare for that.

Finally, one night a skiff of snow fell, and I rode my trap line hoping I might have caught him. I found his tracks made as he came along a path where I'd set a trap very carefully the day before. A few feet from it he had someway located the trap and stopped, then he had circled around it. A few yards beyond, to show his contempt for me and my traps, he had defecated liberally. I knew that if he should come by there again he would stop and smell of his droppings. That is patent dog and coyote nature.

It occurred to me that this might offer an opportunity to fool him. I found an old pine log and got a good sized piece of bark, rode back, got off, and with a stick, scrapped his droppings onto the bark, got on my horse with it and rode back to the trap set. There, without getting off the horse, I deposited the droppings, he had so kindly left me, a foot back of the trap. Possibly he'd think he had deposited it there and consider it safe to take a whiff.

I was right. The next morning the steel trap held him firmly by a front foot. At long last I had outsmarted Old Smarty. His pelt was a large one, well furred and it paid for a couple of the turkeys he had stolen. Despite all the hazards and losses Ethel's turkey project returned a nice profit.

Ranch life was in many ways rewarding, but it seemed there were always unexpected losses of one sort or another that had to be absorbed. Once in the spring some cows got into a pasture where pine trees for saw logs had been cut. They browsed on the green pine needles causing a dozen of them to abort their calves. A bolt of lightning killed three yearlings under one tree, and a grizzly bear killed a cow, her calf and a two-year old steer all in one night. A careless deer hunter shot and killed a big three-year old steer, and another one shot a yearling heifer, in the brush, for a turkey.

All the time we were on the ranch I was an unpaid deputy game warden and, to the extent of my ability required the game laws to be observed in that area. There was a game refuge south of the ranch and it was open hunting area on the north side. During the eleven years we were there the deer herd more than doubled. When we went to the ranch there were practically no wild turkeys left. But with law enforcement and the predator control work I did to protect our tame turkeys and the hunting and trapping for fur value gave the wild turkeys the protection they required to increase their numbers.

And increase they did to perhaps twenty times over in eleven years. Since I left, with very little predator control being done, they are back down to a very low point. Wildlife got to be a great attraction at the ranch.

Driving cattle from winter to summer ranges in spring and rounding them up in the fall was always a big job. Ethel and Roy and sometimes Florence, as she grew older, helped me. Even so, additional riders often were required. We had corrals on the range where we rounded up and branded the calves and vaccinated them against blackleg, usually in June. The kids would keep the fire going and branding irons hot. We usually had help from our neighbors, and we helped them in turn. In emergencies I could always get Celestino Martinez, a top cowboy and brush rider, who lived a few miles from the ranch.

One time when Roy was eleven years old, he, Ethel and I were taking a herd of cattle up the mountain to summer range on Lone Tree Mesa and Beaver Creek. My Airedale hunting dogs were along, but the last thing we could afford to do was to take time out to hunt. Half way up the dogs hit a hot trail of some kind and yelping wildly followed it off into a big canyon where they began barking 'treed'. Roy wanted me to go see what it was. I said no, its just a bobcat and we'll let it go.

But Roy kept nagging at me, and I finally gave him my rifle, I always carried it or my revolver, and told him to go on down there and kill a bobcat. After a bit he yelled back at us as loud as he could, "DAD, IT'S A LION, SHALL I SHOOT IT?"

I yelled back, "Better wait till we get there." I didn't want to take a chance on him wounding it and getting a dog crippled. So we left the cattle to scatter in the forest and rode down to find a nice yearling lion up a spruce tree. There really had been no need for us to go down for Roy put a .32 Winchester Special bullet through the arch deer-killer's heart.

Another time I sent Roy on a gentle, but only half broke, mare to drive some stray stock away from the house. In a little while he came back afoot, limping, all dirty and whimpering. "What's wrong?" I asked.

"Brownie bucked me off and dragged me with my foot caught in the stirrup," he said.

"Oh, come now, Brownie doesn't buck. What really did happen?" I asked.

He said, "The first thing I knew her head went down out of sight between her front legs, her hind end went up and I was looking down on the tops of the pine saplings." That was a mighty accurate description of a hard bucking horse. The tracks verified that she'd bucked.

By the fall of 1925, the financial situation was looking up. Cattle prices began to rise, and it seemed to me there was an opportunity to make some money buying and selling. The banks were good to me and let me have whatever money I needed for that purpose. Beginning that fall I worked hard at it seasonally and did very well. Then I leased two additional ranches, one for summering and one for wintering another hundred twenty-five cattle. For three years we did all right, and got pretty well out of debt.

Ethel was raised on a ranch and she loved to ride the range with me whenever she could find someone to leave with Dorothy. She was a good horsewoman and understood handling cattle as well as I did. We've been married for over fifty-eight years and she still packs into the wilderness areas to camp and fish with me.

143

One fall Ethel went with me to the high country, eleven thousand feet elevation, to help me gather some stragglers we'd missed when we brought the cattle down. We took a pack horse with a light camp outfit so we could stay wherever night overtook us. We camped in a beautiful meadow called Vega Bonita. We had no tent, just a long tarp to put under our bed and double back over us, with three feet extra length to pull up over our head if need be.

In the night it began to drizzle rain and we pulled the tarp over our heads. About daylight I woke up sweating and feeling as if I were smothering. I tried to throw the covers and tarp back but they were weighted down. Ethel woke up in the same fix I was in and we finally threw the tarp back, but in so doing we got great gobs of wet snow down our necks. It had snowed about six inches and really sealed us in tight. Its a wonder we didn't smother.

Roy and Florence learned early to ride and tagged me whenever I could let them. By 1928 Roy was sixteen and could do a man's work horseback, and Florence was close behind him. When Dorothy was six she could follow me all day on my faithful horse Spike if I were riding the trails. The trouble was they had to be in school so much of the time.

One day Florence went with me to pack salt on one of my big work mules for cattle in the high summer range. My saddle horse, Chub, got a bad stone bruise on his heel and went too lame to ride home. I decided to leave him there till his foot got well and to ride the mule back home. We'd packed the mule some but she had never been ridden and was pretty high strung. I was pretty much cowboy in those days and figured I'd get

144

along all right. But Florence was scared the mule would buck me off and hurt me. I remember yet the earnest look on her face when I eased up in the saddle on that mule and she said, "Oh, Daddy, hold on tight!" My new mount resented me no more than she had the five, fifty-pound blocks of salt.

No matter how adverse the circumstances nor how hard we worked, we had fun on the ranch. Friends from nearby and from town would come and we'd picnic. We would catch a mess of fish from the creek that ran the full length of the ranch whenever we took a notion to. But in 1926 when Ethel had to move to town for the school terms it made it mighty hard on everybody. During those times I tried to have a couple with me at the ranch and we managed to get by one way or another.

Once our neighbors, Katherine and Oakley Mc-Cauley, rode with us six miles across the mountains to the Harvey ranch, which I had leased, to help brand some late calves. Just before we got there a thunder shower was threatening. The others rode quickly to the house, unsaddled and turned their horses in a pasture. I stopped for a few moments to repair a break in a fence. When I got to the house it was beginning to rain, but I unsaddled and took my horse, Nig, to the pasture gate a hundred yards from the house and turned him in.

There was a block of stock salt in a little draw fifty yards inside the pasture. Nig kicked up his heels and trotted down to the salt. The other horses were a hundred yards beyond. I shut the gate, and as I turned to go to the house there was a blinding flash of lightning accompanied by a deafening clap of thunder. I looked back to see the reaction of the horses. Poor Nig had been hit squarely by the lightning and was lying stone dead, a strip of hair burned off his back and down his legs. Three horses on one side of him and I on the other narrowly escaped.

Our ranch was beautifully situated in a timbered canyon with a narrow valley of patchy farm land in the bottom through which a clear, willow-banked trout stream wound its way. Ponderosa pine and oak brush rimmed the fields and merged into forests of aspen, fir and spruce up the canyon sides. From the house we had a spectacular view of Lone Tree Mesa, three miles away, rising to an elevation of 9,500 feet, about 2,000 feet higher than the ranch. The lonely foxtail pine on its bald summit was clearly visible.

In summer, meadows and grain fields waving in the breeze were a beautiful sight; wildflowers were everywhere, and life was good. Following summer, gorgeous display of variegated fall colors were dazzling. The evergreen forests with patches of aspen mingled in were especially beautiful. The rich browns of oak brush, where deer come to browse, were eye-catchers too.

When shimmering white blankets covered fields and meadows, and willows bowed and tree limbs drooped with heavy winter snow spectacular scenes greeted one everywhere. Snow-capped haystacks became meaningful when white-faced cattle gathered outside the stack fence to eagerly receive their daily ration, and harvest's toil and sweat were forgotten.

Despite inconveniences, hard times and hard work, in many ways ranch life was good and satisfying. We admired our cattle and petted our horses, we liked our chickens and turkeys and loved the ranch. No more beautiful place will be found in all the mountains, spring and summer, fall and winter than was our ranch on Sapello Creek in the Sangre de Cristo Mountains.

Spring came apace on the heels of melting snow; tender grass and herbs pierced through the fertile soil; pussy willows, plump and fuzzy, adorned the erstwhile naked river brush; aspen crowns turned a rich gray with caterpiller-like pendant blooms; horses shed their winter coats and became sleek; turkey gobblers gobbled and strutted with tails fanned, wattles inflated and flushed; hens having laid a quota of eggs turned broody, clucking defiantly to declare their mood; fruit trees were sprayed with pink blossoms; robins sang lustily at dawn, proclaiming their selection of nesting sites; crows walked proudly in fresh plowed furrows seeking juicy grubs; in bovine maternity wards at the feed lots more pretty, red-bodied calves with snow-white faces appeared daily; in the barnyard a prolific brood sow suckled a litter of pigs.

In the midst of all this, human minds and bodies were revitalized, tensions relaxed and spirits became exalted. Optimism reigned supreme.

Such were the scenes and exuberant emotions on our ranch in the spring of 1929. Prospects for a fine profitable year were never better. To make the most of the generally predicted good times, we expanded our operations to the utmost and stocked our summer ranges to capacity. In addition to our stock cattle, I bought 200 three-year old steers to fatten on the lush mountain range confident of making an excellent profit.

The season was good and all went well through spring and summer. But before I marketed my calf crop and the big, fat steers in the fall the nation-wide financial crash of 1929 hit swift and hard. Calves dropped from forty to twelve dollars a head. The big steers, though hog fat, had to be sold at a heavy loss.

147

It was mighty hard to face, but we were broke again. There was little consolation in the fact that I had qualified as a bona fide rancher—gone broke twice. The desperate and tragic depression that was to last through the early 1930s was upon us.

There was no use to cry over spilt milk. We talked it over and appraised the situation facing us the best we could. Roy was ready for college and Florence was close behind. We had gone through desperately hard times on the ranch once, and it was difficult to face prospects for an even worse situation again. So we leased the ranch, sold all the stock except two fine saddle mares, and I went job hunting. Most fortunately I found one, for work became scarce and salaries poor.

On April 1, 1930, I went to work for Vermejo Park, a 360,000-acre ranch-game preserve in northern New Mexico. I would have charge of game management and predatory animal control. Guest hunting and game law enforcement were included in my assignment. My salary was only $150 per month with a house, some chickens and a milk cow furnished. The work was in my favorite field but the remuneration wasn't much. I spent a year on the job there, the story of which is told in my book titled *"When the Dogs Bark Treed"*," and the highlights of the year's adventures and experiences are told in chapter XI.

9 A COUGAR THE HARD WAY

THE SUN SANK behind Elk Mountain, and November's evening chill set in. In the northern New Mexico Mountains at nine thousand feet elevation, November nights get mighty cold. We were a long way from food and bed.

The dogs were baying on the track of a big mountain lion ahead, and we urged our tired, sweaty horses on. We hoped the pack would tree their quarry before dark, but there wasn't much chance of it unless he'd made a kill, for the track was not fresh.

At dusk we came to a trail leading down into Hollinger Canyon where the big, long-tailed cat had changed his westward course around the hillside and followed the trail and crossed Hollinger Canyon. I knew we could not follow the dogs on the rough, slick opposite mountain side after dark. So I blew blast after blast on my dog-calling cow's horn signalling them to leave the track and come back to us. Pup and Queenie, my Airedales came readily, but Sam, my half Red Bone, half Blood Hound, was hard to persuade. Finally he, too, gave up and came to us.

Captain Fritz VonGontard, a German only a year in this country, was my paying guest hunter. Now we had a decision to make as to what to do. There were but two choices—lay out without food or bed, or make a three hour ride over rugged trails and return in the morning.

The former would be a long, cold, dreary night, but would have the advantage of giving us a day-break start on the track. The latter would mean a night ride, hard on horses and men, but bed and food at my ranch on Sapello Creek. Even with fresh horses it would be nine o'clock before we got back in the morning. The trip would be hard on the already tender footed dogs.

I laid it all out for the Captain to consider and decide, but he said, "Whatever you say is the best way to catch that puma, I do it, and no complaints."

I said, "It's easier on dogs and horses to stay here, and we won't suffer. That way we can start at daylight."

"That is just fine," he said. "I lay in trenches many times in the war, and I think this is better."

We selected a grassy meadow at the base of the trail and made camp. That is, we picked a sheltered spot beside a van-sized boulder, gathered a huge pile of fire wood and built a good fire. By then our horses had cooled off and we unsaddled them and watered them at the little creek. Then I picketed my horse, Chub, with the lariat I always carry, and hobbled the Captain's horse, Chief, with a bridle rein. They would fare the best of all on the abundant, palatable grass.

Of course we were dressed warmly and had heavy coats. We improvised seats of rocks against the big boulder, and used the Navajo-rug saddle blankets, which I use over the sweat pads, as cushions. With a big fire in front we could lean back against the boulder and be fairly comfortable. The thermometer would go down to ten or fifteen degrees before morning, and we'd have to get up now and then and warm our backs.

I knew we need not suffer, but to sit it out for eleven hours without a bite to eat is a mighty wearing pastime. Captain VonGontard said, "We saw deer back there, why didn't we kill one and bring a piece to roast?"

"The season is closed, and that would have been illegal," I said.

"Out here nobody knows," he said.

"I would," I said, but he didn't understand that kind of ethics.

For some unknown reason my hunter was intensely interested in mountain lions, which he always referred to as pumas, the more correct name. Periodically throughout the night he plied me with every imaginable type of question. It was a veritable midnight, outdoor, zoology class-room. Typical questions and answers were:

"How do pumas make their scrapes?"

"They make short, heavy, backward strokes first with one hind foot and then the other leaving a kind of double dig with soil and forest debris pushed up three to six inches high back of it. Females rarely make scrapes."

"Why does he make them?"

"To mark his territory, and perhaps so females can find him."

"How old when they start making love?"

"I believe they mate first at about two years."

"Then every year?"

"No. About every eighteen months."

"How long a time for gestation?"

"Ninety-three to ninety-six days."

"They hurry up. How many cubs do they have?"

"They are called kittens. Two, three and four are normal numbers. Rarely five, but there is at least one record of six. I've never found less than two."

"What month do they have their kittens?"

"In that respect they are like people. New-born kittens have been found in every month in the year."

"What is their principal food?"

"Deer is their choice. But if deer are scarce they will kill whatever is available—porcupines, rabbits, grouse, turkeys and livestock. They are very fond of colts. They rarely eat anything but their own kills."

"How often do they kill a deer?"

"If deer are plentiful, about one a week. Females raising young kill more. Once in a while an old male lion goes on a killing spree. There is one authentic record of a big male lion killing five deer, a porcupine and two grown horses in a thirteen-day period."

"How can they kill a grown horse?"

"Just how I don't know, but I know they do whenever they take a notion to. I observed an instance where a lion killed two big Army mules a week apart.

"Will they kill people?"

"There are very few records where they have, but it is extremely rare. I've climbed trees to make them jump out. One refused to jump and came down on the opposite side of the tree and hissed at me."

"What did you do."

"I just hissed back at him."

On and on my hunter went about pumas. Then went over the same ground about bear, wolves, coyotes and bobcats. Even if we didn't get a lion I figured he'd have his money's worth of wildlife information and rugged experience.

This had started a week before. I was ranching on Sapello Creek on the east side of the Sangre de Cristo range. It was in one of those "depression" periods, and I was as hard up for cash money as one ever gets. I needed $200.00 the worst way to pay my taxes and didn't know where or how to get it. I wasn't desperate enough to rob a bank. My good wife, Ethel, said, "Don't fret, something will turn up." And it did.

The Chamber of Commerce Secretary, in Las Vegas, phoned to ask if I could take care of a lion hunter. Of course I could, as lion hunting had long been my hobby. Two days later I met Captain Fritz VonGontard, a World War I German Captain, who had taken out his first papers to become an American citizen. He had married a Philadelphia woman, and she would stay with my wife while we went lion hunting.

The first three days we hunted from the ranch and my dogs treed a nice bobcat, but we found no recent lion sign. The fourth day we duplicated the first day's trip into the best lion country I knew, thinking that perhaps a lion had come in by now.

By sunrise we were climbing through the shady Sulphur Springs area through six inches of snow. Topping out we rode west to Lone Tree Mesa, and then down into Beaver Creek, and I was sorely disappointed that we had found no lion sign at all.

As we rode down Beaver Creek, ravens and magpies flew up from the willows. The dogs scented something and ran to check it out. We loped our horses over there in hopes it was a lion kill. There was deer hair, scraps of bloody hide and fresh bones scattered around. The dogs bristled up, growled and barked a little.

"Why don't they go get him?" the Captain asked.

"It's not a lion kill," I said. "Coyotes, instead. They kill lots of deer in these mountains, and scatter the hair, hide and bones all over, while a lion makes a neat kill, does not tear up the carcass, and after each meal covers what is left with leaves, tree needles and other forest debris."

I called the dogs and we rode on to some cliffs where the canyon closes in, then took a path around the south-facing hillside above the sandstone cliffs. This was real good lion country, and I urged the dogs to, "Go hunt 'em up." They, like ourselves, were anxious for a lion track. They loved to hunt, and would quit a bear or bobcat track for a lion's any time. They were thoroughly broke against running deer, a requisite for a lion dog.

For a mile the dogs worked hard first above, then below the broken cliffs. Finally from above we could see Sam below the cliff very busily sniffing the ground and showing great interest in some faint scent he had found. His tail-wagging response to his nose findings told me it was something he considered worth thorough investigation.

He would pause at low bushes and sniff them over carefully. Then tail wagging, he'd move on to a rock and press his nose tight to it trying to get the scent which we hoped, and I'm sure he hoped, would be that of a lion. The Captain had never before seen a strike dog work a cold scent, and was amazed at the thoroughness of Sam's investigation. It is, indeed, most fascinating and admirable. Sam had not yet said a word, and I knew he wouldn't until he was sure it was a lion.

Finally Sam worked up hill to a rotted down log near the base of the cliff. There his sure, keen nose told him he'd found what he was looking for. His muscles were tense and vibrating, and his tail wagging enthusiastically. Now I could see that it was a lion's scrape. Sam, that long-eared, red hound, raised his head and uttered a long, drawn out bellow ending on a rising note followed by two short barks as he set out along the rocky hillside. "That's damned sure lion talk," I said.

At the first baying Pup and Queenie knew as well as I what Sam had found and went bounding to him. They were all excited with the find and their initial, enthusiastic barking and baying made the canyon echo with the sweetest and most exciting music than can come to a lion hunter's ears. The greatest joy of a lion hunt is watching the dogs work and listening to their meaningful trail baying.

The pack soon slowed pace and settled down to the difficult task of working out the cold trail.

"How soon will they catch him?" my hunter asked.

"That's hard to say, the trail is old, perhaps made night before last. It might be a long, hard chase," I replied.

"How do you know it is so old?" the Captain asked.

"Sam told me when he made the strike," I said. "They will have to work slow until it freshens. We'll keep above them. You kick Chief along and stay up with me no matter what happens."

"Yes sir," he said, as if responding to a General's order.

For quite a while we had no trouble keeping up. The south-facing mountain side was bare except for an occasional patch of snow. Often on the rocky open slopes the dogs would lose the track and they'd become silent. The Airedales were working silently now most of the time anyway. They would all circle ahead hoping to find the lion scent again. If they failed, Sam, and sometimes the others, would go back to where they had the sure scent last and slowly work forward on the trail, track by track.

Pup was mighty good at guessing where the lion had gone, and would often pick up the scent. Then he'd give a sharp bark or two and his partners would come to him on the run, and they'd be off on the trail.

Finally the pack worked the trail to a deep saddle in the ridge, but instead of crossing it as I hoped he would, the lion had headed right up the ridge toward the awful Hermit's Peak country. This is no ordinary peak rising cone-shaped or knife-edged toward the sky. Instead it is a huge, granite-faced, double hump bulging up crosswise of the ridge that forms the divide between the Rio Grande and Mississippi watersheds. Its 10,500 foot summit is easy of access from the west along the ridge where we were, but to the north, east and south it breaks off abruptly in reddish, granite cliffs some of which drop a sheer two thousand feet.

Occasionally deer ranged on top, and he might kill one there, then we could tree him before he made his get-away in cliffs inaccessible to the dogs. Or he might hole up somewhere in a break in the awful cliffs and we would lose him. I shuddered to think of his turning off either to north or south into deep, rugged canyons at the last possible way down adjacent to the sheer cliffs. We'd just have to follow the pack wherever the trail led.

On the timbered ridge-top there was some snow and the pack moved along at a good pace, Sam trail-baying steadily and Pup and Queenie barking sharply now and then. We put Chief and Chub into a stiff trot to keep up. Suddenly the dogs turned abruptly to the right and headed for the precipitous wall of the rugged, rock-ribbed El Porvenir Canyon.

"That's the last place man or beast can get off into the canyon, and its danged near impossible there," I said.

"If you go, I go too," my hunter said. I was glad he was game.

Soon we were at the rim, looking off into the dark, terrifying, two thousand foot-deep gorge. Our quarry had evidently prowled around here quite a bit before taking off, and the dogs had not yet figured out where he had gone. I called them to us and tied up Sam, the others would stay. It was now one-o'clock.

"We better eat our sandwiches here, rest a bit, then let the dogs find where he has gone," I said.

"Like you said the other day, my belly thinks my throat is cut," the Captain said laughing.

I loosened the saddle cinches, got our lunches and a package of table scraps for the dogs from my saddle bags, and we all enjoyed a half hour rest.

"Do you think he went down into that gorge?" the Captain asked.

"Looks like it," I said. "I think he lay up here yesterday, so the track should be fresher from here on." I sure dreaded the descent into the canyon. It was a perilous route, but I had twice before followed lions off and knew we could make it.

I adjusted our saddles, turned Sam loose and urged all the dogs to go down the steep, rocky hill. I threw a rock away down there where I figured the lion would have gone. Queenie ran to the spot and at once picked up the track. When she yelped Pup and Sam honored her report, and they all set off down that awful mountain.

157

"We must lead the horses," I said. "Follow me, and be careful that Chief doesn't roll rocks on you or on Chub and me."

Many and unforgettable were the haps and mishaps, adventures and rough experiences of the hour-long struggle zigzagging down that awful, trailless canyon wall. We dodged rolling rocks started by the horses, slipped, slid and fell more than once. The Captain lost a bit of skin here and there, but was game and stayed with me. He marveled at the ability of the horses to make it at all. Although many times they literally slid on their tails they never once fell.

When at long last we reached the bottom I said, "Thank God that's over with. Any man who would bring horses down there ought to be jailed." But they made it without injury and drank thirstily from the ice-rimmed creek.

The dogs were now halfway up Cascade Canyon, opposite our descent route. I was afraid they would get out of hearing and we'd lose them. So we quickly mounted and started up the hill, steep but less rugged than the one we had come down. Suddenly it seemed they had changed course and turned west along the mountain side. We stopped and listened intently. No doubt about it now, they were headed back toward the canyon a quarter mile up stream. "Oh, no," I cried. "He musn't cross back over. He can't do that to us!"

We turned back to the canyon and loped up the trail to intercept the dogs. To my great relief they were now heading right up the trail in the canyon bottom. We followed at a stiff pace for a mile and a half to the junction of Beaver and Hollinger Creeks. There the pack headed up the rocky point between the two canyons. After a bit they angled off on the south exposure where the hillside was not so steep or rough. The track seemed fresher and the pack made fairly good time.

It was good deer country, and the lion was hunting on a wandering course along the side of the mountain. We wished him luck, for if he made a kill he would be nearby with a belly full of venison and easily treed. But luck was against him and us. He'd made a run for some deer but they had escaped.

He continued his wandering course along the brushy slope, prowling around an occasional ledge of rock. At last at sundown his tracks came to a cross-mountain trail He had headed down it and crossed the Hollinger Canyon. It was then and there we had stopped and made a lay-out camp. It was, for sure, a long dreary, chilly night for two tired and hungry hunters. Clouds darkened the sky. Hours seemed endless.

When at long last dawn came we saddled our horses, put out the fire, turned Sam loose and set out on the puma's trail once more. The dogs, like ourselves, were gaunt but anxious to go. Sam picked up the trail where he'd left it last night, and broke the wilderness silence with renewed eager trail baying accented by Pup's and Queenie's sharp barks. They seemed to forget that they'd had no supper or breakfast as they vigorously worked the trail up the timbered mountain.

While the trail actually was older than it was the night before, track scent is always easier to follow in the early morning and the dogs worked fast. The Captain and I were put to it to keep in hearing. Half way up, the tracks swung around the mountain to the left, but we angled on up an easy grade. "He is heading to Cascade Canyon," I said. "It's sure rough."

159

"Will we lose him?" my hunter asked.

"The way the dogs are talking only a sudden snow storm can stop them now," I said. "Those dogs won't quit."

During the night low clouds had darkened the sky and the air had become damp. Frost had formed heavily all over the trees. The early morning sun broke through the ominous clouds briefly to bring out the magnificent beauty and glistening sheen of the winter lace adorning the forest. We stopped to breathe the horses and were entranced by the magic scene, while the trail music of my faithful dogs thrilled me as it always does.

"If we get no lion, this is worth the trip," Captain VonGontard said.

On and on the pack went, over ridges, across draws and through timber and brush. We kept above the cliffy country into which the dogs were heading. Around a cliff near the head of Cascade Canyon they killed a lot of time. Baying became intermittent, and I knew they were stymied for the moment. We waited, and the respite was good for the horses. My hunter was worried lest they'd never find the track again.

"Old long-tail likely laid up all day yesterday somewhere in those cliffs," I said. "They'll find where he came out yesterday evening and it will be fresher and easier to follow from there on."

Before long Sam opened up again full blast. He had ranged around the cliffs and struck the tracks where the lion had left them. Pup and Queenie instantly honored the report and enthusiastically joined the chorus. We had a fast working track now! I was elated that they were heading for a saddle in the mountain at the head of Cascade Canyon instead of going down into it.

160

We urged our horses on and were close behind when they topped out through the saddle, a regular lion pass way. We loped our horses to try to keep up as the pack circled south across the flat mountain top. Suddenly they turned eastward and headed up the timbered north side of towering El Cielo Peak.

"If he doesn't kill a deer up there, I think he will cross over to Red Mountain," I said. "So let's go around the Peak and wait."

If he went the other way we'd have a hard climb and be away behind, but if he crossed to Red Mountain we would be right up front. We rode around the Peak and waited. We could barely hear the dogs and the Captain was worried that we'd lose them. As we waited the clouds lifted and revealed the bald pate of 12,000-foot Elk Mountain.

"That's the highest point in the County," I said.

"So what?" the Captain replied. "I'm sitting on the sorest spot in the whole state."

The dogs broke over the crest of the peak and suddenly their trail talk was loud, clear and eager. What a thrill! With Pup in the lead they came down the open slope hell-bent right toward us. In their anxiety they over-ran the track a hundred yards where the lion had changed course. They went back silently to circle for it. Sam soon found the track and told the world about it, and they were off again.

Now they took out toward Trout Gulch which heads between El Cielo and Red Mountain. Trail music told me the track was now hot, at most only a few hours old. Suddenly clouds closed in again and began spitting snow. "Will it cover the tracks and we lose him?" my anxious hunter asked.

161

"Even snow can't stop them now," I assured him. "They will jump him very soon."

Off we went on a long trot for a gap at the back of Red Mountain. After a wild mile ride through timber and brush we stopped in the gap to listen. To get away from puffing horses I got off and went to the canyon rim the better to interpret my dogs' baying and barking down in the gulch. Once more we'd gussed right. The dogs were heading back toward us.

The canine music was ardent, excited and expectant as the dogs raced up out of the Canyon and headed up the steep, brushy side of Red Mountain, passing only a few yards ahead of us. "Trail's mighty hot but they haven't jumped him yet," I said.

We urged the sweaty horses up the hill as fast as they could go in pursuit of the pack. Suddenly the baying became more excited, faster, higher pitched and urgent. "They've jumped old long-tail now," I yelled, "Go git him." But those dogs needed no such encouragement. All hell couldn't stop them now.

There was a few inches of old snow on this slope and we were now following right on the lion and dog tracks. Chub shied as we came squarely onto a freshly killed mule deer buck half covered with forest debris. The dogs had jumped him right off his kill.

Things were happening fast. What excitement! What a chase! What thrills! No time to examine the kill now. Chub became excited, too, and we ran off and left VonGontard. The pack went over the mountain and for a moment were almost out of hearing.

When I topped out the dogs' voices had changed again to sharper, shorter, more insistent tones, with an occasional long, high-pitched bellow from Sam. The climax of the long chase had come with the dogs barking treed!

As I rode down the hill I came in sight of them as they milled about, heads up, under a big pine tree. I got off and waited there for my hunter. Here he came down through the oak brush, brimming with excitement and with a pants leg torn half off.

"Let's hurry, let's hurry," he exclaimed.

"No use hurrying now," I said, pointing to the tree seventy yards below. He looked where I pointed and saw a beautiful sight. On a big sprangling limb some thirty feet up, the big reddish-tan cat crouched, panting heavily and twitching the black tip of his long, pendant tail back and forth as he watched his tormentors below.

The Captain jumped off his horse and jerked my .32 Winchester Special from its scabbard intending to shoot the lion from there.

"No, no," I said. "We'll go down under the tree and enjoy the show for a few minutes." Anyway I wanted him to get over the shakes.

"He will jump out and get away," he protested.

"No, his belly is full of venison and he's winded from the half mile run. He won't jump," I assured him. "Even if he did the dogs would tree him again in a jiffy."

Then the German Captain, shaking like he had ague, grabbed me and gave me a European kiss on each cheek, exclaiming, "God bless you, you got me a beautiful puma."

"Aren't you going to give Sam, Pup, Queenie, Chief and Chub any credit?" I asked.

"God bless them too," he said. "I never thought to see such dogs, such horses and such a man."

We led our horses down almost under the tree to

admire our quarry. He was, indeed, a fine trophy, reddish colored and a bit larger than the usual mature male lion. The dogs became frantic in anticipation of the end. The big cat would lay back his ears, open his mouth wide and hiss at them. It was a good, satisfying show.

Shooting a lion out of a tree is always an anticlimax. The sport and thrills are in the chase. The climax is when one hears the dogs barking treed. I had insisted that the Captain bring my light, half magazine, .32 Winchester Special instead of his scoped .30-06, because it was so much lighter and easier to carry in a saddle scabbard.

When my hunter had fully regained his composure, and the lion was getting restless and was now standing up on the limb, I had the Captain shoot for the heart to avoid spoiling the skull with a head shot.

His aim was perfect, as would be expected at such close range, and the fine old fellow went limp, sank to the limb, slid off and came tumbling down end over end.

The eager dogs pounced on him viciously and wooled the carcass off down the hill. That was their reward for the long grueling chase he had led us. We skinned the puma there, and I cut off piece after piece of the hams and fed the hungry dogs. They loved lion meat and sure had earned their feast. Too bad we couldn't take the carcass home for them.

It was two o'clock, and it had set in snowing in earnest by the time we were ready to start home, otherwise we might have cut some steaks off the lion's back and broiled them to take the edge off our hunger. We had missed three meals and a night's sleep. But if we hadn't lain out the snow would have completely obliterated the lion tracks before we caught up with him and we would have had to give up.

With the lion skin draped across the back of my saddle, and the skull in a bag on the Captain's, we set out on the long, four-hour ride back to my ranch where our wives, food and beds would be waiting for us. My German hunter had proved himself to be of good mettle and game, never once complaining of the hardships of the chase. He was more than satisfied, and I would have a bit more than my $200.00 to pay my taxes. Besides we'd all had fun.

What would Ethel say about my being twenty-four hours late getting home? She had long ago learned not to look for me until she saw me coming when I was on a lion hunt.

THREE RUGGED DAYS ALONE ON A LION'S TRAIL

10

I AWOKE with a start shaking with intense cold. I heard icy breezes murmur through the tree tops. Between frosty eyelashes I saw stars glittering in the blue-black winter sky. Lying there stiff and chilled to the bone I couldn't figure out where I was or why I should be so cold. I stretched out my hand to raise up and felt two of my Airdales curled up at my back. They, too, were shivering vigorously.

The fire in front of me had burned out. Leather jacket over sweater and woolen shirt, leather chaps and a sweat-dampened saddle blanket for cover had not been enough to withstand the piercing, sub-zero breeze of the January night on the high, rugged mountain. Nor did the pad of evergreen branches upon which I lay cut off the penetrating chill of the frozen ground. Pup, my third Airedale, who had chosen to shiver out the night alone beside a log, came over and nuzzled my hands and face. Suddenly awareness came back to me.

Night had caught me very tired from a long, hard day in the saddle on the trail of a big deer and stock-killing mountain lion. I was determined to get him. So, without bedroll or food and despite the severe cold I had decided to lay out the night in order to get a start at dawn on long-tail's trail next morning. That would save a two-hour, trailless ride in the dark to the nearest foot-hill ranch and a long climb back up next morning.

With my saddle rope I picketed my sweaty horse, Chub, in a grassy spot on the south-facing hillside where the snow had melted off. Then I gathered wood and built a roaring fire on the leeward side of a big fir tree. I made a bed mat of small fir branches, and my faithful dogs and I lay down to rest. I had not intended to go sound asleep, but tired muscles and the warm fire enticed me into the arms of Morpheus, who turned out to be a darned cold bed fellow.

I got up with my stiff body shaking as with ague from the severe cold. Clumsily grasping a stick with numb, gloved fingers I stirred up the few embers left in the ashes, put on kindling and with my cap fanned up a blaze. I piled on dead aspen limbs and poles and soon had a good big fire going. Gradually the goose flesh left first one side then the other as I turned about before the roaring fire.

I made Pup come lie down beside King and Queenie. Then I warmed the Navajo rug-saddle blanket and covered them with it. Faithful, hard working trailers, they deserved a good warm rest.

It was then one a.m. I'd slept six hours and almost froze to death. From then until the east horizon paled to herald day I kept a good fire going and tried to keep warm by it. At dawn I brought Chub in, rubbed him of dried sweat with gloved hands and saddled him. In the dim light of dawn we were off for the third day in pursuit of the mountain lion. The Airedales at once took off, a bit stiff and sore-footed, but their anxiety to find the tracks was gratifying.

This rugged lion chase had started two days before when we had come across his track two miles from my ranch on Sapello Creek. A big lion such as this one had been killing a lot of deer in that area and I had lost at least two calves, and a neighbor on Gallinas Creek had lost a saddle horse killed by a lion, likely this same lion. We needed badly to get rid of this lion and there was nothing that I liked better than a lion chase.

I was riding Chub, my top mountain saddle horse, and had my .32 Winchester Special rifle in its scabbard under my leg. My fine Airedale lion dogs were with me and anxious for a chase, so we set out on the two-day old lion tracks. I knew very well that unless the old lion killed a deer along the way it would be a long, hard chase.

From past experience I was sure his trail would lead us through deep, rugged canyons and over wind-swept ridges and cliffy hillsides. But I determined to stay on the trail of this persistent killer until we got him, even if it took a week, which it almost did.

Pup and Queenie were excellent hunting dogs, in their prime and well experienced in bobcat and lion hunting. King was their sixteen-months old offspring, husky and a fighter. He had been in on several bobcat chases, but this was his first lion, and did he like it! Seldom have I seen any breed of young dog take to an old trail as eagerly as he did this one.

It was early January and in these 8,000 to 12,000-foot elevation mountains there was considerable snow on north-facing hillsides and in the canyons which made trailing easy. But the wind-swept ridges and south exposures were partially bare and frozen hard, and what snow there was had crusted so that the dogs had a very difficult time working the old track as it meandered through the roughest country the old bugger could find.

In mid-afternoon we passed a half mile east of the old abandoned Harvey Ranch in a cove on a mountain top. Smoke was boiling out of the rock chimney of the usually vacant house. I wondered who could be there. I tooted my dog-caller cow's horn several times and the dogs left the trail and came to me, and we went up to the house.

A talkative young trapper, who gave his name as Speed Simmons, welcomed me and soon set out a hot lunch of sowbelly and beans, biscuits and coffee which I relished. The dogs were fed some accumulated table scraps, but he had no grain for Chub. Speed begged me to stay the night with him, he was lonesome for someone to talk to but, of course, I had to hurry along if I was ever going to catch up with that lion.

After the brief respite we were off again in pursuit of the wide-roving, long-tailed cat. Down we plunged into rugged Trout Gulch, then climbed out up the slippery side of Red Mountain following the lion's meandering route through steep, brushy slopes, over craggy cliffs and under rocky ledges. At dusk we followed the tracks into deep Gallinas Canyon which they crossed and headed up the other side toward Johnson Mesa towering dark and ominous above. We'd have to stop for the night.

I tooted my cow's horn. When the tired dogs came to me we headed down the road five miles to the Ranger Station where my old friend, Ranger M. M. Bruhl warmly welcomed us. There we had hay and grain for Chub, food and a bed in the barn for my Airedales, and a good supper, bed and a before-daylight breakfast for me.

As soon as I arrived I phoned my wife at the Ranch

and told her, as she suspected, that I was on the trail of a big, old lion and not to worry and not to look for me back until she saw me coming. She begged me to abandon the chase and come on home and attend to business. But I was stubborn and determined to kill that killer lion. Her last words were, "Be careful, Dad, don't let Chub fall with you, and please don't lay out over night, it's just too darned cold." "O.K." I said.

Before sunup next morning we were on the lion's trail again. It was a long, hard climb up the winding route the lion led us. At last we reached the top only to find the tracks led eastward into a series of rough ridges and gulches heading against the *mesa*. If you want to see mountain country rough side out, just follow a pack of dogs on the trail of a roving lion or bear and they will show it to you.

At times we made good headway, then were slowed to a snail's pace on the barren rocky, wind-swept slopes, and where drifting snow had filled the tracks. My Airedales trailed silently when the going was difficult and slow. But when conditions permitted them to move along, they barked and yelped some but not continuously like hounds do.

King was working as hard and faithfully as the old, experienced dogs, often showing a bit more speed. He trailed well and circled sensibly ahead to pick up the track when they lost it. He pleased me greatly for only a small percent of Airedales make good trailers and hunters. Yet when you find one that has the nose, voice, interest, intelligence and perseverance that it takes for any breed to make a good lion dog you can be proud.

Comparatively silent trailing until their quarry has been jumped is a drawback. But they make up for it by getting in quicker than hounds do, and usually tree their quarry in a much shorter chase after its track becomes right fresh. I have found the Airedales I have had to be excellent fighters any time a fight is needed. Anyway, 16-month-old King was proving that he had all the qualities inherent to a great lion dog and I was elated.

We topped out on a snowy ridge and the lion tracks showed plainly how he had stalked four deer to within fifty yards of them, then he had made the typical quick dash for his prey with sixteen-foot leaps. The deer had bounded off down the hill and the lion had missed which seldom happens. He had followed the tracks of the fleeing deer only a short distance, then turned off to hunt for another bunch. I was real sorry that he missed, for had he made a kill we would have caught him right there.

About noon we stopped briefly on the cliffy rim of a rugged canyon while I ate my sandwiches and Chub ate the grain the Bruhls had insisted that I carry along. There were table scraps for the dogs too. I had rejected fresh meat for them because it is not conducive to the best trailing.

In a half hour we took up the lion's trail again which headed southwest in an erratic course through the roughest kind of country where Chub was put to it to stay right side up. I remembered my wife had said, "Don't let Chub fall." So I walked and led him in some of the worst places.

The old lion was hunting diligently and finally found a big mule deer buck bedded down beside a pine tree. Tracks in the snow were an open book. He had cautiously stalked by scent, then when within thirty yards of the buck he lunged from a clump of fir saplings and made a mad rush.

171

The buck had made two desperate jumps but the lion caught him and they went skidding together for a few yards down hill, then a great wrestling match had taken place. It looked as though the lion was first on top then the buck. Deer hair was scattered all over the place, and the snow was spattered with blood. To my amazement the buck had finally broken away and bounded off down the hill leaving a blood-spattered trail. For the second time the lion had let his prey escape, which I have not often seen. Oh, how I'd been hoping he'd make a kill!

The butter-clawed lion did not follow the buck, but continued across the hillside leaving spots of blood beside his tracks. Soon he had climbed up on a big, flat boulder and lay down, and left a saucer-sized patch of blood-stained snow in his bed. Evidently the buck had scored with a sharp tine but not seriously injuring him, for he went on as before.

The sun dropped behind the range to the west. We passed some cliffs where it seemed the lion had lain the day before, for the tracks leading away noticeably freshened. I wished for a couple of hours more of daylight for it looked like we could over take our old lion in that time. We hurried on, but darkness overtook us too soon and we had to abandon the trail for the night. Then it was that I made the decision to lay out for the sake of a daybreak start on the track next morning. Why not? I had done it several times before and spent the long night beside a good fire, but never before in zero weather.

We crossed a rugged sidecanyon and swung around on a bench to try to pick up the tracks ahead of where we had left it last night. Queenie, the best strike dog of the three, picked up the trail scent and joyfully gave tongue. Pup and King ran to her and they were all off on the third day on long-tail's trail. This was the freshest track we had had and it seemed certain we would overtake the old bugger by noon or sooner.

The morning was bitter cold and I had to pull down my cap ear flaps. Frost formed on my eyelashes, and I had to keep rubbing my nose and cheeks to avoid frostbite. Chub's head and breast were soon snow white from the freezing of his breath. But nothing could stop us.

We followed up the mountain side, around bench lands, over and under cliffs, ever in an erratic course for Mr. Lion was hungry and hunting. To our knowledge he had not eaten for three days. King was working more enthusiastically than ever as the tracks freshened. The faithful dogs all seemed to realize that the end of the long, arduous chase must come soon.

Up and around rocky Bear Mountain we went, then down into and across Blue Canyon. The snow became deeper making trailing much easier, but traveling for Chub and the dogs much harder. Chub was lathering with sweat as we tried to keep up with the pack.

Finally, as if he had sensed that we were on his trail, the old fellow set out on a straight course toward the top of the Bull Creek divide. This country is covered with a vast forest of spruce and fir timber and runs to a high elevation. The snow became deeper and deeper the higher we went, but it was soft and not crusted.

The snow was now two feet deep and the Airedales could hardly get along even in the drag-like trail broken by the lion. Chub was put to it to keep in sight. I saw that King was now in the lead. I knew he could outdistance Queenie but he had to be good to make stout-hearted Pup accept second place. Thus they forged ahead single file, now in full cry on the hot track.

According to all my previous lion hunting experience it seemed certain that the dogs would soon force the lion to take a tree, and normally, I would have taken my time to get there. But this time I wanted to see King's actions and reactions at the finish. It certainly looked as if he would develop into a top flight lion dog, and that made me very happy.

I touched spurs to Chub's sides and urged him on in a desperate effort to keep up with the pack which I could glimpse now and then through the open forest a hundred yards ahead. Suddenly I was amazed to see the big, old lion plunging through the deep snow only a few yards ahead of the dogs. Why didn't he tree? Surely he wouldn't let the dogs overhaul him on the ground! Would he, out of character, turn and fight as a bear often does? Only once before in all my experience had I seen a lion refuse to tree when pressed by a good pack of dogs.

The short distance between King and the lion was closing. I knew the danger of my dogs getting hurt badly or killed if they caught him on the ground. Chub was winded and a-lather with sweat. With bridle reins and spurs I urged him to make a last ditch spurt. As if sensing the desperate situation we were in, he nobly responded.

The eager, excited barking and baying of the dogs made the woods ring in a manner to frighten the daylights out of any ordinary lion. But not this one! He kept on and on, lunging through the snow in the open forest disdaining to climb a tree even as the dogs closed in, barking viciously and eager for a fight. I knew it was useless to try to call them off.

Then my dire fears became reality. King lunged

ahead and grabbed the seat of the lion's pants. Like a flash the big lion turned snarling and lashed out with deadly sharp claws at the brave young dog who dodged back then went in again.

Pup was on the lion instantly and Queenie followed as the lion turned over on his back to fight as a cat does. From then on a writhing mass of dogs and lion in a whirl of flying snow was all I could make out as Chub, with heaving sides, galloped right up to the fray.

"Get back! Get back, damn you!" I yelled at the usually obedient dogs, but they had a fight on their hands and paid no attention to me. I sure didn't want to get a dog hurt or killed. I jumped off and, rifle in hand, tried my best to get a shot without hitting a dog before they got torn up by the clawing, snarling beast.

My heart sank when I saw that King was already hurt, I hoped not too badly for he was still in there fighting viciously. But his flank looked bloody and crimson splotches appeared in the snow. Through the first opening I saw between the dogs and the snarling beast, I took a chance and fired from only six feet away. Things were happening and everything moving too fast to take aim and the bullet only broke the lion's shoulder.

The dogs dodged back when the shot was fired so close to them, and the lion instantly turned right side up and attempted to bound away on three legs, still refusing to climb one of the many nearby trees. He didn't get three jumps until the dogs downed him again. King, strong-hearted and brave, went in there quickly and was fighting as viciously as the others.

As King went after the lion I saw a terrible sight that made my heart very sick. Yet I was filled with admiration for the grit, stamina and strong heart the young

175

dog displayed. His left side just back of the ribs was torn wide open. The long, needle sharp claws of the lion's front foot had been sunk deep into his loin and swiped downward with lightning speed.

A piece of his side almost as wide and long as my hand was hanging down. His intestines had been cut in two and pieces a foot long were hanging out. Despite this mortal wound he plunged without a whimper into battle with the snarling, clawing lion.

Quickly recovering from the awful shock of what I had seen, I rushed into the middle of the melee, rammed the muzzle of my rifle against the lion's breast and let him have it. Pup and Queenie continued to chew on and shake the now lifeless beast, but King backed away into the edge of the unbroken snow. He looked around at his bloody, open side and licked at it a few times. Then he looked at me pleadingly, but without even a whine.

I realized that there was no possible way of saving his life. Even if it happened in a Veterinarian's hospital I doubt if anything could have been done for him so badly were his intestines torn up.

There was just one thing that I could do for the strong-hearted young dog, and there was no use to procrastinate. It was one of the hardest things I ever had to do, but when he looked the other way I placed a mercy bullet behind his ear and instantly ended his suffering. He never knew what happened. Even if he had known I think he would have understood.

There was no way to dig a grave to bury King. So I laid his body on the snow under a low-limbed tree and piled a great mound of compacted snow over it. The snow would get deeper and deeper and stay frozen hard until late spring.

While I was happy to get that bad, stock-killing lion, it was with a sad heart, indeed, that I rode down the mountain side with his skin dangling from the back of my saddle. The grueling hardships of the three-day chase were forgotten. Following behind, tired and sore-footed, Pup and Queenie seemed as depressed as I. I'd have to spend the night at a friendly ranch for we were forty miles from home.

To put up with such things as this a ranch wife has to have a lot of mettle, patience and devotion. Mine surely has.

GAME MANAGER AND PREDATOR HUNTER

11

Vermejo park, a huge 360,000-acre cattle ranch and game preserve in the mountains of northern New Mexico, belonged to the Vermejo Club of which Harry Chandler, owner and publisher of the Los Angeles *Times*, was the mainstay. The eastern three fourths is on the Canadian River drainage, a tributary of the Arkansas, and the remainder on Costilla River watershed, tributary of the Rio Grande. Elevations range from 6,500 to near 13,000 feet. It is good cattle country and excellent deer, elk, and wild turkey habitat.

When I was employed April 1, 1930, to have charge of wildlife management and predator control, Mr. Chandler told me that the deer population was steadily decreasing and my first job was to find out why and, if possible, remove the cause.

The Club held a Class A Park Permit which permitted taking of game and fish with permission of the owner, regardless of State seasons and limits (law since repealed). However, only a limited number of guests hunted and their kill was not enough to cause a decrease in deer numbers.

Leaving my ranch I drove to Vermejo Park in my

178

Durant car, taking bedroll, camp equipment and my three excellent Airedale hunting dogs, Pup, Puse and Queenie. My top saddle mares, Brownie and Dixie, were brought up by a ranch cowboy. My wife, and my daughters 9 and 16 would come when school was out, and we'd ship by truck meagre household necessities. We would have a comfortable house at Castle Rock seven miles from ranch headquarters.

The Ranch Manager, Tom Talle, assigned to me five good saddle horses which, with my two, meant a fresh horse each day of the week. It didn't always work that way. Frequently I rode one all he could stand from daylight till noon, and another equally hard in the afternoon.

I immediately began riding the principal deer ranges to try to find out what was happening to the deer. I asked Tom Talle and the cattle foreman, Skeet Williams, about mountain lions and they said there were not enough to amount to anything. Yet, everywhere I rode I found carcasses of deer killed by lions.

A lion covers his kill with whatever forest debris is available, and even if the carcass is old that sign is evident. I also found lots of "scrapes" on their runways. Scrapes are made by male lions with short, backward strokes of their hind feet, leaving a double dig with a 3- to 6-inch pile of debris back of it.

Within the first ten days my dogs twice came near treeing a lion but were stymied when the long-tail cat took refuge in the vast stack rock area of Ash Mountain where it was impossible for dogs to follow. The excessive amount of lion sign and number of old lion kills convinced me that an over-population of lions was causing the decrease in deer. My job was not to exterminate the lions, but to drastically reduce their numbers.

179

With the amount of lion sign I found almost everywhere I felt sure I would quickly catch several. Such was not to be. When I told Talle about the amount of lion sign I was finding he kidded me, an old lion hunter, for not catching one. In mid April I told him I'd bet my job I'd get one before the end of the month.

My luck was all bad. We lost several more in the Ash Mountain stack rocks. Once when we were about to tree a lion a hard rain washed out the tracks. Another time things were looking very good when I was called off to handle a game law violation case. April 30 came and I had no lion.

At daybreak I rode to the "Wall," an upheaval of rock extending north and south across the ranch, which was a favorite passway for male lions. This time we hit old, but workable, tracks of a medium size female. It was hard, slow trailing for the dogs where the hunting lioness had meandered over the rugged country. Deer were scarce and she had no luck finding one. Finally in late afternoon we followed her tracks around a steep hillside into Leandro Creek and up it past some beaver dams.

Suddenly the dogs became excited, noses to the ground and milling around fast. Puse took off in high gear across the creek yelping eagerly. Pup and Queenie followed, and in a few minutes they were all barking treed. I pursued in a lope over logs and through brush, and there she was up a spruce tree, looking down and hissing at her tormentors. Shooting was an anticlimax, but late the thirthieth day I had a lion.

Upon field dressing her I found she had killed and eaten a large beaver, fur, feet — all but the skull. I also found that she was carrying three fetuses.

Upon being advised of my findings Mr. Chandler encouraged me to reduce the lion population, but there was much other work to be done — checking wildlife spring migration, supervising the planting of 300 acres of oats for hay, and law enforcement for there were some bad poachers.

Elk were seen daily when I rode in the high country, their summer range. Once exterminated from the State, elk were first restored here by the ranch owner in 1911. One day I ran onto a dappled elk calf less than an hour old. Its mother moved slowly away as I dismounted to examine her baby. Suddenly she turned and, with long, black neck-hair bristled up and chewing ominously, she charged me. She looked as ferocious as a grizzly bear. I took refuge behind my horse.

May 6 we had a four-inch snow and I found a turkey hen sitting on a clutch of eggs sheltered by a snowberry bush. A bit farther on we crossed hot fresh tracks of a huge black bear, and I had difficulty in preventing Pup and Puse from giving chase. Later there were tracks of a mother bear and two small cubs. Mamma had been foraging diligently for green shoots and turning over rocks and tearing up rotten logs for insects and grubs. The cubs had constantly romped and played and wallowed in the snow which could be read like a book.

And so it was month after month. One adventure after another with wildlife and the great outdoors in a magnificent country. Enjoyment and thrills justified the extremely long, hard hours of riding.

In April when I was losing lions in the stack rocks, I had trapped one but he pulled two toes off and got away. I set no more lion traps. I bought two hounds to help the Airedales. One proved worthless and was returned. A big, red female named Kate showed signs of

181

developing into a lion dog. I saw the lion's tracks again and dubbed him "Cripple Foot."

Early in June after my wife and daughters joined me, I left Castle Rock at daybreak and rode west toward the lion passway at the Wall. It had rained during the night and we, the dogs and I, were elated when we came across Cripple Foot's tracks and a scrape made after the rain — it had to be fresh. Instantly the dogs were all off on the trail in high gear, and the woods rang with their yelping and baying. I put spurs to Cyclone, my snorty mount, but we couldn't nearly keep up.

They turned north at the Wall, topped the ridge, raced down into a rough canyon and out over the next ridge, and out of hearing. I rode on stopping now and then to listen, but heard nothing. Circling around some headers I came out on a high ridge and then I heard them. There was no doubt about it, they had Cripple Foot treed. Kate was there bellowing along with the others.

When I got there the lion was standing quietly on a big limb only twenty feet up a pine tree. It was with regret as well as satisfaction that I drew my .45 Colt revolver, for he had beat me fairly many times. When he came tumbling down with a bullet through his brain I said, "Old Cripple Foot, it's too bad that it must end this way." I loped Cyclone three miles to Castle Rock, and Ethel came back on Dixie to help me pack him in. The girls were tickled speechless with my success. Fortunately, my women folk have always backed me in all my undertakings.

To spend June in New Mexico mountains is a delightful experience. Days are warm and sunny, nights cool and refreshing. Wildflowers adorn the landscape and their fragrance pervades the air. Birds are nesting,

streams are clear, and gamy trout feed at top water. Wild and domestic animals have shed winter coats and are sleek and fattening on lush herbage. Along mountain trails one runs onto new-born fawns and elk calves, a coyote den with pups inside, a turkey hen with poults in grassy parks, a grouse with chicks in alpine glades. All nature is virile and active.

Riding from daylight till dark every day I saw and enjoyed these and many other things. Also, I learned the area well enough to do effective work from then on, including game law enforcement.

One day I saw some fishermen with stringers of fish. They saw me coming and ran, and when I caught up to them they were a few feet across the Colorado State line. Regardless of the fact they had caught the trout in New Mexico without a license or permit from the Club, I could not arrest them. I had no authority to make an arrest in another State and they knew it. So I had to let them go.

Trout came up Costilla Creek to spawn but were stopped by a water storage dam and congregated there. That was a favorite place for poachers. I camped a mile below the dam one night, and after dark an old Ford car went by. I supposed it probably was the water regulator to open or close the outlet gate, but decided I'd better check whoever it was when they came out. At daybreak next morning I stopped the car of a man and woman. Also in the car was a gunny sack of nice trout. Of course I arrested them. They were known to be habitual game law violators, I'd been told to look out for them.

The Justice of the Peace was twenty miles down stream, and I had another job to do that day. So I asked the fellow if he would bring the sack of fish and meet me at the J.P.'s office at ten next morning. He was astonished and said, "Would you turn me loose and trust me that way?"

I said, "Yes, provided you give me your word you'll do it."

He studied over that for a minute, then said, "You know you are the first officer that ever trusted me to do anything. You're damn right I'll be there." He was, and was fined a hundred dollars, and the trout were given to some needy families in the village.

Some pretty tough elk poachers occasionally came from Colorado villages into the upper Costilla River area. I never had the fortune, or misfortune, to catch them. The cattle foreman, who was a deputy game warden, caught three of them dressing an elk they had killed. He placed them under arrest and told them they would have to go with him. They were affable and he didn't expect any resistance, and failed to take possession of their guns which were leaning against a nearby tree.

While discussing where they'd have to go, one of them had edged, unnoticed, over toward the rifles. Suddenly he grabbed one, covered the foreman, made him drop his six-shooter and get off his horse. They unsaddled and turned the horse loose with a whack on the rump that sent him galloping off down the canyon. Then at rifle point they ordered the foreman, afoot and unarmed, to get going. It was eight miles to the first cattle camp, and no chance to catch his horse. Next day he recovered his horse, saddle and gun, but the poachers got away.

On a cold winter day a cowboy under similar circumstances had been disarmed. He talked them into building a fire so he could warm his feet before taking off. He astutely watched his chance, grabbed a rifle, covered them and brought them in. I handled a number of game law violation cases but always was cautious and never had any trouble.

On the C. S. ranch a dozen miles south of Castle Rock a Biological Survey trapper-hunter was stationed. He sent me word that he was having trouble getting his young dogs to keep a lion treed till he could get there, and wanted me to help him. Before daylight one morning I headed that way. Enroute my dogs hit a very fresh lion track and treed him within a half mile. Tingling with anticipation I rode toward them.

Soon I saw a beautiful, tawny lion coming down the tree and I knew he would jump out and it was too far to shoot with my revolver. He jumped and the dogs gave chase as he raced over the ridge. Soon they again barked treed, but when I got within a hundred yards he jumped out again. I could now see he was trying to get to the stack rock country. The pack treed him for the third time, but now if he made one more run he'd be able to get into the slide rocks. How to prevent it was a dilemma. He had been jumping out only when he saw me coming. So I must not let him see me this time.

I tried stalking afoot, but I could not keep under cover. So I decided to play dog. I left my hat and crawled toward the tree on my hands and knees, yelping steadily in imitation of the Airedales as best I could. The ruse worked and I got within easy pistol range. Did you ever have your dogs call you a damned fool? Mine sure did me! Anyway the Survey trapper-hunter was happy that I'd got his aggravating lion.

Tom Talle planned a big Fourth of July picnic on Costilla Creek for ranch employees and their families. Everybody brought fine food, and we spread it out on my six by fourteen-foot tarp in a beautiful aspen grove. Tom said, "If nobody else is going to say Grace, I'll just say good bread, good meat, Good Lord let us eat." Then Ted Paddock, a late arriving cowboy, loped up on a sweat-lathered horse. He jumped off and said, "Mr. Talle, we've got a bad forest fire going."

"Where?" Tom asked.

"Between York and Caliente Canyons." It was 20 miles to headquarters and that would be 15 miles beyond.

Tom knew of my experience with the Forest Service and said, "Barker, you had better take charge."

"All right," I said. "But you know as well as I what has to be done."

He said, "You give the orders."

I said, "We must get on it as soon as possible, but it is unwise to go to a fire on an empty stomach. Let's make haste and eat this grub, then drive to headquarters and get tools and water. Someone can bring the left-over food for our supper at the fire." We ate a lot of fine food but the picnic was smothered by smoke.

From the Costilla Divide we could see dark brown smoke boiling up some 30 miles away, and it looked bad. At headquarters we got axes, shovels, heavy rakes and hoes, a keg of water and some canteens, and hurried in pickup trucks to the fire. There were eight of us and we got within a mile with the trucks and walked on. By four P.M. we started cleaning breaks to surround the hundred-acre fire.

It had been started by lightning, but was not in too bad country. The mild breeze wouldn't interfere much. We worked furiously and at dark two cowboys came on horseback. We put them to work and sent Tom horse-back to bring more water and the food. By exerting every effort by nine o'clock we had a pretty good break around

187

the entire perimeter. Tom came back, and put the two late-coming cowboys on patrol. The rest of us had a good supper from picnic left-overs. The patrolmen came in and reported everything O.K. So Tom and the others, except Ted and I, went back to the trucks and on to headquarters to be ready for tomorrow's jobs.

Ted and I patrolled all night and until mid-afternoon next day. The wind came up, and there were several breaks over the line, and it kept us jumping to control them. To our delight, in mid-afternoon there came a hard rain and hail storm which put the fire completely out. After forty hours on the go, at 9 P.M. I got back home dead tired and grimy. That was the start of the rainy season, and ended fire troubles.

Throughout the summer other work prevented lion hunting, but wherever I rode I saw lion sign — some fresh, some old. They'd killed lots of deer, two turkeys, beavers, porcupines and one saddle horse, but no elk. In widely separated areas I saw tracks of a lioness with the outside lobe of her left hind foot missing, and named her Scar Heel. She had some husky kittens following her. I promised my impatient dogs we'd get a run after her some day.

In September elk came out of the high country for mating season, and bulls were bugling all over the place. They broke through fences and damaged the oat fields. One night we drove through a valley and saw many elk in the car lights, and bulls bugled all around us. One day I rode into a narrow old log skidway in which there was a huge bull elk with massive antlers. I rode toward him, but he didn't run. Suddenly he bristled his neck hair, began chewing and came right at me. I put spurs to Dixie and plunged into the adjacent thicket. The bull snorted

...r Barker has served as the American Forestry Association's representative in charge of 25 of its ...y wilderness trail rides in five different states. The trips have drawn thousands of people over the ...who come from many different life styles and locations to experience the splendor of the Great ...west. Today at the age of 88, the frontiersman still makes pack-in trips into the wilderness.

Horses and riders take to the bushes in the Pecos wilderness north of Santa Fe, New Mexico. The ride, like the others offered by the American Forestry Association, provides a majestic mountain vi...

A rushing mountain stream quenches the thirst during a trek in the Pecos wilderness.

Packing their horses with duffel, bed rolls, tents and other gear, wilderness trail riders break cam

A cold brook provides relief for hot feet.

serenity and beauty of a mountain lake make it a favorite lunch stop.

A weary rider on Colorado's San Juan wilderness trail ride is caught napping.

Gathered around last night's still-smoldering bonfire, a group of wilderness riders enjoys a trout breakfast before starting the day's ride.

Experienced anglers as well as novices find the fishing good.

Heading home after 11 days in the wilderness.

as he passed just behind me. I had trapped him, for his antlers would not permit him to go into the thicket and he had no choice but to run over me unless I got out of his way.

My son Roy came to visit us, and he and I afoot cornered another bull the same way in a little glade, and we were blocking the only way out. He bristled and charged us and we ducked aside just in time.

The cattle outfit had an arrangement with the Club to use a few elk for meat to compensate for their continual damage to fences. Beginning in September it fell to me to kill a young cow now and then for them. Once I couldn't resist taking a big bull, but he was tough.

Late in September a few guest elk and deer hunters began to come, and it was up to me to guide as many as I could and send others into good hunting country. That took precedence over all other work. These were mostly wealthy people, some experienced hunters and others novices. Most were good sportsmen, but I had to ride herd on a few to keep them within the law and Club rules. Good hunters sometimes wanted to kill for a less-skilled partner. That was not permissable.

A young novice hunter and I trailed a small herd of elk to a sharp ridge top that formed the property line, beyond which hunting was taboo. It was in open timber and when I saw that the herd had crossed the line I said, "Well, that's that." A fine bull bedded right on the line heard me and sprang to his feet and stood broadside not forty yards away. The young hunter dropped him in his tracks. As if by design he had waited, for two steps farther would have been out of bounds.

Walt Smiley, a Club employee, and I took four deer hunters out one afternoon. We separated, each taking two hunters. Very soon one of his hunters shot a fine buck, and thirty minutes later the other one shot several times and got his. That buggered a bunch that we had been trailing and they turned and came straight to us. One of my men shot a very large buck, and the other what looked to have barely legal antlers. We found that it was a big cactus buck with the antler bases and between covered by a velvety growth several inches thick. From it hung dozens of tublar strips of velvet-like skin from one to six inches long. The hunter was delighted with this most unusual trophy. We had been exceedingly lucky to get four bucks because deer were quite scarce.

The next day we took the same hunters out after elk and they were successful in bagging two medium-size bulls. We field dressed them and left them there over night. Next day we found that my Scar Heel lion and near-grown young had come by one bull and laid claim to it. While they had not eaten a bite, they had clawed up what grass and debris they could up against it. Pieces of bark from a nearby pine log had been leaned up against the back and legs of the carcass. That's rare feline ingenuity. I might have brought the dogs and gotten her but there were other hunters to take care of.

By November 10, sportsmen were gone, and I could get on with the job of reducing the predator population. In the first week I took three lions and four bobcats with the dogs and trapped three coyotes. The lions were Scar Heel's yearlings, but she had skillfully eluded us.

Some readers will protest so much killing, but when predators become over abundant, as they certainly were here, it is just as important to reduce their numbers as it is to reduce deer and elk over populations back down to the carrying capacity of the ranges. There was no extermination involved, and my year's work here resulted in the deer population building up to the carrying capacity of the range and remaining so to this day.

Trapping is cruel, but unlike poison, it can be made selective by releasing unwanted animals such as dogs, foxes, badgers etc. Poison is an indiscriminate killer, and I have never used it in taking predators.

Trapping a coyote is no more cruel than he is to his prey. He will chase a deer, even a big buck, for hours until it is exhausted and stops, perhaps in a creek, to fight. He worries his prey nipping its legs, flanks and nose until it is forced to give up and is killed by a neck hold. A coyote will kill a hen turkey and leave the poults to suffer and perish. Sometimes he catches young poults and grouse chicks and gulps them down whole. I know of authentic instances where three small poults were found in a trapped coyote's stomach. On the ranch a heifer was having difficulty giving birth to her calf. When I approached a coyote was eating on the head and neck of the half born calf, while at the time the heifer was helpless to fight it off. I've seen lots of predator cruelty to prey but there's no use telling of more.

On November 19, a terrific snow storm broke. In the forenoon I rode ten miles to a cow camp with a message from Mr. Talle. It was cold going, and colder and miserable facing the wind-blown snow coming back. It seemed that we might be snowed in, so that afternoon I drove down to headquarters for supplies. It was foolish for me to let Ethel and Dorothy go with me for six inches of snow had fallen and more was coming. When we started back at dusk there was a foot of snow at headquarters.

They begged us to stay the night there, but I thought we could make it, we nearly didn't.

199

We drove four miles up the main canyon, then turned up Rock Creek where the road paralleled a deep *arroyo*. Now it was snowing so hard I couldn't see the road. I'd walk ahead with flash light and mark a track to follow, then go back and drive to the end of my tracks. That was slow, and as the snow got deeper we had to rush the grades, back up and try again and again to get up.

Then the lights went out, and it looked as if we'd have to spend the night there. I had an extra can of gas and knew I could build a big fire in the woods and not freeze, but the outlook was not pleasant. I checked the wiring and found nothing wrong. I put in a spare fuse I thought was all right, but still no lights. Finally, with tinfoil chewing gum wrappings, we made a fuse-size roll and inserted it in the fuse slot. To our great relief, the lights came on. In another hour we had battled our way to Castle Rock.

Next day there was a foot of snow at Castle Rock, eighteen inches at headquarters and as much as thirty inches in many places on the ranch. I dragged in and chopped firewood, and did other chores. The ranch foreman with a squad of cowboys came and moved into a nearby house to gather cattle still in the area.

The following morning the sun came out, and I could get back to my lion hunting. Trailing would be perfect. In the upper field I saw a magnificent sight. Six or seven hundred elk had come out of the high country and were bunched up there in the field. To my dismay, I soon found that some had broken into one of the long haystacks, and I spent the day rebuilding the fence instead of hunting.

From that time on I had many high adventures

with my fine dogs and horses in quest of lions and bobcats, but only the high spots may be told here. The snow
was hard on horses, but when we hit a track we could
usually count on getting our quarry.

On my first day out we had taken three bobcats.
With skins back of my saddle, the dogs had jumped another and were running heads up on his trail. Suddenly I
saw Puse and Pup put on the brakes, turn back and begin sniffing at something else — a strange thing to do.
Before I could get to them the four dogs took off up the
hill at right angles to the bobcat's course. I found they
had picked up a ten-to fifteen-hour old lion track. I
marveled that while running with heads up in bobcat
pervaded air they'd caught the scent of an old lion track.
They were correct in shifting to it.

My horse was tired but I'd have to follow the big
lion's track. I couldn't let the pack down. They topped
the ridge and headed east along it in the opposite direction of home. On and on they went meandering back and
forth across the ridge and, with a very tired horse, I was
put to it to keep up. Just at sundown I heard the pack
furiously barking treed. From the frantic baying I knew
the lion was low in the tree and in sight. Sure enough
the huge, long-tailed fellow was lying in the crotch of a
pinon tree only ten feet up. I approached cautiously with
my .45 Colt ready for a quick shot should he start to
jump out. He was panting heavily and showed no signs
of trying to get away. From twenty-five feet away I sent
a heavy lead slug through his brain. He was the largest
of the sixteen lions I took during the year.

I left him there; we'd get him tomorrow. It was getting dark, we were fifteen miles from home, the snow
was a foot deep, the thermometer would hit zero before

morning and my horse was completely worn out. I hung my chaps on the saddle and set out afoot leading the tired horse, with the equally-tired dogs strung out behind him. I walked all the way except for a couple of down grades when I rode to rest my legs.

Arriving at the barn a little before midnight I found Skeet and his cowboys saddling up to go hunt for me. Ethel had become worried and rousted them out of bed to do that. Putting up with me and such escapades, no wonder Ethel's hair prematurely turned gray!

A few days later we hit a good trail of Scar Heel, and she led us a merry chase for a while. Then, trying to get away from the dogs, she plunged over the cliffs that rim the ridge-top southeast of headquarters. The pack found a way to get down and treed her two hundred yards below. I was riding sturdy, faithful Dixie but no horse could go down over those ledges. I left her with reins dragging in a barren spot on the wind-swept ridge.

I finally found a break in the cliffs where I could slide off, then waded through two-foot deep snow to the dogs to end Scar Heel's career. Tomorrow I would come from below and get her. I wallowed through the brush-laden snow back up to the rim rocks. They were snow-covered and slick and I just could not find a place to scale them. I was stuck below and my horse was on top.

At last I gave up and waded through the snow a couple of miles down to headquarters. I was sopping wet to my waist, but dried out before a fireplace. Mrs. Talle fed me and Tom got me a horse to ride back to Castle Rock. I got home at dark and would have to leave Dixie until next morning. When I got to her she was right where I had left her. I had broken her myself and taught her to stay wherever I dropped the reins.

We moved to a house at headquarters so I could hunt and trap the winter range where predators would be concentrated. Snow soon melted off of south exposures and bottom lands, and I put out a string of coyote traps and took 46 that winter. That would save some deer and turkeys and young calves in the spring. Bobcat hunting was fairly successful also and I took 39. Two incidents are worth recording.

My dogs were well trained and fearless. They would watch me set a trap and scent bait it. If we passed it next day or a month later they would circle around it. They would run a coyote only when he got away with a trap, then they'd trail him up for me. Their fearlessness sometimes got them in trouble. Once they chased a bear and as he started up a tall pine, Puse grabbed him by the seat of the pants and didn't let go until he was twenty feet off the ground.

One day they treed two half-grown bobcats and went on after the mother. I followed leisurely expecting to hear them bark treed at any time, but no, and it puzzled me. When at last I came upon them a real big female bobcat was stretched out on the snow stone dead. Pup and Puse were rubbing blood off their heads on the snow. Instead of treeing the cat had gone in a hole extending six or seven feet back in the rocks only big enough for one dog at a time to go in. It seemed that Pup had gone in, faced the cat and absorbed all she could give with teeth and claws to get a neck hold. He had dragged her out and Puse helped finish the job. That took nerve, but I had to sew up their cuts.

On another occasion I got into a ludicrous situation. We were chasing a bobcat with three two-thirds grown young ones in foot-deep snow. I saw where one had taken

a tree, so I got off Dixie and shot for his head with my
.45 Colt revolver. He fell limp and I picked him up and
tied him on the back of the saddle, got on and hurried
along.

Suddenly Dixie flinched and threatened to buck. I
put a stop to that with bit and spurs. In another moment
she kicked up and started to buck in earnest. I tried to
hold her head up. Then I saw the bobcat had come to
life. I'd only grazed his skull and stunned him. Now
struggling to get loose, he was raking front claws up
across Dixie's left flank, and kicking down across the
other with his hind feet. Oh, my! The bullet had just
grazed his skull, knocking him out.

While trying to control Dixie with my right hand,
I grabbed for his neck with my left, but OUCH! He bit
me. Then my right knee got bumped against an aspen
and knocked me partly out of the saddle. The cat grabbed
that part of my anatomy below the waist that chaps
don't cover and hung on. I grasped his neck and squeezed
with all my might as we went bobbing around and
around. The cat was first to let go, and I hung on till he
went limp and Dixie quit bucking. What a merry-go-
round that was! Neither Dixie nor I were injured seriously. Ethel and Dorothy sure had a good laugh at my
expense when I told them about it.

A serious accident happened once when I was riding
hard after the pack on a lion trail. I was riding Buster, a
big, snorty horse, and turned him too sharply in a canyon bottom on an unnoticed sheet of ice formed from
melting snow. His feet went out from under him and he
fell flat on his right side with my leg under him.

I had on boot overshoes and it flashed through my
mind that my foot might hang in the stirrup when Buster

got up. I grasped the right bridle rein and took a wrap around my right hand. I knew I must hold on to it at all costs. Buster lunged to his feet and, as I feared, my foot was hung in the stirrup. If Buster got his head I knew I'd be dragged and kicked to death. He kicked at me and tried to get away, but I held the rein and jerked his mouth unmercifully to control him.

He went around in a circle dragging me on my behind as I tried every way to free my foot. I couldn't get my knife out to cut the stirrup straps, and couldn't get back in the saddle. Buster became more jittery by the second. I was facing a horrible death but, fortunately, did not panic. At last I saw I might get loose by unbuckling my overshoe.

I lunged up again and again and finally jerked the one buckle open. My boot slipped easily out of the overshoe, and I was free! I got up and quieted Buster, then led him a hundred yards before getting on. When I did start to get on I couldn't. My knees were weak and I was trembling all over. I had to sit on a log and get over the reaction. Finally, going on and killing another lion was an anticlimax.

My total predator take that year was 16 lions, 46 coyotes and 39 bobcats. The Survey hunter took 3 lions. There were five or six left. A lion will kill an average of 50 deer a year. The annual deer kill of the lions we took and left would be 1,200. That was more than the annual increase of the deer herd, hence the necessity for this reduction.

I worked very hard on this job and had many adventures and lots of fun. I also learned much about wildlife and its management.

Effective April 1, 1931, the State Game Commission

appointed me State Game Warden of New Mexico (Director, Dept. Game and Fish).

The change was most welcome; the job was a challenge. My family had followed me deep into the woods, and it was time to bring them out.

12 STATE GAME WARDEN

I took the oath of office as State Game Warden of New Mexico (Director, Department of Game and Fish) on April 1, 1931. When I declared that the Department thenceforth would be operated free of partisan politics there were many who considered that date prophetic of a short tenure. There was some basis for it because, under political appointments there had been ten Game Wardens in 27 years, an average tenure of 2.7 years.

On the other hand, I knew that I had full backing of the State Game Commission. I also knew that the chairman of the Commission, Colin Neblett, a Federal District Judge, was a strong man of high principles whom the politicians respected. The showdown wasn't long coming, and it was double-barreled.

First, the Governor was pressuring me to employ some political friends whom I did not consider qualified. Second, it was the policy of the party in power to assess all employees of the State two percent of their salaries to support the political organization. The Democratic State Chairman was insisting that I pay and require all of the Department employees to pay that two percent, and threatening to have me fired if I didn't. I positively refused to pay political tribute; instead, I'd do the best job possible. Within six weeks the situation was really getting hot.

The Game Commission met and I told them of the situation. Commission member, James B. McGhee, said, "Mr. Chairman, I move we recess for an hour and go work the Governor over." Gilbert Espinosa seconded the motion. They went and had it hot and heavy, for the Governor had strong feelings about it. At one point the Commissioners all tendered their resignations. They were all well known and highly respected men and the Governor knew it would be politically most unwise to accept them. When they came back they assured me that I would have no more trouble on those scores. What a relief that was!

Actually as long as the two per cent assessment policy was in effect I was nagged at to get in line. Other departments saw us refusing to pay and, since we were getting by with it, some began resisting also. That vicious policy was later renounced by both parties. Often Governors, State and County party chairmen urged me to employ political friends, but no threats of having me fired were made when I refused to accede. During my twenty-two years tenure no one was ever hired or fired for political reasons, nor did I ever drop a Game Law violation case for political reasons.

We prosecuted high and low offenders alike. My list of prosecutions for violation of game laws and regulations included a lieutenant governor, a governor's son-in-law, a democratic state chairman (in a democratic administration), a legislator, Armed Services privates, majors and colonels, a chief of State Police, State policemen, various State employees, preachers, a priest, prominent lawyers, doctors, businessmen, sheepherders, cowboys, farmers, school teachers and even a member of the State Game Commission. The public supported that policy.

Often there was political pressure brought to bear from high and low to get game law violators off. Once a field warden arrested a Spanish-American friend of mine. He was a very small man, spoke broken English and was quite a precinct politician. The charge was fishing before the season, without a license and taking a double limit of trout. He insisted upon conferring with me to try to get off the hook so he wouldn't have to go to court.

He said, "Meester Bark' you know I ees good sportmen, and I always buy license and do what the law say. Thees times I forgets and don't get license to feesh, and I go just one leetle day too soon, and them damn feesh they bites so good I can't stops and catch only two limits."

I said, "Tito, that is pretty serious."

He said, "Now Meester Bark', I am good democrats and you are good democrats, why you not just forgets eet?"

I said, "My friend, you know I can't do that." But he continued to argue that he worked hard for the party and got out the votes on election day, and that I should for get it all because I was a good democrat. When I told him that he definitely would have to let the judge settle the case just like anyone else he got awfully mad at me.

Later in telling a mutual friend about it he said, "I tell Meester Bark' how we both good democrats and ask heem to forgets thees leettle things, but he won'ts listen to me, but say I have to go to courts. He makes me mad, he makes me so mad I wants to fight, and I would fights and wheep heem too, but the sonama beech ees twice my heavy."

209

I had long wanted this position, and my name had been discussed in 1918 when Dennis Chavez, later a long-time U.S. Senator, was Acting Warden for a few months. Then in 1926 the position was offered to me. Dr. Aldo Leopold, who had sponsored me, urged me to take it. Regretfully I had to decline because of the situation at my ranch. Now that I held the responsible position I found that it was the greatest challenge of my whole life.

Dr. J. Stokley Ligon had just made a thorough game survey of the State which emphasized the need for building up deer, turkey and antelope populations, and restoring bighorn mountain sheep, elk and sage chickens. Waterfowl was at an all-time low and its habitat required attention. The 1931 Legislature had just passed a long-sought law giving the State Game Commission full regulatory powers to manage the wildlife resources of the State. Prior to that the Legislature set hunting and fishing seasons and bag limits, and made laws to regulate all hunting and fishing activities and management policies. A ridiculous situation.

The drafting of rules and regulations to replace laws for approval, amendment or rejection by the Game Commission was a tremendous undertaking. Sportsmen's conservation organizations made helpful recommendations, but they were often conflicting, adding to other difficulties. The Game Commissioners worked hard with me on it, and someway we got the job done. They stood the test when challenged in court.

We found that eight cents a mile was being paid the field force for use of their personal cars and an average of about 25,000 miles a year was being driven. We felt sure we could save money by using State-owned cars. The field men all objected, claiming that they were losing money at eight cents. One man became so belligerent about it that I had to dismiss him. We bought Ford and Chevrolet cars and pickups, and for many years operated them for a total cost of four cents and less per mile. That included depreciation, gas, oil, repairs — everything. Cost of car was charged and trade-in price credited. On seven vehicles we saved $7,000 a year.

We were soon beset with financial difficulties. The Department's revenue, its sole support, had built up to $135,000 a year, but with the great depression, it dropped to $100,000 and then to $92,000. Salaries were meagre anyway, but now had to be cut to a mere existence, not a living wage. When I wrote all employees and told them that we would either have to lay off a number of employees or drastically cut salaries, my own included, and asked them which they would recommend, everyone said, "Cut salaries, don't lay off anybody." I was proud of them, for times were as hard as they have ever been, and there just were no other jobs to turn to.

Our revenue then was only one twenty-fifth of what the Department has to operate on today — over two and a half million dollars. Taking into consideration a 250% increase in cost of everything the revenue is still ten times as much as we had then.

My total force for a few years was 27 to 30 men and women. Yet with Federal WPA and PWA funds (work relief), we built two new trout hatcheries to replace two. Those replaced were strictly politically-located hatcheries built during the previous administration where the spring water supply was wholly inadequate and only a fiftieth of that at the new locations. Then in the 1940s, when revenues had materially increased, a third trout hatchery on Red River was built which now produces 200 thousand pounds of trout each year.

Deer populations were low, estimated by Dr. Ligon in 1927, to be sixty thousand. Yet there were a few spots such as Black Canyon in the Gila National Forest and spots on the west side of the Sacramento mountains where they exceeded the capacity of the range. The New Mexico Game Protective Association and its affiliated chapters had worked hard to get the regulatory power law passed so that such situations could be properly corrected. Despite that fact, when the first doe seasons were set to correct those situations, many of the sportsmen were up in arms protesting it.

Black Canyon was badly over-populated and damaged, so in the fall of 1931, hunters took a total of 26 deer per square mile from a hundred square mile area, about four fifths of the population. So badly was the range over-stocked by deer and cattle that it would have been better to have removed all of both for a time. But many sportsmen in the area, ignoring habitat conditions, protested bitterly about removing what we did. Drouth followed — the dust bowl era — and browse plants were slow to recover. It took several years to convince many sportsmen and other conservationists that does had to be killed here and there to keep the herds within the carrying capacity of the range. I believe we did finally convince ninety percent of them that occasional doe killing is a necessary game management tool.

Generally, deer needed to be increased. We controlled no lands and had no means of improving habitat. The only available tools we had to work with were a system of game refuges, strict law enforcement and predatory animal control. Dr. Ligon did much of the work of selecting and laying out refuges. My five District Wardens with the help of a large number of unpaid, voluntary deputy wardens — in many cases ranchers — and Forest Officers did a pretty thorough job of enforcing the game laws and stopping illegal killing of game. We put on a half dozen predator hunters and trappers in areas needing such work. The U.S. Biological Survey assisted in this field also, but they worked principally where damage was being done to domestic livestock. Anyway, in twenty-two years the estimated number of deer increased from 60,000 to 200,000.

Law enforcement was not always pleasant, sometimes it was difficult, but often had its humorous side. One time a District Game Warden with binoculars saw a businessman and his plump wife, while hunting doves, shoot down several quail and put them in their game bags. Quail season was not open. He went to them in a weedy abandoned field to check their game bags but found no quail. They denied having shot any quail. The warden suspected they had seen him coming in time to throw the quail away, and was about to start hunting for them when his sharp eyes detected three bulges in the lady's blouse where nature provides only two.

He accused her of having the quail there and asked her to produce them. They vigorously denied having any quail there or anywhere else, and the man got mad and threatened to whip the warden for accusing his wife of any such thing. The warden had seen them shoot the quail and he put them under arrest, then took their guns. He said, "Now Madam, bring those quail out or I shall be forced to go in after them." She cursed him, turned her back and took seven blue quail out of her blouse.

Pronghorn antelope had been reduced from an estimated hundred thousand or more down to the mere seventeen hundred head estimated in 1916 by Dr. Aldo Leopold. As the result of a cooperative program of the Department of Game and Fish, the ranchers, and New Mexico Game Protective Association, by 1931 the herds had been built up to about four thousand head. In a few areas they were abundant, but in many areas of suitable habitat there were none at all.

Since these animals are highly polygamous, we decided in 1932 to have a mature buck hunting season with the number of permits limited to 300. Thus, in specific areas we would utilize the surplus bucks for sport shooting and, we hoped, scatter the herds to nearby uninhabited areas. It certainly was sound game management, but again sportsmen rebelled, claiming we were out to destroy the herds they had helped to build up.

Of 300 permits offered only 49 were taken. Otherwise the season was a great success as every permittee got a trophy. The next year 150 permits were authorized and 149 were taken. Since then there have always been more applicants than permits and public drawings are held annually to determine who gets the permits. When antelope herds increased satisfactorily despite the mature buck seasons, sportsmen agreed we were right. They continued to object, however, to our charging $5 for the permits and $10 for elk permits in addition to the big game license specified by law for deer, bear and turkey. The legislature came to our rescue and provided a $5 antelope and $15 elk license.

Despite these differences with sportsmen's organizations, in practically all other major matters I always had the support of organized and individual sportsmen. Certainly there were some who made a lot of noise over small matters, but they were a small minority. Over my desk as this is written hangs an unusual, framed scroll highly laudatory of my twenty-two years work which was presented me by the New Mexico Wildlife and Conservation Association when I retired.

The eleven western States (now 13) have an organization which was formed in 1918 called the Western Association of State Game and Fish Commissioners of which New Mexico was a charter member. I attended my fourth annual meeting in Portland, Oregon in June, 1934. Judge Colin Neblett, Chairman of the Game Commission, my wife and daughter, then 13, accompanied me. It was in the depths of the great depression and attendance was poor.

At that time the U.S. Forest Service had come up with a regulation, called G-20-A, which purported to give the Forest Service authority to set seasons and bag limits on big game in National Forests under certain circumstances. The Western Association felt strongly that this was an infringement on State's rights, and Judge Neblett and I had taken the lead in opposing it.

At this Western Association meeting, it was the principal item under discussion, and I presented the resolution that was adopted opposing it. We had to leave before the meeting was over and officers elected. When we took our leave, I was asked which route we would take. I said through California's interior route. The Oregon Department Director then told me to stop at Stockton, California to pick up a wire.

I asked, "What about?"

All he would say was, "You will have to wait and see."

We received the wire in Stockton the next day noon and it read, "Congratulations upon your election as President of the Western Association." I was completely flabbergasted, for I had no inkling that they had even thought of such a thing. Judge Neblett got a kick out of my confusion for he had been in on the deal.

While that would add to my heavy work load, I felt pleased and honored, and wanted to hurry on home and get with it, but the Judge said, "Barker you haven't taken a day off in three years, you must take a vacation. I'll go back by train from Los Angeles, you and Ethel go to Catalina Island. Don't come back to Santa Fe for ten days, that's an order." We really enjoyed the first vacation we'd had in three years.

The Association presidency meant lots of work, and the next year they re-elected me — the first man ever to succeed himself in that position. In September that year, 1935, I went to the annual meeting of the International Association of Game, Fish and Conservation Commissioners in Oklahoma. New Mexico had been a member but, due to lack of funds, we had not paid the $25 annual dues for two years.

The Taylor Grazing Act, passed in 1934, brought the Public Domain lands under government supervision and regulated use for the first time.There was much activity by stockmen and wildlife interests throughout the west in working out the governing rules and regulations. Now on some issues, the livestock interests and wildlife conservationists were opposing each other. Ranchers fearing that wildlife would be given too much consideration and conservationists fearing, with reason, that they would not be given enough.

I was on the program to present the wildlife and

216

conservation standpoint, and Captain B. C. Mossman, a very prominent New Mexico sheep and cattleman, was to present the stockmen's position. The evening before I left for Oklahoma, Captain Mossman phoned me that business matters would prevent him from going. I urged him to send someone in his place, but he said it was too late for that. I said, "Well, what will we do? A one-sided discussion is no good."

Mossman said, "Barker, you know our position as well as I do. You just go ahead and make my speech for me."

So I made the two speeches, presenting both sides as fairly as I could. It was nice to know the ranchers trusted me despite disagreements.

My surprise at being elected President of the Western Association was dwarfed when I was nominated for President of the International. I declined as I was already overworked and, since New Mexico had not paid its dues, I said I was ineligible. The Treasurer, Ray P. Holland, long-time editor of *Field and Stream,* took issue with me declaring that New Mexico was paid up and produced his books to prove it. I knew we had not paid for two years. They overruled me and my protests, and elected me President of the International Association of Game, Fish and Conservation Commissioners. (Ray Holland had personally paid our dues.)

I am the only man who ever has served as president of both organizations at the same time until Harry R. Woodward, who served briefly in 1970. On my wall there is a large plaque which says, "In Recognition of Elliott S. Barker for His Service as President of the International **** 1935-36."

We got some pretty good rules for wildlife adopted

for the Public Domain lands under the Taylor Grazing Act. Seth Gordon, my successor as president of the International, finished the fight we had been carrying on against Regulation G-20-A, and the Forest Service came up with a satisfactory cooperative substitute which restored harmony.

In January, 1936, I was appointed by President Roosevelt as a member of a 25-man committee to arrange for and set up the first National Wildlife Conference. The conference was held in Washington, D. C. February 2 to 7, 1936. I was one of the program speakers and served as chairman of one session.

On the closing day of the conference the National Wildlife Federation was organized with J. N. Ding Darling being elected President. I was honored by being elected as a member of the Federation's first Board of Dirctors. I have worked with the organization through the years and was its New Mexico representative from 1959 to 1966.

Let's get back to New Mexico wildlife administration. The need for restoring pronghorn antelope to a great many areas from which they had disappeared was urgent. How to do it was the problem. Other states, Canada and the U.S. Biological Survey had failed in efforts to trap and transplant them. Despite that fact, in 1935, Judge Neblett, Chairman of the Game Commission, passed the buck to me by saying, "Barker, it's up to you to find a way." I in turn handed the package to District Game Warden Paul Russell, stationed at Magdalena adjacent to our best antelope country.

In the spring of 1937, after two years study during which time I often conferred with him and gave him all the asisstance I could, we made wildlife restoration history. We successfully trapped and transplanted 34 head of pronghorns, moving some of them long distances. We made a lot of mistakes and killed too many, but in doing so we learned how to get the job done.

We revised our equipment and methods, and late that fall began thoroughly successful operations with minimum losses. From then until I retired in 1953 we trapped and transplanted 2,800 head to start about sixty new herds. Texas and several western states sent their wildlife technicians to observe our methods and get specifications on our equipment, and went ahead with the program in their respective states. This pioneering restoration project was one of the outstanding accomplishments of my administration.

Elk were indigenous to all mountain areas of the State, but by 1890 they had been exterminated — not one remained. Initial restoration was by Vermejo Park in 1911. The next major planting was in the Pecos Wilderness by the Game Department in 1915 when 37 head were released. The herd thrived and we have had seasons there starting in 1933. The TO Ranch near Raton and the GOS Ranch near Silver City stocked elk in 1917. Ranchers made these plantings at their own expense.

During my administration we stocked several other areas, one of which, near Tres Piedras, quickly developed into a huntable herd. The others are coming along, also. Additional stockings since I retired have resulted in practically all suitable habitat areas being re-populated with these magnificent animals.

Sage chickens were brought in from other states to stock their original habitat areas, but they have not prospered. The Dust Bowl era in the early 1930s almost exterminated our prairie chickens from the sandhill country of eastern New Mexico. We did all we could, under Dr. Ligon's supervision, to effect a comeback. He originated a type of water-catchment units, and we installed some. We set up Game refuges where they would not be disturbed by quail and dove hunters.

Then, after Federal Aid to Wildlife Funds became available, we bought about 30,000 acres of prairie chicken habitat lands in scattered units and fenced them to permit restoration of natural food and cover, and planted some crops for them. We again have some chicken hunting.

In the drouth and depression era, Dr. Ligon and I, while inspecting the prairie chicken situation, spent the night with a dry-land farmer. Despite the drouth he had raised a fair crop of corn. I was stunned to see him using ears of corn for firewood! He said he couldn't sell a ton of corn for enough to buy a ton of coal. While at breakfast a prairie chicken in flight crashed through the kitchen window into our midst. We looked out and a perigrine falcon was perched on the yard fence. He had evidently pursued the chicken and it hit the window as it desperately tried to escape.

Another wildlife restoration project that I initiated was restoration of beaver to areas from which they had been exterminated by early day mountain men. Beavers could be spared from some areas to restock many unoccupied streams. The first transplant was in 1932 when Bert Baca, a District Game Warden, and I packed three pairs in boxes — a box for each beaver and two boxes on each pack horse — and released them far up on the Mora Fork of the Pecos.

We built a small dam of logs and brush to make a pool for them, and felled aspen trees to provide food and dam-building material. Then under the dirt bank we dug out a den at water level and released the beavers in front of it. They went right in and made themselves at home. While we were eating lunch on the opposite bank they came out and combed their fur with the unique comb-claw on their hind feet, and then swam about in the pool and seemed pleased with their new home. In the months and years since they have multiplied and built many fine dams nearby. During my tenure we transplanted 630 beavers to establish about a hundred new colonies.

In 1939, 1940 and 1941, I obtained each year three Rocky Mountain bighorn sheep from Banff, Alberta, Canada, and released them in the Sandia Mountains just east of Albuquerque. The herd is now very well established there. In 1932, I obtained six head from the same source for restocking bighorns in the Pecos Wilderness Area, but the planting was unsuccessful. In recent years they have been restored in goodly numbers there and in the Taos Mountains and the Gila National Forest.

Our initial acquisition and development of land and water for wildlife and fish habitat, and incidentally for public recreation, was in 1940 when the Fenton Ranch in the Jemez Mountains was purchased and a dam to create a 20-acre trout lake was built. Game Commissioner Hugh B. Woodward, now deceased, got the Commission embarked on such projects.

As funds became available this kind of program was greatly expanded both during my tenure and since I retired. Outstanding examples of which I am proud to have had a part in acquiring and developing are the 33,000-acre spectacular Cimarron Canyon wildlife area, water and recreation rights at Bluewater Lake, the

2,100-acre American Metals Company property, including five miles of stream on the heavily used Pecos River, the Charette Lakes, renowned for good fishing, building Wall Lake, buying Jackson Lake, the Rio los Pinos property and others.

By the beginning of World War II the Game Department revenue had increased to about $185,000 annually. Contrary to all our predictions, it continued on an accelerated upward trend throughout the war years until by 1946 it had reached $335,000. The larger income at last began to provide funds for much needed salary increases and expanded programs. When I retired in 1953, the revenue had reached $713,000 a year, or seven times over during my tenure. This does not include Federal Aid to Wildlife funds which have helped materially in the acquisition and development of fish and wildlife habitat and, incidentally, public recreation areas.

It was my policy to spend half of my time in the field so that I could have personal knowledge of wildlife and fisheries situations all over the State, particularly in problem areas. That meant a lot of both car and horseback travel. In off-the-road areas I inspected game and range conditions and predatory animal situations horseback, accompanied by a member of the field staff. On National Forests, one or more forest officers would accompany us, and local ranchers and representatives of sportsmen's organizations often went along. Thus I tried to work out solutions to problems that would be both effective and acceptable to all concerned.

I drove approximately 660,000 miles and had only two very minor accidents. I rode 11,000 miles horseback, had no accidents but came close to having a serious one.

A game trail in the Gila Forest along which I was riding followed a narrow break in a long strip of steep, slick, granite rocks. I started to ride across, then decided to walk and lead my rented horse. Halfway across he fell and slid and rolled a hundred feet to the bottom. He was skinned some and my saddle still bears the marks, but no serious damage was done. I certainly would have been injured or killed had I stayed on him.

I attended as many meetings as possible — sportsmen's, cattle and sheepmen's, regional and national conservation organization's and miscellaneous others — often appearing on the programs.

When I went to work as State Game Warden, finances were so limited that I had no assistant warden, nor chiefs of divisions. I had to wear the hat of the Chief of Law Enforcement, Game Management, Fisheries, and Public Relations. I was not well versed in fish culture and had to make use of one of my hatchery foremen, John P. Bengard, part-time to help me out. The first month I visited the five hatcheries to meet the personnel and learn as much as I could about the fisheries activities.

Mr. Bengard and I visited the little Chama Hatchery, later abandoned, in mid-April. It was still snowed-in so we had to walk two miles from the highway to reach it. When I was introduced to the foreman and his wife he said, "Well, Mr. Barker, I'm sure glad to see you, it gets so damn lonesome here, snowed-in all winter, that we are glad to see just anybody."

Throughout my tenure, even after we had a chief of fisheries, I tried to visit every hatchery once every three months. It stimulates and encourages personnel for the boss to show an interest in them and their work.

223

I kept a close check on predator control work for that was a field in which I had had ample experience. One day I was riding with lion hunter Homer Pickens, hoping to get some moving pictures of a lion. The dogs treed one, but he stopped in a brushy place in the tree. A little farther up, the branches were open enough for a picture.

To make him go on up I climbed the tree with my Colt .45 on my chaps belt. The lion refused to go higher, instead he decided to come down head first, as cats do. I waved my hat in his face but he came on. I could have shot him, but we wanted pictures. He was on the opposite side of the tree and when his head was even with mine, he peeked around the tree, opened his mouth wide and hissed right in my face. I just hissed back at him and he came on down a few feet and jumped out.

Once a Forest Officer and I apprehended an habitual game law violator who had four quarters of deer meat stored in a big carton. I opened it and started to take the quarters out, but suddenly changed my mind and sealed the box with railway car seals. He saw that he was caught red handed and agreed to appear in court the next morning and bring the box of meat as it was without opening it. We had suspected that he had killed two deer but he vigorously denied it.

Next morning in court I filed charges of killing two deer, and he raised hell about it. I had him put under oath for questioning. He said, "Judge I'll plead guilty to killing one deer, but I positively did not kill two deer."

The Judge told me I'd have to prove that a second deer was killed or reduce the complaint to one. I said I'd prove my case. I questioned the defendant and he agreed that the box of meat was the same one I'd found at his house and that it positively had not been opened. I took the four quarters of meat from the box and laid them on papers on the Judge's desk. I called attention to the fact, which I had seen yesterday, that there were two right hind quarters and no left hind quarter. "For one deer to have two right hind quarters is incredible." I remarked. Caught red-handed perjuring himself, the defendant was the worst nonplussed and embarrassed of any defendant I've ever seen.

Handling game cases in outlying areas sometimes gets touchy. Once a Forest Ranger, Lee Wang, saw a man deliberately shoot an antelope fawn during a buck season and go off and leave it. He recognized the man as being one of two reported criminals who had purchased some land in the area, on which they were camped while building a house and an earthen water tank. They were supposed to be tough characters and this was sixty miles from the nearest town.

I was in the area and Wang notified me, and we went to arrest the fellow. We'll call him Buck and his partner Jim. We met them in a car and told Buck he would have to go with us to court to answer a charge of illegally killing a fawn. The local justice of the peace, Mr. Moore, was building the water tank for them, so we said we'd have to go to Reserve sixty miles away. Buck objected to going and wanted to be tried before Moore. I knew Moore would handle the case according to law, but figured that would get him fired and I did not want that to happen.

They agreed that it would not affect Moore's job no matter what his decision might be, so we set the case for that evening at 7:30 when Mr. Moore would be there.

We had some misgivings due to their reputation but had to go through with it.

By the camp fire in front of a tent with door flaps closed was a small table and four blocks off of a log for seats. On the table was a pile of dishes covered with a small table cloth. The Judge, Buck, Wang and I, all unarmed, sat down and I drew up the complaint. While doing so I pushed the pile of dishes back a little to make room and glimpsed the butt of an automatic pistol under the cloth a few inches from Buck's right hand.

At this point a neighbor of theirs, called Aaron, appeared on the scene with his six-shooter on. He had a bad reputation and later killed a man near there in cold blood. He called me aside and warned me that these men simply were not the type to submit to prosecution for a game law violation, and advised me in a threatening manner to forget the case. We talked for a few moments, then returned to the table. Meanwhile Wang and Buck had got up and were standing by the fire. I quickly sat down where Buck had been seated, with my hand now within inches of the automatic pistol.

If that gave me any sense of security, it was short lived, for as Buck passed the tent he threw the flaps back and there lay two young women with their heads toward us and each with a sporting rifle at her side. It was all bluff to make us drop the case, but neither we nor the Judge budged an inch.

The complaint was read, Wang testified to what he had seen and the defendant entered a plea of guilty. The Judge fined him $50 and $5 costs. Buck produced a roll of bills as big as a beer can and the smallest he could find was a hundred dollar bill. The judge accepted it

226

and said he would credit them with $55 on what they would owe him.

We felt that there was less danger of trouble starting if we left our side-arms in the car, and I believe that was correct, but in any event those gals in the tent had us covered.

An event took place in 1950 that was to have nation-wide repercussions and do many millions of dollars worth of good in the conservation of forests and wildlife. L. W. Simmons, one of my District Wardens, while assisting the Forest Service in fighting a serious forest fire, found a whimpering, five-pound cub bear clinging to the charred bark of a pine tree in the fire-scorched area. His fur was singed, the pads of his feet badly burned and he was almost starved. His pitiful, faint whimper was heard across the nation.

The cub was given first aid at the fire camp, and next day was flown to Santa Fe by Ray L. Bell, Game Department pilot, and nursed back to health. When his feet had heeled and he had gained some weight, we gave him to the U.S. Forest Service with the provision that his life be dedicated to forest fire prevention and wildlife conservation. That was the now famed Smokey Bear who for years has been the greatest single attraction at the National Zoo in Washington D.C. I am proud to have had a part in this, and proud that Smokey is a New Mexican.

There is much more to tell, but there is no more room here. I may say, however, that whatever success I may have had as State Game Warden is due to Judge Colin Neblett, the hard-working, loyal staff that I maintained and to working 12 to 16 hours a day for 22 years. My staff, for the most part, were not the highly-educated type but made up for it with their devotion to the cause of wildlife conservation and ingenuity in finding ways and means of getting difficult jobs done.

Indicative of their fitness and abilities is the fact that today three of them are heads of State Departments, one an assistant head, and five are division chiefs.

THE BIG ONE

FOR AN HOUR I had been sitting hunched up against a snowberry bush in the grassy, aspen-rimmed East Beatty Parks waiting for a bull elk to come out to forage for his supper. It was not for just any bull that I waited, but for a special monstrous one whose bed, tracks and droppings I had found the day before both here and in the Big Beatty Park across the canyon. It had been a tossup when I left camp which park to wait in as he'd been using both.

The sun had slipped behind timberline peaks. There was not more than twenty minutes of legal shooting time left. I was looking through a pair of 10X binoculars, which a Texas hunter had insisted that I try out, when suddenly my pulse quickened. Some cows and young elk were coming out of the timber. It was a thrilling sight as the calves and yearlings frisked about kicking up their heels while the cows began grazing ravenously.

For ten minutes I waited for a bull, hopefully the big one, to follow. Then a rack of antlers appeared at the edge of the timber. The bull was cautious. He waited there several minutes, turning his head this way and that looking to make sure it was safe to come on out. At last with his head swaying from side to side he walked slowly out toward the cows.

What a huge, black-necked, gray-sided bull he was! His antlers were simply enormous — high, long-tined, wide and heavy. No doubt about it, he was the out-sized bull I was waiting for. I was tensely absorbed in determination to have him. The 10X binoculars seemed to bring him right up in my lap. Instinctively I reached for my .32 Winchester rifle lying beside me.

To my chagrin, when I lowered the powerful glasses I realized that the elk were in Big Beatty Park across the canyon, much too far to shoot, and it was too late to get over there before sunset. Disappointed that I had picked the wrong park, I watched a while with the glasses. Then I got my horse, tethered in the timber, and rode slowly to camp in the nearby Pecos River Canyon.

Forest Ranger J. W. Johnson and I were camping together in the Forest Service's administrative cabin at the old Beatty's Cabin Site in the Pecos Wilderness. He was reroofing the cabin and repairing the pasture fence and postponing his elk hunting until the last of the season. Four Texas elk hunters were camped a mile below us, and besides them there were only a few other hunters in the immediate area.

When I told Ranger Johnson my hard luck story he said, "Don't fret, they'll bed down there tonight, then graze from dawn to sunup. We'll be there at daybreak and get him."

I had killed a half dozen elk while employed at Vermejo Park, 360,000-acre ranch and game preserve in northern New Mexico, but had not taken a worthwhile trophy. Now I had special reasons for craving that remarkable trophy. This was one of New Mexico's first public elk hunts with only 100 licenses available and hunting was hard. I was then State Game Warden (Director,

Dept. of Game and Fish) and to get such a trophy would greatly enhance my prestige as a hunter, which many considered a necessary attribute of a good game administrator.

Historical records show that originally elk were abundant in the major mountainous areas of New Mexico, and even in the foothills where they came down to winter. But, unfortunately, by the turn of the century, every last elk in New Mexico had been killed. Not one was left.

The greatest tragedy was that the Merriam elk, a subspecies of the northern elk, found only in southern New Mexico and southeastern Arizona, was completely exterminated. Unlike the northern variety it can never be restored. Thousands of years of nature's work was destroyed by man in a few decades.

Restoration of the American Elk, *Cervus candensis*, to New Mexico began in 1911 when the owners of Vermejo Park imported 15 head from Wyoming, supplemented by a second planting two years later. About that time the Game Department made three plantings of four head each. Then in 1915 the Game Department stocked 37 head of Wyoming elk in the upper Pecos River Country.

In 1917, A. J. Meloche stocked his big *T O* ranch east of Raton with elk. Then in 1926 the *G O S* Ranch north of Silver City imported 25 elk which for years were confined in a 5,000-acre elk proof pasture. Since then the Game Department has made releases to supplement these and stock new areas, so that elk are again well distributed over the State with liberal open seasons. Northern elk have been stocked in the original Merriam elk ranges. It is certainly a notable fact that cattle ranchers pioneered in the restoration of these noble animals.

In the early thirties we began hunting the Pecos Wilderness herd which was started in 1915. Restoration began paying off, and has since paid big dividends. Now, I thought, what a restoration symbol this big, royal trophy would be.

Up at four next morning, I got breakfast while Ranger Johnson brought our saddle horses in from the pasture and put their morrals on so they could eat their grain while we enjoyed our breakfast of bacon, eggs, pancakes and coffee.

Breakfast over, we at once saddled up, put rifles in scabbards and set out for Big Beatty Park long before sunrise. The late October dawn here at 10,000 feet elevation was chilly despite there being no snow yet. We were confident my big bull would still be somewhere in the twenty-acre hillside opening and took every precaution not to disturb him as we approached it.

In the alpine forest a hundred yards below we got off, tied up our horses and took off our chaps and spurs. It was still a quarter hour before legal time to shoot. Slowly and quietly we eased up the trail. The loud flutter of wings of a blue grouse cock we flushed broke the quietude of dawn.

We did not show ourselves at the park's edge until time to shoot, and even then the light at a half hour before sunrise was still not very good.

"They will likely leave the same way they came in," Johnson whispered. So we gave attention to that area first. Sure enough, there were the antlerless elk grazing toward the timber. We searched for the bull and at first could not see him anywhere. Then we glimpsed his huge antlers over and beyond some bushes that hid his body.

232

I was ready when he moved a few steps into the forest but the brief glimpse of his big, white rump gave me no chance for a shot.

"Oh, damn," I exclaimed, "I muffed my chance."

"No, he's just pretty smart," Johnson said. "You've still got a chance."

"How, by following him?"

"Not now, wait a couple of hours until they bed down, then if you are good enough stalker you might get a shot."

"I've stalked a lot of deer, so I'll try it," I said.

We got our horses, rode back to the cabin, warmed up the coffee, washed the dishes and cleaned up the place. The Ranger went about his work and I got in a supply of firewood.

About nine o'clock I rode back to the park, left my horse, chaps and spurs there, and took up the trail of the elk. They were easy to follow for they stayed on a game trail that was headed toward an old blow-down, a favorite elk day-bedding type.

Watching every step, I walked very, very slowly and avoided making any kind of noise. I stopped every few yards and squatted to search under the tree branches for a sleeping elk. The spruce and fir forest was so dense that one could not see more than fifty or sixty yards. So I knew I'd have to be good to get that close to the shy old bull.

At last I saw a yearling lying by a log placidly chewing her cud. I looked for a long time but could see no other elk. I slowly took off my hat and left it there. Slowly, cautiously I crawled forward on my hands and knees, moving the rifle beside me a yard at a time. Not far beyond the heifer I spied an old cow lying head toward me. I couldn't go any farther without flushing them, so I just lay there and waited hoping something would happen.

It did. A little gust of wind swirled through the trees carrying my scent directly to the drowsing herd. Instantly about twenty elk sprang out of their beds and elk legs were all around me. The cow I had been watching sniffed the air for a brief moment, then took off down the hill and the others followed. At the same instant there was a big ruckus beyond as the big bull unseen went crashing through the forest straight ahead instead of following the cows. He had used the cows as a buffer for safety.

That was that. No use at all to try following him now. I'd have to depend on finding him somewhere in a park late evening or early morning. But with dozens of meadows and parks in the nearby area which one would he choose? Ranger Johnson, super woodsman and wildlife observer, would have to serve as my crystal ball.

Frustrated for the second time that day, I went back to my horse and rode to camp. My companion was just sitting down to a mid-day dinner when I got there. He had cooked for two and put my plate on the table.

"I calculated you'd be here about this time," he said. "What luck?"

When I told him my sad story he said, "You did a fine job stalking. When you saw the yearling you should have backed away and crawled around the herd. A big bull always beds down to one side or beyond the cows, never with them."

"Now you tell me," I said. "So now tell me where he will come out to feed this evening or in the morning."

"That's hard to say. But the Cebadillosis Canyon

parks are next the way he was headed, so I'd say that's your best bet."

Beatty's Cabin is at the site of a cabin built by an early-day prospector named George Beatty, and is in the center of the very best elk area of the Pecos high country. There are scores of well-vegetated parks and meadows interspersed in the alpine forests and aspen woods. Lush, well-watered feeding grounds with adjacent dense cover makes it meet the ideal environment often mentioned by Aldo Leopold.

My big bull had the choice of a score of parks to feed in while I could be in but one during the few minutes before sunset when he would be most likely to show himself. I chose the Cebadillosis Canyon whose mouth is only a half mile from Beatty's Cabin. I saddled up and set out at 2:30 p.m. to make the hard mile and a half climb from 10,000 feet at the Cabin to 11,500 feet at the cirque at the head of the canyon.

The upper half of Cebadillosis is one continuous grassy park bounded by dense alpine timber on the ridge to the north and along the water course on the south. Jutting fingers of spruce along the south side make it possible to hunt a segment of the park at a time by hugging the timber's edge.

I would make the late evening hunt from the cirque down, so I rode up to the canyon head, tied my horse in the timber and sat at the edge of it watching the surrounding area carefully until only twenty minutes of shooting time was left. Then I rode down along the uneven edge of timber to keep under cover as I worked the long park a piece at a time.

Four fine mule deer bucks offered tempting shots but it was not deer season. With but a couple of minutes

235

left of shooting time I came upon a bunch of cows, calves and yearlings, apparently the ones I had spooked that morning, but the big bull was not with them. So again I rode into camp empty handed.

That evening one of my patrolmen, Bert Baca, dropped in and spent the night with us. He reported few bulls had been taken. Most hunters were inexperienced and were getting out late and riding the parks and meadows in midday and getting back to camp long before sundown. One just can't get elk that way.

The Texas hunters, one of whom had killed a good bull, came to visit and we got a game of penny ante going, but big bull elk dominated the conversation. Plans for the next day's hunt were made so as not to interfere with each other.

"Where will I find my big 'un?" I asked.

"Seems to me Cebadillosis is still your best bet," he said. "As he was spooked today he may have stayed under cover this evening, but he will likely be out in the morning."

One of the Texans wanted to go with me, but Johnson knew I was a loner and saved me by telling him of another even better place to go. So next morning on a fresh horse I got started forty minutes before shooting time. That put me at the lower end of the long park at just the right time. This time I hunted up instead of down.

Soon two whopping big bucks stood and dared me to shoot them. A little farther on a black bear ran away from the carcass of a cow (victum of larkspur poisoning) upon which he had been feeding. I had to hurry to be at the cirque early enough. Finally with my horse lathered with sweat I reached the canyon head, a most beautiful place to find an elk.

As we rounded a clump of spruce saplings the horse stopped and pricked up his ears. He'd seen something. For a moment I was unable to see what it was. Then I saw it, a fine bull elk grazing placidly, oblivious to our presence, on the steep slope above. I eased out of the saddle, drew my rifle from the scabbard and trained my binoculars on the bull, and by golly there were two of them not twenty yards apart.

I studied them carefully and they were both fine specimens, but to my disappointment neither was my big 'un. But what a really thrilling sight there in the amber sunrise light. It truly was an unusual scene in a magnificent setting. Now, oh, how I wished I had brought that Texan along. I felt selfish for he would rather have one of those bulls than to bring in another oil well.

Now I had to make a decision. I could easily have either one of those fine bulls, and their racks were right good, too. Should I settle for that or spend my remaining four days trying to find and get a shot at my big fellow? Toss a coin? No. It had to be a free choice made with deliberate speed. I wanted that big one like I'd never before wanted one of any kind. All right then, I'd try for him until my last afternoon and then settle for a lesser one if I could find it. I felt real good when I slipped the .32 Winchester Special back in the scabbard.

I remounted and started on. Not till then did the bulls see me. They threw up their heads and for an instant stared in amazement, then took off in a long trot toward cover.

When I mention my .32 Winchester Special, open-sight rifle I can see a lot of hunters' eyebrows raised. All I can say is that in a dozen years I took seven elk with eleven shots with it. Then I got a .270 Winchester with a K-2.5 scope and I haven't been able to equal that good record.

It was now too late to hope to find my big bull in open country anywhere. So I decided to go afoot and work the many likely bed grounds in the deep timber between Cebadillosis and Beatty Parks area. For four hours I prowled stealthily up and down and across those loggy woods, but not a sign of the big fellow could I find.

I got back to my horse at noon about pooped out. I picketed the horse out to graze, ate my lunch and stretched out in the sun for a snooze. Two hours later the chattering of a chickaree squirrel in his nearby nest tree woke me up. Tree shadows had now crept around over me and I was quite chilly.

I saddled up and rode over the ridge to the north and hunted out the south and north Azul country, checking as carefully as I could for tracks or droppings of the coveted bull. I found none. I got to camp at dark.

Four more days and then I had to get back to the office, bull or no bull. Next day I hunted out the East Beatty Parks and the Hamilton Mesa country, and ran into more hunters than I had seen elsewhere, but they were not having much luck. Not a track could I find big enough to be my bull. Now I was thinking of him as *my big bull*.

That evening Ranger Johnson told me of a little hidden park on a bench some distance above Big Beatty Park where we had last seen old Biggy.

"He could be feeding there undisturbed," Johnson said. "Get there at dawn and you might find him."

"That sounds good, and I'll sure give it a try," I said.

Next morning I tied up my horse a hundred yards

below the little open area and eased up as cautiously as I ever did anywhere to a vantage point in the timber's edge. It was still forty minutes till sunrise and I'd have to wait ten minutes, till legal time at half an hour before sunrise. Anyway it was not light enough to shoot yet.

I waited for a half hour, but no game showed. Then very cautiously I circled the lower side of the park so as to see into every nook and corner of it, but no bull was there. When I walked up through the lush five-acre opening I was delighted to find fresh tracks and droppings to match those of the big fellow. There were a couple of night beds in the tall grass that matched his size, too. He had used this secluded, lush feeding ground last night but left before I got there. He was still playing it smart. I wished for snow as elk normally come out early and stay out later when it is stormy.

I got away from there quickly, determined to come back and lay for him under cover that evening. I rode back to camp and helped Ranger Johnson most of the day.

Sunset would be at five thirty and end shooting time. Four o'clock found me sitting under a droopy spruce tree by a log with some currant bushes in front of me over which I could watch unseen. Time passed slowly. Finally a cow and calf came out and fed across the park and went on below it. Three deer came and fed for a while. At five thirty my big bull had not ventured out. He was still playing it mighty crafty. I decided to wait a while longer just to see if he would come out at all.

At ten minutes to six, when it was getting pretty dark to shoot anyway, the big one showed at the upper side of the park. He came out only a body length, stopped and turned his head from side to side searching for signs of danger. At a hundred yards with binoculars I could see him quite well and his antlers were simply magnificient, by far the best I'd ever seen. He was truly a royal trophy bull.

To say that I was tempted to shoot him regardless of it being twenty minutes late is no understatement. But as a sportsman I have always tried to play it square, and as State Game Warden it was completely out of the question to fudge that way. I waited until good dark then crawled out of there without disturbing him. Thus I had high hopes that he would still be there next morning.

Next morning before it was light I crawled up to a spot where I could see the park to best advantage. I searched the area with and without binoculars until sun-up but there was no bull there. He was simply making a habit of feeding at night and staying under cover of the forest during shooting hours.

I decided against trying to follow him to his bed ground. Maybe, I thought, he will be less astute this evening and venture out a few minutes before sundown. That day I rode the Jack's Creek and Baldy Lake area to size up game conditions in general. I ate my lunch on top of the 12,000-foot divide that runs between the famous 13,100-foot Truchas Peaks and 12,600-foot Pecos Baldy. From there the view of the Pecos Wilderness Area is breath-taking. The mosaic pattern of meadows, parks, aspen woods and spruce forest rimmed by timberline peaks is magnificent and inspiring, and it's all elk range.

Four o'clock found me back at my lookout behind the currant bushes waiting for the big 'un to show up. Some cows and calves came and fed up to within fifty

feet of me. I was afraid they would scent me and spoil
my chances, but they finally turned and grazed back
the other way. At a quarter to six the bull had not come
out so, greatly disappointed, I rode back to camp. Tomorrow would be my last day.

That evening the Ranger and I discussed at length
the strategy for the morrow. The fact that I'd not spooked
him at his hidden feeding ground made us decide that
he might be there next morning. In case he had spent
the night there and left before daylight I would try to
trail him to his day bed ground, which Johnson assured
me would be back toward the Cebadillosis Canyon. If
that didn't pay off I'd make a desperate effort to find
another acceptable bull before sundown. It just would
not do for the State Game Warden to go home empty
handed.

So at dawn I crawled up to my currant bush station
and for a long time looked hard for my big bull. He just
had to be there this time. At last the morning sun bathed
the park. No bull. I walked to the game trail at the
timber'd edge where he had again come and gone.

I gave him an hour to bed down, then followed his
tracks along the game trail as cautiously as possible to
the bed grounds Johnson had told me about. He was not
there and I lost his tracks in the hard, needle covered
forest cloor. I hunted at random for a while but failed
to find him. Dejectedly I went back to my horse.

The big bull had outsmarted me all the way, or
else my reputed skill as a nimrod was skidding badly.
It was now ten o'clock. Where in the seven and a half
hours left could I find a decent trophy? I asked my horse
that question as I tightened the saddle cinch, but he only
stretched and gave me the bronx cheer.

Elk would not be out grazing until near sunset. So I'd hunt the Jack's Creek and Azul Canyon parks and meadows to find where elk had fed last night, then follow them and try to get a shot at a bull at their bed ground. Then an hour before sundown I'd work the South Azul parks, cross the Chimayosis Canyon and finish the few minutes before sunset in the beautiful aspen and bunch grass slopes of Rito Padre.

Twice I found where elk had grazed in open country and followed them to their day beds and flushed them. But all I got to see was a flock of legs dancing away through the timber. Then the South Azul parks yielded nothing but a bunch of fat mule deer.

With but twenty minutes left I crossed the Chimayosis Creek and, as planned, headed for the Rito del Padre slopes. I'd ride fast, cover as much territory as possible and take a chance on riding up on a bull for a quick shot. I was desperate. My chances were fading fast.

With sweaty sides and heaving nostrils distended my horse carried me up over the edge of a bench land park interspersed with clumps of aspen and spruce trees. Just ahead was an old sheep camp site at a spring where bluegrass, a favorite elk forage, had supplanted the native bunch grass. I looked at my watch—ten minutes left. I touched spurs to my horse and he took me around a clump of trees in a hurry.

Whoa! There a hundred yards ahead were five bull elk—two spikes, a pair of two-year-olds and one with a fine rack of antlers. He was not *my bull* but he would do nicely. I jumped off, jerked the rifle from its scabbard and levered a cartridge in. I'd have to hurry, for the bulls were taking off fast. A few yards and the big one would be gone.

I drew a bead on the only target the bull offered me—his big, white rump patch. If I could break the pelvic bone that would down him and the coup de grace could follow very quickly. My shot went about eight inches to the left and took some hair off his thigh and his ribs, and a bit of hide off of his shoulder and then smashed square into the point of his jaw.

That turned him broadside to me and he took off down hill in a long trot shaking his head violently. No better running shot could one ask for. Taking it instantly I aimed for his neck, and scored. The fine fellow tumbled head over heels with a broken neck.

I caught my horse which had run off a hundred yards or so and rode to my quarry. It was now five thirty, time to quit shooting and I had. I was under the wire just in time.

If I had not seen my *BIG BULL,* I would have thought this one a real prize trophy as everyone does who comes into my office where it graces the wall near my desk. The brown, ivory tipped antlers have 12 points and a total length of 48 inches and a spread of 42 inches, and they are as symmetrical as one will ever find.

I got a picture, then field dressed the bull and turned him up on his back with little poles under withers, back and hips to break contact with the ground so he would cool out thoroughly. It was dark when I finished and I rode the three miles to camp by moonlight.

"I heard the shots, so figured you'd be late," Johnson said. "Was he the big one?"

"No. But he'll do," I said.

"Supper's ready, go eat, I'll take care of your horse." Johnson was as pleased as I was.

Next morning two of the Texas hunters went with

Ranger Johnson and me to skin, quarter and pack out the bull. After throwing away 20 pounds of neck, the quarters weighed 120 pounds each, or 500 total.

At the cabin I grabbed a sandwich, put my bedroll on one of the packs and headed for home as it had begun to snow. So ended my quest for the big bull, except that there is an interesting sequel.

On the trail I met Ellis Bauer and two friends packing in to hunt the last five days of the season. Their eyes sparkled with anticipation when I told them about the big bull and the area he had been using. Now with two inches of snow, they would have a good chance to find him. I suggested that his friends take the pack outfit in to camp and that Ellis follow a little path to East Beatty Parks that branches off two miles before they would get to camp.

Ellis followed my tip and half way to the parks found where a band of elk had just left their beds and headed up the trail toward the parks. From the size of the bed of one and the tracks and droppings he was convinced that my bull had made them. He followed quietly in the new snow, leading his horse.

At the first opening he flushed the elk in a patch of willows along a spring branch. Some cows came out on the opposite side, then two nice bulls ran out, stopped and offered perfect target. He was sure they were neither one the big one he wanted. Yet a bird in hand—he thought. When they ran toward cover he was about ready to shoot when all hell broke loose in the willows, then out came the big one. There was no mistaking it, but he was going straight away as mine had, and he tried the same shot. His bullet went high and caught the magnificent bull squarely in the back of the head and he dropped in his tracks.

In a half hour Ellis had accomplished what I failed to in eight days of hard hunting. At that time I believe his bull rated in the Boone and Crocket record book.

PRONGHORN ANTELOPE AND BEAR STEAKS

14

MY GOOD FRIEND, A. T. Cap McDannald, who has now passed on to happier hunting grounds, was one of the finest men I have ever known and truly a royal host. Some years ago he had twenty-two guest hunters at his big Adobe Ranch for the mature-buck, pronghorn antelope hunt. I was State Game Warden of New Mexico and was there to supervise the hunt and, perhaps, get a buck, also.

After a fine dinner, including unusual steaks, on the eve of the season's opening, Howard Olmstead, who had hunted big game all over the world, told me he wanted an outstanding trophy or none.

"That's just fine," I said. "Whatever type you prefer, the Adobe Ranch has got 'em."

Howard said, "This is my first pronghorn hunt, and I am ignorant about the trophy types. Tell me about them."

"There are several variations from the typical horn pattern," I said, and went on to explain. "Some horns are quite long and straight—high horns we call them—with very little top curve, and almost no fork. Others of normal size and shape lie out almost flat, with a spread of thirty inches or more. The exact reverse are those that have little or no spread. I've seen some with points actually overlapping. Another attractive type is the horns that rise in typical fashion, but have inward and downward curves six or seven inches long."

Cap McDannald and other hunters had become interested in the discussion and Cap said, "Elliott, we'd understand better if you would describe a typical, prime trophy. I believe the horns are prime now and will be shed in November and December."

"You are right, Cap, I should have done that first," I said. "I recently measured a good typical set of antelope horns and the tape readings were: length around outside curve, 16 inches; height to top of curve, 13 inches; curve about 3 inches; length of prong from fork to point, 5 inches; spread between points, 8 inches; maximum spread 12 inches; and girth of horn at base, 6 inches. Typical horns stand up straight, angling back just a little from right angle to top of the nose line. A trophy of those measurements won't come near making the record book, but it will grace any den."

Bob Snow said, "So now, Howard, what type of trophy do you want? As for me, I'll settle for any good one."

"If I had my 'druthers' I'd 'druther' have the high-horn type," Howard said.

Someone else asked, "Barker, what kind of steaks did we have for dinner?" The steaks were good and tender but a bit sweetish.

"Cap said they were bear steaks, that's all I know about it," I said.

In his quiet, drolling way Cap said, "Yep, Skeet killed a bear yesterday, and we thought bear steaks would just suit you hairy-chested antelope hunters." Skeet Williams was Cap's ranch foreman.

"Where's the hide?" Otis Watkins asked. A good question.

"Skeet hung it on a pole, and when he went back with a pack horse for the meat he forgot to bring it," Cap said.

More talk of bear steaks, pronghorn trophies, and some wild hunting tales, then we spread down our bed-rolls in a circus-type tent that Cap had set up and hit the hay. Alarm clocks were set for an hour before sunrise. One thing about big game hunting, it gives one the opportunity to see the sun rise as he seldom does at home.

Seated on benches at the long table in the dining room the jolly nimrods enjoyed a hearty breakfast of coffee, orange juice, cereal, bacon, eggs and toast. Then hunters in groups of three and fours were assigned to various parts of the hundred thousand-acre prairie and rolling-hill ranch in quest of pronghorn trophies. Mostly they went in jeeps and pick-ups, but I took Howard, Bob and Otis with me in my Buick. We could drive over most of the ranch but, of course, were not permitted to chase the antelope, and had to get out and away from the vehicles to shoot.

Only a mile from headquarters I braked the car to a stop like a roping horse. "The left one is a high-horned trophy, the type you want," I said. They had drawn straws and Howard would get first shot.

Howard got out and sized up the trophy with binoculars. "Is he good enough?" he asked.

"He'll be hard to beat," I said. To my surprise the high-horned buck, a small buck and a doe with stubby, ear-length horns stayed there on the sky line two hundred yards away, their sleek sides glistening in the rosy sunrise light.

Howard continued to study them. The doe walked, light-footed, past the bucks and stopped. "Better Hurry! They're ready to go," I said.

Howard aimed, hesitated, then aimed again and fired. At the crack of his .30-06 Winchester the doe fell in her tracks.

"Damn it, you killed the doe," I exclaimed.

"Oh, no." Howard wailed.

"With a four-power scope how could you make such a mistake," I scolded. I'd warned them all that such mistakes would have to be atoned for in court with a stiff fine.

"I've hunted the world over, and that's the first time that ever happened to me. I'm so sorry. How could I have done it?" Howard said near tears.

Undoubtedly he had moved the scope off the buck when he hesitated and brought it back on the doe and fired without checking the horns. Bob and Otis thought their good friend's misfortune was funny, but not Howard, nor I.

We drove over to the dead doe and Otis broke the tension. "Of all the trophy types the Warden told us about he never mentioned a stub-horned head like this one," Otis said. "This will be tops in your den."

"You guys have my permission to go straight to hell," the unhappy hunter said.

I quickly field dressed the doe, and put her on a tarp in the trunk of the car. Then I sent Otis and Bob to hunt in nearby rolling country where they could ease up over one little rise after another and maybe get some shooting. I'd pick them up later.

With my crestfallen hunter I drove to headquarters and turned him over to a Deputy Warden Bert Baca, to

249

take him to a Justice of the Peace and get the case settled. Then Howard could resume his hunting.

I went back and found Bob dressing out a nice buck. Otis was disgusted that he had missed several shots.

"Don't worry," I said. "We can find another, another and another."

With Bob's buck in the car trunk we headed across the valley toward the foothills beyond. Topping a rise we flushed a nice band of antelope. They ran parallel to the road a little ways, then crossed ahead of us within range.

I stopped the car, Otis jumped out and began firing at a large buck that, so typically, had fallen behind. He emptied his .270 Remington, speeding the buck up a bit with bullets kicking up dust beyond and behind him. Otis came back to the car exasperated.

"Like most hunters," I said, "you didn't lead him nearly enough."

"I've had no trouble with deer, how much more should I lead these critters?" Otis asked.

"That depends on bullet velocity, speed of buck, his distance from you and angle at which he is running." I said. "For example: A buck can run forty-five miles an hour, but suppose he is a hundred yards away doing forty at right angles to you. With a .30/30, whose velocity is 2,200 feet per second, you should hold eight feet ahead of the target spot, or six feet in front of his nose.

"At two hundred yards you'd lead more than twice that much due to the bullet's loss of velocity."

"My .270 is much faster, how much do I lead with it?" Otis asked.

"Right. With 130 grain bullets the .270's muzzle velocity is 3,120 feet per second. So at forty miles an hour, a hundred yards away you should hold just over five and a half feet ahead of the target spot, or about three and a half feet in front of the nose. At two hundred yards it would be about twelve feet, or ten feet in front of the nose."

Bob said, "that sounds easy, but you have to estimate the distance, speed and angle."

"Sure. But just remember that you have to lead an antelope a hell-of-a-lot more than most hunters do until they have wasted a lot of ammunition," I stated.

The hunt was right in the mating season, and bucks were chasing the does all over the place, which is part of the ritual. When not chasing a doe, the big bucks were busy protecting their harems from rival bucks with ideas of their own. Fortunately, pronghorn meat is not unsavory as are buck deer at mating time.

As we continued along the dim road white rumps flashed a mile to our left. I backed the car into a depression out of sight. Then we crept up to where we could study the herd with binoculars. They had not seen us and a stalk was in order. I sent Otis down a draw to stay out of sight, and pointed out bushes to use for cover to get in shooting range.

Bob and I sat watching hunter and antelope with biniculars. In thirty minutes Otis crouched behind the bushes waiting for a buck to get in the clear. When he stood up the firing sounded like Cox's Army. The herd took off like the devil had bit 'em. Otis stood there a moment, turned and headed toward the car. Again he'd missed. We drove across the prairie and picked him up.

"What happened?" I asked.

"Just too damned much prairie space around him," Otis said, trying to smile.

"Don't feel bad," I said, "It happens many times

251

every year. We'll cross to the base of the Wahoo Hills where there are openings on low timbered ridges and get rid of some of that space. Antelope buggered by prairie hunters will be coming that way."

We drove up a draw and left the car concealed by juniper trees. Then we hunted afoot under cover of trees and taking advantage of draws and low ridges. Pronghorns love the prairie but seek adjacent timbered areas to elude hunters.

"Down," I whispered. A doe was leading her band our way in a lazy lope. We crouched behind Apache plume bushes. The pronghorns went through an open park a hundred yards away.

"No bucks?" Otis asked in subdued voice.

"Must be; wait," I said *soto voice*. Sure enough, a buck came poking along. "There he comes! Be ready, Otis," I said. "When he's opposite I'll whistle, he'll stop, then get him."

I whistled. The buck turned facing us and stopped. "No excuse for missing this one," I cautioned.

The .270 banged, and the buck dropped with a slug in the sticking place. Laying his rifle down, Otis ran to his quarry. "He'd be in a hell-of-a-fix if his buck got up and took off," I said.

But the rifle wasn't needed, and Otis was jubilant over a clean kill at last. We dressed the buck, carried him to the car and headed back to headquarters. We'd had enough action for one day.

We were the first to bring in bucks, but during lunch three more were brought in. Good enough for the first half day for no doubt others still out had been successful also.

That afternoon I just cruised the hunting area checking hunters here and there. Back at dusk, I was highly pleased to find that fourteen of the twenty-two hunters had been successful, and that no more violations had occurred.

Bert and Howard were back. The fine was a hundred dollars, but that hurt less than the ribbing of his fellow hunters.

We had roast "bear meat" for dinner. Despite many red hot stories of the day's adventures in quest of the speedsters of the plains, comments about the meat persisted. Skeet stood firm that it was bear, and Cap backed him up. It didn't taste like any meat I'd ever eaten.

Next morning Cap asked me to take his elderly banker friend from Texas with me and try to get him up on an antelope. He had never hunted any kind of big game and had missed several good chances the first day, and was becoming discouraged. I assured Cap I'd do my best.

I took him to a hilly, lightly-timbered area where, by stalking with trees and bushes as cover, we got in range of a small band of antelope. A lone buck was chasing a doe who, it seemed, was not ready to accept his favors. We waited, crouched behind oak bushes, for the buck to offer us a clean, standing shot.

Suddenly fortune favored us. The ardent buck chased his doe toward us, unaware of our presence until within forty yards. Then he skidded to a stop and stared our way unbelievingly.

"Let him have it," I whispered.

The novice nimrod sent a .30/30 bullet through the buck's heart.

"Congratulations, you've got yourself a nice trophy," I said.

That old banker was shaking like the ague. "I'm an old man," he said. "I've had a full life with thrills in many fields, but Warden, this is the most exciting experience of all."

Cap McDannald would never hunt until every guest had filled out, but that afternoon he insisted on taking me out for mine. Driving toward our chosen hunting area we glimpsed a band of pronghorns in a distant fence corner. We maneuvered the car to within a half mile. Then, with scattered pinon trees for cover, we stalked within range unseen.

It was always a pleasure to hunt with Cap. I wanted a typical trophy for my den to replace a non-typical one. In the herd he'd found was a reddish buck with an excellent set of horns. We waited and waited, but he stayed in the midst of the does.

Cap said, "Let's show ourselves, they'll take out along one fence or the other and maybe you can get a shot."

Antelope seldom jump a barbed wire fence and are reluctant to crawl under or through it. When they saw us they bunched up tightly, then a doe led out along the fence to our left with the others stringing out behind her. Luckily my typical buck lagged behind offering me a perfect running shot.

There was too much space around him, I reckon, for the first shot from my .32 Winchester Special missed. Quickly I levered in another cartridge, led him four feet and pulled the trigger. With a broken neck, the fine buck took a nose dive. Cap was delighted, but kidded me about my practice shot.

The trophy, exactly what I wanted, graces the wall back of my desk bringing back many fond memories.

I was pleased that evening that no more violations had occurred, and that twenty of the twenty-two hunters had gotten bucks, with trophies ranging from fair to excellent. Everyone was satisfied.

Dinner, with home-grown beefsteak, would have pleased the most fastidious gourmet. But "bear meat" remained a half-jesting topic.

Next morning Howard reluctantly went with Bert to try for a good trophy. We learned later that he took the first legal buck they saw.

At last Cap went with Bob and me to try for his buck. Soon after starting, a band of twenty pronghorns, including a large,heavy-horned buck, crossed ahead of us.

"He's good enough," Cap said. But there was no opportunity to shoot. They ran down a low ridge, then into a valley where they stopped. We eased the car out of sight, then crept to the ridge crest and watched the band unnoticed. They grazed back up the valley, then they topped out on a low *mesa* about a half mile away and stopped.

"If they stay there, Cap, you can keep behind this ridge, to the valley, then slip up to the *mesa* rim and get that old fellow," I said.

As we watched an old doe bedded down, then several others followed suit. "O. K. Cap," I said. "You've got it made."

"I'll try it," Cap said, and set out on the half hour stalk.

"Look back now and then. If they leave we'll wave you back," I said. "Good luck."

With binoculars Bob and I watched the now quiet herd. Soon the old buck singled out a sleek doe. Nudging her gently he drove her a few yards from the others.

255

There in five minutes he covered her three times. Then they both slowly returned to the band.

Right soon the buck drove a yearling doe away from the herd and covered her five times.

"What a man!" Bob exclaimed.

In a few minutes the buck drove a third doe out and covered her three times. As before they walked slowly back to the herd.

Surely that will be all, we thought. But, no! After a few minutes rest he gently nudged an old doe with a horn and made her get up. She played around him, then left the band voluntarily to welcome the virile old buck's favors three times. Fourteen times in the space of thirty minutes! !

Absorbed in this first-hand biological demonstration, we had forgotten Cap. Turning binoculars we saw he was ready to fire at the fine, super buck who now stood offering a perfect broadside target. Before the rifle report reached us we saw the buck collapse, and the others take off in high gear.

We drove over there before Cap finished dressing his quarry. When we told him of the astounding spectacle we had witnessed, Cap said, "If I had known that I wouldn't have had the heart to shoot the old son-of-a-gun."

Bob asked what buck pronghorns eat.

Back at headquarters Skeet was spinning yarns with contented hunters. Cap said, "Skeet, let's go get that bear skin."

Seeing that he was cornered, Skeet said, "Cap, there ain't no bear skin."

"What do you mean, no bear skin," Cap ejaculated.

"It's this way. I thought it would be fun to make the

hunters think they were having bear steaks. Something to write home about, you know," Skeet said.

"If it wasn't bear what the heck was it?" Cap demanded.

"Just a nice, fat, two-year-old burro," Skeet said, turned and walked to the corral where his saddle horse was waiting.

Cap was furious, and I can't describe the reaction of his guests.

"Anyway, Cap," I said, "twenty-two hunters and twenty-two trophy bucks is, also, something to write home about."

15

LADIES' LUCK

THE LAST PERIOD of New Mexico's 600-permit antelope season was set to open at noon, October 12. It was still a few minutes of 12 o'clock. We had eaten our lunch at the car and walked a couple of hundred yards up the rocky, grass-covered slope toward Baldy Mountain. There we sat down to wait until legal time to shoot.

The terrain was entirely too rocky to use a car, as is customary, to find the antelope and maneuver within shooting range. Besides the ranch owner did not want cars running all over the tall dry grass. So we had driven to the end of a dim road near a windmill a mile from U.S. Highway 85, parked the car and started out afoot.

As we waited the remaining 15 minutes of a long pre-season forenoon, I stretched out on my back in the luxuriant grass that covered the whole landscape. As I watched the high, fall clouds drift slowly across the sky I wondered which was the worst, being unlucky in the drawing for antelope permits or having to act as guide for a couple of women hunters neither of whom had ever hunted antelope before.

Then it occurred to me that it made no difference which was worse for I had been drawn out for the second year in succession and on top of that it had fallen to my lot to take Ethel and Recie, otherwise known as Mrs. Barker and Mrs. Evans, out on their first antelope hunt.

Ethel was armed with my trusty .32 Winchester Special rifle, and Recie carried her new .30-06. I was armed with a pair of good binoculars to better locate and identify antelope, and a hunting knife which I had promised to loan the ladies to dress their antelope if or when they got them.

"I didn't think there used to be any antelope here or anywhere on the Fort Union Ranch," Ethel remarked

"Well," I said, "there weren't until 1939 when the Game Department trapped and trucked 22 head in here from the Roswell area."

"How many are there here now?" asked Recie.

I explained that we did not have an exact count but that our fieldmen estimated not less than 150 head in the whole Turkey Mountain unit and that we could let sportsmen harvest about 20 mature bucks this year without imparing the breeding potential of the herd. In fact, it has been demonstrated that removal of old mature bucks actually improves the herd's ability to increase.

"That's surely providing new hunting where none was found before, I'd say," exclaimed Recie.

"Yes, and I'd say it is one minute past 12 and we better get going if you fair nimrods are to get your bucks."

Cartridges were quickly injected into rifle magazines, sights were checked, binocular lenses cleaned and we were off afoot in quest of America's fleetest-footed animal, the wary pronghorn antelope.

"Now Ethel," I said, "remember I told you you must get yours by one o'clock." I found long ago that whenever anyone is given a dead-line to meet, they are far more likely to get the job done than if the allotted time is indefinite.

"Fifty-nine minutes ought to be a long enough time in which to kill a buck," I said, and then she checked it right back to me and I was on the spot as usual.

"O.K., but you agreed to find me one within shooting range."

We headed on up the slope fifty yards or so to a little rim above which the country flattened out a bit toward the base of the steeper slopes of Baldy Mountain. We stopped, with only our heads showing to scan the area ahead which had been out of sight until now. Within a few seconds I glimpsed the white rump of an antelope a half mile away.

"Wait! I see one," and I quickly focused the binoculars on the spot. Sure enough there was a band of five or six feeding right on a little ridge and headed away from us.

"How many? Any bucks? Where?" exclaimed the girls almost in unison. "Oh, yes, there they are away over there."

As the glasses were passed from one to the other for a better view, the little band fed on over the ridge and out of sight. Antelope usually get up and move around and feed for a while in midday.

"If we hurry we can top out over the ridge within shooting range," Ethel said.

"I saw no bucks, but there should be one around. Let me have the glasses for a good look-see before we go on."

I carefully scanned the slopes of Baldy Mountain a mile away and searched the area where the band had been, but could spot nothing. Then I fixed the glasses

260

on a flat half way between us and where the antelope had been.

"Be still," I whispered. "I see two nice bucks, they are feeding, heads this way, over there about 400 yards."

"Where? Where? Let me see."

"Better take my word for it and get out of sight."

"Let us see, we want to see." So I slowly handed over the binoculars and the girls each got a good look. Excitement in anticipation of some shooting ran high.

We slowly eased down out of sight and steathily, but without losing any time, skirted to the right keeping below the little rim around to the slope of a draw which headed against the very flat the bucks were on. We followed up the draw to its head then slowly and cautiously peeked over near where the bucks should be. No bucks in sight. We straightened up and took a few steps forward and stopped to look around.

"Wait, I hissed. "There he is over to the left."

"Oh! Oh! Shall I shoot?" Ethel whispered.

"Sure. He's only a hundred and twenty-five yards away. Steady now."

The buck was standing broadside watching us and ready to run. The gun cracked and down he went, kerplunk. Now Ethel doesn't drink. She doesn't smoke. And she doesn't swear. But what my earphone recorded sure sounded like, "By Gee Sus I got him."

Reice and I started to congratulate her, but congratulations had to be deferred. The buck got up and started a wobbly lope off down the slope. Ethel shot a couple of times but missed, and as she did so the second buck broke from cover of a little header to our right. He successfully dodged a couple of bullets from Recie's .30-'06 as he high-tailed it around the slope.

262

Ethel's buck was pretty hard hit but just a little too high in the shoulders to keep him down. He soon sickened and lay down and we tried to sneak up on him but there was no cover and he jumped up. Just as he went out of sight over a little ridge, Ethel missed another running shot at 200 yards. That's nothing unusual even for seasoned hunters. Perhaps it's because out in these wide open spaces there is so much space around these streamlined speedsters.

When we started on, Ethel was in front. I was next and Recie was behind. We were passing over a very rocky place when Recie called out "A rattlesnake bit me."

"Oh, my God!" I exclaimed and we rushed back to her. She was pale and trembling. I made her sit down to examine the wound, and we were all most happy to find that the fangs had not penetrated through her boot top. It was mighty fortunate that she had worn high topped hunting boots.

Ethel said, "I heard him rattle, but didn't realize what it was." We searched the area but the snake got away.

Recie was shook up a bit but got over it very quickly.

We followed Ethel's buck slowly and soon jumped him again without getting a shot. He went out of sight running very unsteadily. The next we saw of him he had crossed a draw and was walking head down and wobbling a little about 300 yards away.

"Think you can hit him?" I asked. "It's a long way."

"I can't if I don't try," she surmised.

The first shot raised dust at the right elevation but three feet to the left. The second shot was the same elevation but less than two feet to the left. The buck didn't run but walked on away from us.

"You're pulling off every time; try once more and hold steady." I realized that is a hard thing to do, shooting off-hand at that distance which by now was at least 325 yards.

At the crack of the gun down he went. This time with a broken back and he didn't get up. We hurried on over there and as I started to stick the dead buck, Ethel said, "Wait, what time is it, did I get him by one o'clock?"

"My watch says twenty minutes until one. Now can I stick him?" I asked.

"I knew I could do it!" She almost shouted. Such confidence.

The buck was a nice fat four year old with fair horns. While I was dressing him two more dandy big bucks came over the shoulder of Baldy Mountain and stopped more than a quarter mile away to watch. At the same time high on the ridge near the top of Baldy Mountain three other hunters appeared and waved congratulations at our buck.

After drawing the buck I turned him over belly down to drain out, and cut some red stemmed sage and covered him over to keep off the warm afternoon sun. All the while the two big bucks were watching first us then the hunters higher on the hill.

Recie asked, "Is there any way we can get closer?"

"There is no cover," I said, "but if we go straight toward them, stooped over and in single file we maybe can, and they probably will come part way to meet us."

So we set out, bent way low, and went nearly a hundred yards, then sat down in the high grass to rest. The bucks stood like statutes, and watched us. Again we went on fifty yards and stopped. Then while we were sitting there the larger of the two bucks trotted toward us maybe forty yards. We went a little way farther right toward him. Then he came on again through curiosity for he could not recognize us as human beings in our stooped and sitting postures.

When within a hundred and fifty or sixty yards, he indicated that was about all the cooperation we could expect from him, and trotted off to our left. Recie pulled up the heavy rifle and tried a couple of shots but failed to connect, and the two bucks high-tailed it out almost to the highway fence a mile and a half away. As we watched with the glasses they circled back where our car was parked and on up the slope past where Ethel had first shot her buck.

We went back and dragged Ethel's buck off across a rough little draw to a point where we thought maybe I could get with the car. We went on back away toward the car. Then I sent the girls on up the slope the way the two bucks had gone, telling them about where they might expect to jump either those or another buck.

Recie took my .32 Special that Ethel had used and I took her .30-'06, which was pretty heavy for her, on back to the car. I drove very slowly and carefully over the boulder strewn slopes meandering first this way and that to get through to where Ethel's buck had been left. On the way a band of eleven head of antelope including three nice bucks passed just ahead of my car. I wished Recie were there, for it would have been a grand opportunity to get the big buck that was trailing the herd.

After I loaded Ethel's buck in the trunk of the car, I drove carefully back to the ridge up which the ladies had gone. They were not in sight so I picked a very crooked way through the rocks up the ridge for a quarter mile or so until the slope became so rocky I could take the car no farther. I got out to look around and wait for the girls when I saw them a couple of hundred yards back down the slope of the draw to my right. They were stooped over doing something when they raised up, to my astonishment, I saw that their sleeves were rolled up and their hands and arms all covered with blood.

Although I admit I was anxious to hear how it all happened I took time enough to turn around and in getting back down there so that they would have finished dressing the antelope. Sure enough it was ready to load when I got there. It was an older buck with considerably bigger horns than Ethel's, but both were nice ones.

It seemed they had gone up on the ridge where I had told them to and sat down. Three bucks appeared on the slope above. While they watched them a bunch of eleven head including three nice bucks came over the ridge and passed within thirty yards of them. The bucks were intermingled with the does so closely that they realized it was not safe to shoot, so they passed them up. That bunch was the same one that had come down past my car.

The three bucks they had been watching separated, two going around the hill out of sight. The big one came down the slope as if to go and join the bunch which had passed them a moment before. When he came within range, Recie fired and badly wounded him. He came on by on the run, though wounded, and dodged two or three bullets. Then he lay down and a more deliberate shot finished him off.

"This time I asked, "What time was it."

"Just twenty minutes to three," Recie replied.

And so there we were. The hunt was over. It had taken less than three hours and hunting had been done afoot. Two fair nimrods with two fine pronghorn bucks, and an old worn-out guide whose luck is better in finding and getting others an antelope than it is in drawing a permit himself. After all, that is the greater satisfaction. I was glad to have had the opportunity of acting as guide for the ladies and proud of the ladies' luck which was made possible only by their good sportsman-like effort.

Another thing, it was a mighty gratifying for the old Game Warden to personally see the direct, concrete results of the Game Department's untiring efforts in restoring one of our finest game animals, the pronghorn antelope, to new ranges. While it was a satisfying thrill to see two fine ladies bag their first bucks, it was made doubly so because they, as many other sportsmen, were getting their bucks from a herd established only a few years ago under the Game Department's trapping and transplanting project.

BATTLE
OF THE
BUGLING BULLS

16

DARKNESS enveloped the alpine wilderness. Quiet solitude prevailed. My tired companions, Tommy and Walter, Explorer Scouts, with only their shoes off dozed in their sleeping bags spread out under the sparkling stars. I was glad for a respite from their myriad questions about wildlife. I sat on my bedroll screened by a fallen spruce tree at the spot selected for our nocturnal vigil.

Off across the deep Pecos Canyon a coyote set up his weird yip-yip-yieu-ee-e yapping. Another answered from not far away. Now and then from near and afar melodious bugling of bull elk broke the night's quietude.

At last a big, red moon, a bit past full, rose boldly over the Sangre de Cristo Range. Ever so slowly its light had crept down the hillside and on across the big, grassy park below us, dispelling the erstwhile gloom. The bright moonlight on the dry, straw-colored, bunch grass was almost like daylight.

A hundred yards below I could easily distinguish a herd of 35 or 40 elk grazing contentedly. It was, indeed, quite a harem for the lone bull with them, but he was a real monarch. As I watched he sought the favors of first one cow and then another only to be rejected. Finally a cow became the suitor. They nuzzled each other's flanks and necks amorously for a moment. Then she turned away, stopped and accepted his eager culmination of the affair.

I shook the boys awake. "Sh, sh, quiet," I cautioned. "Here is a chance to see elk by moonlight."

They rubbed the sleep out of their eyes and crawled up to the log blind beside me. There was bugling of elk here and there some distance away but none close.

"Any bulls?" Tommy asked a bit too loud.

"Just one big fellow," I said. "But boys, you must speak only in whispers. Watch it."

"Why don't this bull bugle?" Walt asked. "Those others are challenging him aren't they?"

"That old monarch is smart, he doesn't want to reveal the where abouts of his harem," I explained.

"So that's it. Then we won't get to see a fight?" Walt asked.

"I'll bet one or more bulls find this herd before dawn and we just might see some action," I said.

For an hour or so the boys watched this rare sight, taking turns with my binoculars. When the herd had grazed some distance away and began to bed down, I suggested that we all get some shut-eye, and resume our vigil at the first sign of dawn. So for the second time that night the boys crawled into sleeping bags with their clothes on to be ready for quick action when called. I hit the sack, too.

We were on an elk count in cooperation with the New Mexico Department of Game and Fish. I'd asked my young friends to come along to get a lesson in wildlife conservation and management, and possibly some real thrills. We had packed in twelve miles that day with several Game Department men to a headquarters camp at Beatty's Cabin site. Now the others were lying out as we were in strategic spots over the area to get as good a classified count of elk as possible at dusk, by moonlight, and at dawn.

A little while before sunset my young friends and I had packed our bedrolls and some sandwiches on a mule and walked and led him a mile up to this big park to watch for, and get a classified count on, whatever elk might show up there. We unpacked the mule and turned him loose, and he set out for camp in a long trot. He would be too noisy to keep with us. We had come a bit early to avoid disturbing any elk that likely would come out at sunset.

We spread our beds down behind a fallen spruce tree which would serve as a blind at the upper edge of the park. We munched sandwiches and drank coffee from a thermos bottle. I remarked that it would be a long vigil.

"We won't mind if we get to see a bull fight like you told us about today," Walt said, "You think we will?"

"We may, but I can't guarantee it," I said.

"Well, why don't you tell us about elk while we wait," Tommy said.

"Okay, but we must keep our voices very low," I said. "What do you want to know?"

Many questions then tumbled out as though from an assembly line.

"Were elk always here?"

"Originally they were found here, and in most other mountains of New Mexico. But by 1890 every one had been killed, so elk had to be restored."

"Where did they get them?"

"Wyoming mostly. In 1915, 37 head were shipped

in and released down below to get this herd started. But some ranchers and the Game Department have made plantings in many localities since them."

"How many are in this area now?"

"That's what we are here to find out. Maybe a thousand."

"What do elk eat mostly?"

"Mainly they are grass eaters, but they eat forbs and some browse, especially in winter. They are fond of green aspen leaves."

"Do they shed their horns every year?"

"They have antlers, not horns. Yes, bulls shed their antlers every spring along about March usually. Cows do not have antlers."

"How old must they be to have a calf?"

"Usually they calve first at three years, but sometimes at two."

"Do they have twins like deer?"

"Normally they have just one calf, but occassionally have twins."

"The mating season is about now, isn't it?"

"That's right. Mid-September to the last of the month is the peak period."

"When are the calves born?"

"The gestation period is about eight months, so most of the calves come during the last half of May."

"About their horns, I mean antlers, how can they grow them so big, so fast?"

"That's one of nature's wonders. But from the time the new antler starts as a ball, looking like a ripe tomato, in five months the antlers are mature, the velvet rubbed off, and they are ready for battle."

I thought the *sotto voice* questions in this unusual

wildlife classroom would never end. We had been on the go since five that morning and were pretty tired. When it grew pitch dark I had suggested that they turn in. "I will wake you at the crack of dawn, or before if anything happens," I assured my young companions. And so I had when the herd of elk had showed up in the moonlight.

I was awake when the east horizon paled to herald day and got up. I was delighted to hear a lot of elk bugling going on a quarter mile west of us. I nudged the boys smartly and said, "Come on, crawl out of those sacks. Day's breaking, and it sounds like all hell's about to break loose around yonder."

We put on our shoes and hurriedly laced them up. Then we put on our coats, for at 10,500 feet elevation the mornings are cold even in September. The Explorer Scouts were wide awake, excited and ready to go, for elk were bugling like mad. I told them, "It's not just one but it sounds like three or four are ganging up on our monarch to run him off and steal his harem."

It was not yet daylight and I felt sure the elk would stay in the open until sunup. So, despite protests from the boys who wanted to get going, I got out the remaining thermos bottle and we had coffee. Walt said, "Gee whiz, Mr. Barker, we are missing the show!"

"Okay, let's go," I said. "But damn it, keep quiet, stay behind me and do as I do."

The elk herd had moved westward and the commotion sounded nearly a quarter mile away. I knew every acre of the area intimately and figured that they had crossed a little spring branch, along which there is a narrow strip of timber, and were now in a bench-land park just beyond. We headed around the open hillside that way.

Walking in the dim light through the tufts of bunch grass was difficult. A third of the way there I stopped and listened to the almost continual melodious, thrill-packed bugling. The excited boys came close and I whispered, "If they are where I think, we'll get a grand-stand seat." We then continued along the bench out of sight of the slope below toward the other park. "Watch carefully, we must not spook them," I said.

Tense and trembling with anticipation the boys followed at my heels, stopping when I stopped, crouching when I crouched, with hearts pounding almost hard enough for elk to hear them. We stopped and searched the area with binoculars, for the light was still dim. A young bull bugled close below, but he had not seen us. We slowly squatted and waited. He paid no heed to us and slowly walked through the strip of timber to the park beyond.

"They're right there in that park," I whispered. "Follow me."

I angled up the hill to the end of the narrow, dense strip of timber to get above the elk. Slowly, cautiously we crept into the dark timber. Soon we could see the big park, and there were elk all over it. "Get down. Let's leave our hats here, and crawl."

Just ahead was a freshly wind-thrown tree with lots of green limbs sticking up. We squirmed to it. We'd watch through the branches from there. Softly I whispered, "Watch. Don't talk. Don't make any quick moves. We'll see action."

There were about forty elk there at close range. My primary interest was in getting a count of bulls, cows, yearlings and calves. For the boys this sight and sound was the thrill of a life time. But they wanted to see action — a real bull fight. It now looked as if they would get their wish.

Our lordly monarch was in the midst of the herd. With fearless hatred he glared at a majestic, but younger, worthy-looking antagonist approaching from the west a few steps at a time. When he stopped he would bugle an exciting challenge. The old monarch would paw the earth and answer. At a hundred yards the raucous, explosive grunts culminating the bugle were quite awesome.

Up the hill a fine, but somewhat smaller, bull stood, giving out with an occasional bugle, as if waiting for the outcome of the imminent battle before committing himself. Below the herd was another bull waiting and bugling now and then in like manner. He had a red streak on his shoulder and ribs, and when he moved I could see that he was lame. Evidently he'd been in a fight but was ready for another.

To our left the two-year-old bull we'd seen earlier was lurking about but making no fuss. Perhaps he felt that his younger legs and agility would get him out of danger if charged. His intentions of courting a cow near the edge of the herd were obvious. Never before had I seen such intensive thrills and enjoyment as my young companions were experiencing.

The stage was set. The actors were steamed up and ready. The unseen audience lay shivering on the cold ground peeking over a big log. The curtain was drawn when the first rays of the morning sun bathed the park in its amber light.

The challenger, now close, gave a final sharp bugle call to battle. The lordly monarch stood waiting with legs rigidly braced, facing his adversary without fear.

Now the challenger came on, swaying his big, high antlers from side to side. When but twenty feet separated
them the challenger stopped and shadow boxed with his
antlers for a brief moment. The other in defiance shook
his head viciously as if to say, "Come on, and I'll rip you
apart." Tommy murmered, "Oh, lordy."

The challenger came on a few steps, then lowered
his head and rushed into the old bull head on, and they
locked antlers with a crash like a falling tree. They rattled their antlers together, grunted and strained and
pushed each other around. But it seemed as if they were
just feeling each other out. Then suddenly the challenger
sidestepped and quickly broke off the engagement. The
calves in the herd seemed frightened. Some nearby cows
stopped their grazing to watch, others paid no attention.

There the bulls stood for a moment, heads down and
ready, glaring hatred and defiance at each other. Like a
flash, as if by a starting signal, they rushed forward and
banged their heads together with a fearful clatter of
ivory-hard antlers. No mistake, this time they pushed
and shoved, grunted and groaned in dead earnest. The
banging, clanging and rattling of antlers together made a
terrific din.

Furiously back and forth, around and around they
raced. Each was trying desperately to throw the other off
balance enough to gouge him in ribs or flank, but they
were evenly matched and neither one seemed to gain any
advantage over the other. By now the two other bugling
bulls edged in a bit closer. The two-year-old had boldly
taken advantage of the situation and cut a willing cow
out of the herd to sire her offspring.

The battle continued to rage with such fury that the
battlers were becoming exhausted. Again, as if by mu-

tual consent, they broke contact briefly to rest. There they stood ten feet apart with lowered heads and tongues lolling out of their frothy mouths. Each was intensely vigilant for an opportunity to launch a surprise attack to gain access to the other's side. Equally alert were they to ward off such an attack.

After they had rested a little while, they banged and rattled their antlers together again. Straining, heaving and pushing was even more furious than before, and grunts and groans louder. I was put to it to keep the boys from rooting for the monarch, and to keep them down out of sight.

The bulls plowed up the soft earth with their hind feet as they alternately launched attacks and braced against them. Once the challenger got the old monarch off balance almost enough to score a vicious thrust with sharp tines in his ribs. But with incredible skill and speed, the big one recovered and whirled to meet his antagonist head on instead.

With determination and desperation they fought, banged and raged with heaving sides and clanging antlers, then broke off briefly a half dozen times to rest. They were wearing each other down, but which would weaken first was impossible to predict. Would the endurance and agility of the younger challenger ultimately give him the advantage? Or, would it be the old one's experience and his determination to retain his harem prevail? Lolling tongues, clanking antlers, grunts and groans gave no clue.

Finally the fury of the battle carried them down the hill to where the slope became steeper. Fortunately, we were high enough to still see the show. There they went at it hammer and tongs. For a second the monarch was pushing the other down hill when the challenger's heels shoved back under an aspen pole that was a few inches off the ground. He couldn't free his feet to back up and rebrace himself, nor could he push the big fellow back up hill. He was forced to turn sideways to get out of his predicament. He tried to break off contact clean, but couldn't back up enough. He had to turn to get away and the pole threw him off balance for a half second. With the speed of a magician the monarch proved himself to be an opportunist.

In that instant the monarch caught his unfortunate antagonist in the ribs with a vicious thrust with sharp brow and bez tines, and knocked him flat, back down hill.

He let out a hoarse bleat of distress and, kicking and pawing, tried to get up. The monarch lunged at him again, but the antlers caught the flailing feet in such a manner that he rolled him over instead of ripping his belly.

The challenger sprang to his feet like a flash. Quick as he was, he was not in time to turn and meet the big one head on. His ribs and flank were exposed and he knew it. His lightning decision was that he had had it. Quick as a flash bulb he took off down hill at top speed with the victorious monarch after him.

How far he ran we couldn't tell; he didn't bugle any more. The victor very soon came slowly back up the hill mouth agape and tongue hanging out. He joined the cows but showed no interest in courtship. He rested a little while watching the two other buglers which were now engaged in a furious fight. When he'd got his breath back he suddenly made a vicious rush at the two fighting bulls, and they both took to their heels leaving the monarch in full charge again.

I had gotten my classified count. The boys were

about to burst, but we still watched the herd before us. An old cow had come up behind us and was not fifteen feet away when we saw her and she saw us. "Be still and quiet," I whispered. She looked long and hard at the prone figures by the log trying to make out what they were. Finally the breeze shifted and she knew. Head high and nose extended she stalked around the log, then ran through the herd to give the danger signal. They all took off into the forest on a lope, that is, all but our old monarch. Still king, but looking pretty well done in, he was content to trot along behind.

We got up, stretched and kicked the kinks out of our numb legs. I had tallied 6 bulls, 15 cows, 9 heifers and 11 calves — 41 total.

"I'll be a monkey's uncle," Walt exclaimed! "That was the best darned show I ever saw!"

"I'd call it a heavyweight prize fight," Tommy said. "Oh, how I wish a lot of the other kids could have been here."

The boys were happy, exuberant and thrilled to the bone. I wished for a tape recorder to record their conversation about the experience and how OUR BIG OLD BULL won.

Walt said, "Mr. Barker, we can't ever thank you enough or begin to pay you for giving us this show. It is worth a million dollars."

"That goes for me, too," Tommy said.

"It was my pleasure," I said. "If you have learned a good lesson in wildlife habits, their conservation and management, that's pay enough for me." I, too, wished that many more boys could have like experiences. What an antidote it would be for juvenile delinquency.

Jubilantly we walked back to Beatty's Cabin camp

where some of the others had breakfast waiting. If ever two boys did a meal justice, they did while bubbling over with stories of their thrilling experience.

After breakfast I said, "I'll catch up a saddle horse and pack mule and go get our beds. You roosters stretch out and have a nap. You must start back at noon so as to be in school tomorrow." From their moans you would have thought they were dying.

The other Conservation Officers and I would have three more days on the elk count before we'd go in. The Explorer Scouts envied us, but they would go back with a fine memory keepsake.

With many thank you's, Tommy and Walter had taken their leave and ridden down the trail aways when Tommy turned and trotted his horse back and said, "Mr. Barker, how would you describe an elk's bugle call?"

"I'll try, I said. "Bill Rush in his *Wild Animals of The Rockies* says, 'The bugle call starts low and clear, rises in pitch and volume for a half minute, then falls away suddenly, and ends in three explosive, raucous grunts.' In my book *When The Dogs Bark 'Treed'* I describe it this way, 'The bugle call starts low with bell-like clearness, waveringly rises to higher, musical notes and increases in volume for five seconds, suddenly ending with two or three explosive grunts', so take your choice."

"Will you please write that down for us?" Tommy asked.

"When I get home I sure will," I said.

THESE HAPPENED TO ME-BELIEVE IT OR NOT

17

JUST ABOUT every outdoorsman that I know has experienced at least one rare coincidence. Such coincidences, or rare one-in-a-million incidents, make good talk around a camp fire. But barring past presidents of the Ananias Clubs, I'll challenge anyone to beat my record of unbelievable, long-odds incidents that have happened to me. Perhaps the challenge is a bit unfair because of the fact throughout my long life my vocation and avocation have been that of an outdoorsman.

Considering the countless billions of unborn, perhaps the most amazing coincidence, among the many, many weird ones that have happened to me, is that I was born at all. Yet I was, and, in so doing, made the one chance in three hundred sixty-five by being born on Christmas day. Anyway that is how it all started eighty-four years ago.

Here are a few of the inexplicable coincidences and incidents — happenstances as we mountain-raised kids used to call them — that have been experienced through the years. There is the risk, of course, of not being believed in relating some of the rare ones, but I swear this is the way they happened. Fortunately, in many instances, there were witnesses who are still around and available to testify.

Let's start with one whose background dates back more than three score years. In 1908, while alone in my favorite bear-hunting camp in the Sangre de Cristo Mountains at nearly twelve thousand feet elevation, through a hole in my pocket I lost a silver dollar in a grassy, alpine park where I had my horses picketed. I hunted and hunted but could not find it. It was a real coincidence that I had a silver dollar, but that is not the point.

In 1958, just fifty years later, while in charge of twenty-five Wilderness Trail Riders on an eleven-day pack trip, we had lunch in that same park. After lunch while hunting for Indian arrowheads, which occur there, I found a tarnished silver dollar. Considering that very few people ever visit this spot, I have no doubt at all that was the same silver dollar that I had lost fifty years before.

In 1925 I was operating a mountain ranch west of Las Vegas, New Mexico. One spring day when I had finished plowing a ten-acre field I discovered that my billfold, which I carried in the left hip pocket of my Levi's was missing. If it had worked out and dropped from the plow seat it would have fallen in the furrow, or on the unplowed edge of it, and would have ben plowed under the next time around. To go look for it seemed ridiculous.

Then I remembered a spot about six by ten feet where an old burned-off stump made it necessary to lift the plow and skip over that tiny patch. The number of square feet in that spot compared to the number in the field meant there was only one chance in seven thousand of its being there. But, because I was terribly broke and the billfold had my last twenty-five dollars in it, I went and looked anyway, and there it was!

Other findings I have made are astounding, but true, nevertheless. For instance, in 1960 I was in charge of a Wilderness Trail Ride trip in the Maroon Bells — Snow Mass Wilderness near Aspen, Colorado. One of the good-looking gals lost a tiny little compass, about the size of a quarter, in a big meadow where grass was knee high. She had no idea where for she had wandered all over looking at wildflowers, butterflies and humming-birds. She could not be tracked because some forty head of horses had grazed there overnight.

Just to humor the young lady I said, "Don't worry, I'll go find it for you." I knew, of course, it would be like looking for the Lost Dutchman gold mine. I strolled down across the big meadow, then turned and started back to camp a different route. Something glistened deep in the tall, tangled grass. It was the little compass.

Once my wife and I were returning from a trip to California when out in the Arizona desert the timing gear of my Chevrolet went out. A passer-by pushed the car about nine miles to a garage in a little highway town. It would cost twenty dollars to fix the car. We had overstayed in California and spent all our money except barely enough for travel expenses to get home. The mechanic refused to take my check despite my identification cards.

I jay-walked across the highway toward a store where I though I might cash a check. In the gutter next to the curb a greenish something caught my eye, and I picked it up. Folded tightly into about an inch and a half square were two ten dollar bills. It looked as if they had been there a long time. All the same, it was just what I needed to pay the garage bill.

Twenty years ago I drove from Santa Fe to Albu-

querque early one morning. Albuquerque was then a
city of about sixty thousand. At our office I met District
Game Warden, J. W. Peckum, and we set out afoot for
the Court Cafe to get breakfast.

Enroute I noticed an envelope on the sidewalk, address side down. It appeared to be an unopened letter so
I picked it up. To our amazement the address was, Elliott S. Barker, State Game Warden, Santa Fe, New Mexico. That was me! Upon opening it I found that it was
from one of my hunting and fishing license vendors and
contained a check for a thousand dollars in payment for
licenses sold. It would take a mechanical brain to figure
the odds on that one. The witness, Mr. Peckum, just retired from the Game and Fish Department and lives in
Santa Fe, New Mexico.

Not long ago I wanted the address of a friend, Mr.
Wm. H. Brady, of Houston, Texas, who, a few years before, had hunted antelope with me here in New Mexico.
I looked in my card indexes and correspondence folders
where it should have been but failed to find it and, after a
diligent search, gave up.

Later that day I took a folder out of my closed files
to get some information on an entirely different subject.
As I went back to my desk a tiny piece of paper fluttered
to the floor. I picked it up and started to put it in the
wastebasket. Then I saw it was the corner of an envelope
torn off bearing the name and address of my friend, Wm.
H. Brady. The deep mystery of how it got to where it
had been and how come it to appear as if by magic right
when I wanted it is bizarre, to say the least.

Five years ago my wife and I were visiting a
daughter in Long Beach, California. We learned that a
grandson from El Paso, Texas, was selling magazine sub-

scriptions in Los Angeles. The only clue we had as to where we might find him was that some months before he had stayed a few days at Hotel California. We drove up to Los Angeles one evening headed for that hotel to see if we could find him or get a clue as to where he might be staying.

While we were stopped at a traffic light five blocks from Hotel California, my grandson walked across the street in front of my car, recognized us, came alongside and got in before the light changed. He hadn't known we were in California. With six million people in Los Angeles the one we were looking for met us as if it had been planned to the second.

In the early 1930s Paul G. Reddington, Chief of the U.S. Biological Survey (predecessor of the U.S. Fish and Wildlife Service), and I, accompanied by several others, were on a wildlife inspection trip in the rugged west side of the Sacramento Mountains of southern New Mexico. That morning we had had a rather heated discussion regarding the damage done to game by golden eagles, and the need for controlling their numbers. I was for it and he against any eagle control at all. There was no law then against killing golden eagles.

As we rode along someone called attention to two golden eagles soaring round and round, perhaps twenty-five hundred feet above us — mere specks against the clear, blue sky. Reddington said, "Elliott, since you are so keen on controlling eagles, let's see you control one of those."

"All right, I believe I will," I replied, realizing that it would be easier to hit a tossed-up dime at a hundred yards. Anyway, I got off my horse, drew my .32 Winchester Special rifle from the saddle scabbard, aimed

285

straight up toward one of the tiny moving targets and fired with no thought whatever of hitting it. A couple of seconds after the bang there was a puff of feathers and the eagle plunged to earth over a nearby cliff. John Gatlin, who is still in Albuquerque, rode over and said in *sotto voice*, "Elliott, you'd better pretend your are out of cartridges." Why try again?

In 1934 I was in New York City attending a Wildlife Conservation Conference. At 5 P.M. one day with three friends I walked from the Pennsylvania Hotel toward Times Square just to see and mingle with the tremendous mass of human beings hurrying and pushing their way along at that rush hour. No one seemed to notice anyone else or to bother to say, "I'm sorry," when they bumped into one another.

One man did look at me as he passed, and seconds later came back and tugged at my arm. "You are Elliott Barker, aren't you?" he asked.

"Yes," I replied. "But I can't seem to remember you."

"You certainly should remember me," he said. I was your assistant when you were Forest Ranger at Panchuela Station in 1910, and you fired me."

"Sure, I remember," I exclaimed. "I said your talents might bring you success in New York but they weren't worth a tinker's dam in the West."

After 24 years, seven million people, a splitsecond passing, what are the odds of us meeting and him recognizing me?

Eight years ago with four buddies I packed into the Pecos Wilderness to hunt the big, timberline mule deer bucks found there. The second morning, instead of making a clean kill, I had the misfortune to wound a very large, unusually chunky, fat buck. There was a bit of

hard-crusted snow on the ground making it easy to follow his bloody trail, except that it was very slick walking.
I tried hard, first on foot, then on horseback. But, in
character, he took to a steep, loggy, timbered hillside and
if he adhered to all precedents he would stay in that sort
of country and avoid all open areas.

At 76, and hampered by an old knee injury, it was
simply impossible for me to follow his trail. Through the
years I had helped scores of hunters retrieve wounded
game, but this was the first time I ever had to have help.
I'd have to get two young hunting companions to follow
up my buck for me. It's unthinkable to leave wounded
game in the woods.

I turned back, dropped down to a trail at the base of
the steep, densly-timbered hillside and headed for camp.
In about a mile and a half the trail came out into the
lower side of an opening that extended all the way up to
the top of the very steep hillside.

At the very instant that I rode out into that opening
I saw a big buck, obviously badly wounded, stagger slowly out of the timber some three hundred yards up the hill.
I stepped off my horse and shot him. It looked like mine,
but mine or not, he was wounded badly enough to have
to be killed. Had he been five seconds sooner or later I
never would have seen him. He proved to be my buck,
all right, and the coincidence saved me the humilation of
having to have someone follow up to administer the *coupe
de grace* for me. Actually it was a double coincidence—
the split-second timing, and his violation of all buck laws
by leaving cover.

The longest odds of all involved an incident that happened to my disadvantage thirty-nine years ago which I
still can hardly believe. In the crash of 1929 I went broke

ranching and took a job hunting mountain lions on the 360,000-acre Vermejo Park ranch and game preserve in northern New Mexico. One big tom lion was giving me trouble in eluding my fine pack of dogs by taking refuge in the vast slide-rock areas of Ash Mountain around whose base he killed deer for food.

So I set a number four-and-a-half New House traps for him on a regularly used runway, and I caught him too. The trap was not anchored solidly because a trapped lion in his first mad, powerful lunges will pull out of the trap. Instead the trap is equipped with a six-foot-long chain with a double-hooked clog, back-to-back, and each about four inches across. The hook points are sharpened and one bent up and the other down so as to leave a mark even on hard ground.

The trapped lion had hung up briefly on some brush, then on a fir sapling. When the clog came loose from the sapling the lion had plunged hell for leather down an open slope of about five acres. On that hillside there was only one log — a solid, blackened, pitchy log resulting from an old forest fire. Midway along the top of this log was a little knothole about an inch in diameter. The sign showed that the lion had bounded down the hill at full speed jerking the clog in erratic bounces after him, and crossed the log right where the knothole was.

Incredulous, but it is God's truth, the point of one clog hook came down right in that little knothole in the solid log! The force of the fleeing beast was so great and the stop so sudden and solid that he jerked a toe off and got away. It was a bad luck coincidence because I needed that lion to hold my job.

There are about 31,000,000 square inches in a five-acre tract and the knothole was only about one square inch. Besides the hook had to be in just one position to go in. Page a computer.

The sequel was that in a few days my luck changed and, after a fine, thrill-packed chase with my faithful dogs we treed the lion in a big pine tree, which is the method I prefer in taking them anyway.

If you are a strong believer in clairvoyance then this incident may make sense to you. To me it is a most perplexing enigma.

My wife was in the habit of using my little old 'trap shovel' puttering around flower beds in our back yard. I'd made the tool myself back in the 1920s, when I was doing quite a bit of coyote trapping, by chiseling the center section out of a common long-handle shovel and cutting the handle to six inches in length. It was stout enough to pry rocks out of a 'trap hole' and heavy enough to drive a trap pin. It had no value except as an item of my old equipment that I wanted to keep.

One day the little shovel disappeared. Stolen? There were many more valuable articles around the yard that could have been taken instead. We really missed the handy little tool, but time went by without our hearing anything about it.

Five years later we were visiting some friends forty miles from Santa Fe and there was present a fine lady who was reported to be clairvoyant. In the course of the evening there was a discussion of vandalism and thefts, and I mentioned the disappearance of my 'trap shovel'. That lady became interested and said, "Tell me about it." I told her what little there was to tell, and emphasized that it was not the value of the shovel at all but the sentiment that I attached to it that made me want to get it back.

She looked me straight in the eye for a moment and said, "Don't worry, you will get it back soon." The subject was dropped and I thought no more about it.

A week later when I went out to get into my car parked in the driveway I was utterly flabbergasted to see my 'trap shovel' lying on the front seat. Who had had it, where it came from, and why it was returned after five years, we have no idea. That one kind of haunts me.

So much for that sort of thing. But, in a different category, perhaps it was another coincidence that I held the position of State Game Warden of New Mexico (Department of Game and Fish Director) for twenty-two years—three times as long as anyone else has ever held that position. And that I am the only man ever to be President of the Western Association of Game and Fish Commissioners and the International Association of Game, Fish and Conservation Commissioners at the same time, except Harry R. Woodward who served briefly in 1970.

Also, that I was one of a committee of twenty-five appointed by President Franklin D. Roosevelt in 1936 to arrange the First National Wildlife Conference out of which came the National Wildlife Federation — largest conservation organization in the world — and that I was elected as a member of its first Board of Directors.

There is more, but that's enough.

RIDING WILDERNESS TRAILS

18

A SCORE of horses with empty saddles and reins dragging, nibbled the short timberline grass atop the twelve thousand six hundred-foot peak while men and women riders wandering over the narrow crest were enthralled by the breath-taking panoramic view of willdderness scenery. Northward, the majestic Truchas Peaks towered above 13,100 feet. To the east across the mosaic pattern of alpine forests, aspen woods, bunchgrass parks and steep rock slides the east fork of the Sangre de Cristo Range formed the horizon. On the south lay the myriad lovely canyons merging into the Pecos River with plains beyond extending as far as the eye could reach. Westward, the rugged mountains dropped off to the foothills and thence to the Rio Grande valley, with the Jemez mountains rising hazily in the distance beyond.

On one side of the timberline peak there was a deep, rugged, slide rock gorge, and on the other, snuggling close to its base, lay a charming emerald lake. Around the shore, when one looked carefully, could be seen several other members of the party who had chosen to angle for cutthroat trout instead of climbing the mountain. A quarter mile beyond the lake blue smoke spiraled up from the camp where we had spent the night.

Here on the peak some were taking pictures, some looking through binoculars and others standing or sitting around spellbound by the inspiring vistas. One couple, who had wandered out to the escarpment at the north end of the crest, suddenly called out, "Sheep, bighorn sheep!" Every one scrambled over the rocky terrain to join them, for the sighting of bighorns is a rare trail ride experience.

Sure enough, there were thirty-four contented bighorn mountain sheep, some lying, some standing on a little bench with tall cliffs above and below. We crowded up on the lookout spot, and those who had binoculars passed them around so all could get a close-up view. Shutters clicked, but at an eighth-of-a-mile it was too far without telephoto lenses. But the sight of bighorns, wily denizens of rugged, timberline peaks, was intriguing enough to hold our attention for a long time, and the bighorns, indifferent to our presence, remained there unafraid.

Watching the band of mountain sheep provided a rare and thrilling experience, and the Wilderness Trail Riders were reluctant to leave the fascinating scene. But magnificient scenic views in other directions which had been glimpsed were so entrancing that they could not long be ignored. By ones and twos, the Riders withdrew and wandered about the narrow crest, stopping to gaze first in one direction, then another.

The Riders were awed by the craggy, timberline peaks towering above green alpine forests interspersed with parks and meadows. They were amazed that the clear, clean atmosphere permitted them to distinctly see horizons more than a hundred miles away. They marveled at the deep, rugged gorges and canyons radiating from the high ranges. They were inspired and humbled by the overall marvelous scene, and made to realize how small man is in the midst of a vast, alpine wilderness as God made it untrammeled by man. Those two hours atop the majestic peak, 200 feet above timberline, they would never forget nor regret.

Finally, as ominous thunder clouds began boiling up out of nowhere, as they do around the high peaks, I called boots and saddles suggesting that it would be well for us to get off the peak before lightning flashed or static electricity began buzzing around our, and the horses', ears. As soon as saddle cinches were tightened and riders mounted, I led them down the steep, rocky trail which zigzags around twenty switchbacks to a meadow at the halfway mark.

There we stopped to wait for stragglers to catch up, to rest a bit and take pictures. (Kodak could well afford to subsidize these trips.) It began to sprinkle, and we put on our ponchos and saddle slickers and set out again. The lower half of the trail was not rocky or so steep, and in a half hour we were at the lake letting the horses drink. The light shower had passed on and the sun shone through a deep blue sky. The Riders were thrilled that the half dozen fishermen had caught enough beautiful cutthroat trout for us to have a big fish fry that evening.

In another ten minutes we were greeted at camp by the cook who had hot soup, coffee and sandwich makings ready for lunch. Wranglers unsaddled the horses, hobbled some, belled some and turned them loose to graze in the nearby lush mountain meadows.

This was the fourth day of an eleven-day Wilderness Trail Ride in New Mexico's Pecos Wilderness Area in the Santa Fe National Forest. It was one of more than twenty such rides sponsored by the American Forestry Association annually in Wilderness Areas of the western States. There were sixteen women and fourteen men riders, including the Medical Officer and myself, the AFA representative in charge. In the service crew were nine men and women — the outfitter, cooks, wranglers and packers.

The Riders were from 14 to 77 and hailed from a dozen different States. There was a doctor, banker, lawyer, executive, governess, secretary, salesman, chemist, life insurance agent, biologist, teacher, pathologist, two librarians, two students, two unspecified, three retired persons and five housewives. As usual, housewife was the dominant calling represented. These riders of the wilderness are just average American citizens with the love of the great outdoors and wilderness in their hearts.

The American Forestry Association contracts with a reliable outfitter to put on the ride. He provides everything but your bedroll — horses, saddles, sleeping tents, packers, wranglers, good food and a good cook to prepare and serve it. The AFA provides a doctor to take care of any sickness or accidents which might, but usually do not, occur. The AFA also sends along its representative, in this case myself, to have overall charge of the trip. It has been my privilege to be on 33 of these rides, and to have been the AFA's representative on 23 in five different States.

The cost of this eleven-day wilderness trail ride is $270.00 and the outfitters—one of the best—are Wesley and Margie Adams, Mountain View Guest Ranch, Cowles, New Mexico. There are five camps with two nights at each camp, thus providing a layover-day at each camp. On layover days a good ride to some scenic spot, lake or high peak is provided, but riders are free to stay in

294

camp and rest up if they choose. The daily rides are from seven to eighteen miles and a total of about 125 miles of wilderness trails are explored.

This ride was September 5 to 15, inclusive — September because July and August are too rainy. The Riders rendezvoused September 4 at La Posada Inn in Santa Fe. That evening they attended a get-acquainted banquet, courtesy American Forestry Association. As the M.C., I briefed them on the trip ahead, throwing in some humorous trail Ride stories. Then I had each one rise, state name, where from and occupation. Forest Service officials present spoke briefly welcoming the Riders to the Forest and Wilderness, telling them something of the policies and programs and wished them well on the trip.

The Medical Officer (doctor) assured the Riders that he was well equipped to take care of any emergencies, and would be available for consultation anytime day or night. He cautioned against sunburn, for in the high, clean, clear atmosphere it can be severe and distressing. The outfitter gave some miscellaneous instructions about handling the horses, equipment carried on the saddle and the schedule for tomorrow. In conclusion, The Department of Game and Fish showed a most interesting color film entitled *Wildlife World*.

Next morning by 7:30, duffel bags and bedrolls were loaded on a truck and taken to Mountain View Ranch. At 8:30 the Riders left by cars on the interesting trip to the Ranch where gas burners would be traded for grass burners. Upon arrival, horse and saddle were assigned to each Rider, stirrups adjusted, and lunch bags supplied. To riding novices instructions were given on horse handling, mounting and dismounting and tying coats and raincoats on the saddles.

Then after a fine buffet lunch we mounted and took off on the seven-mile trip to our first camp in beautiful Horse Thief Meadows. We rode a mile and a half to road's end at Panchuela Ranger Station, and a mile beyond entered the fabulous Pecos Wilderness Area, marked by a large attractive sign. I deposited a list of the Riders in the registration box. The ride in the Wilderness had begun, and for eleven days we would be out of touch with civilization.

We were riding in a big canyon timbered with ponderosa pine, Douglas and white fir, aspen, Gambel oak and mountain mahogany. We rode along noisy Panchuela Creek, then crossed it and continued up Cave Creek. The outfitter, with a string of ten pack mules loaded with our bedrolls and duffel and some supplies, overtook and passed us. Food, tents and kitchen equipment and grain for the horses had been packed in the day before and camp would be set up for us.

A rest stop, which I call about every hour and a half, was called at the cave from which the creek gets its name. The creek flows into a huge cave, surrounded by banks of moss on the limestone, and comes out a half mile below. The cave is unique and interesting and there were many questions asked and considerable shutter clicking.

From there we climbed up, and up beside the tumbling brook through forests of Douglas fir gradually giving way to alpine forests of cork bark fir and Engelmann spruce with fine aspen woods intermingled. We topped out in a lovely aspen-park area on the divide between Cave and Horse Thief Creeks. A mule deer doe with twin fawns beside her stood for a few moments staring in wonderment at the motley cavalcade, then bounded away into forest cover.

296

We rode through one mile of rather steep trail through a dark forest to emerge suddenly into the charming Horse Thief Meadows, adorned with blue and fringed gentians and other wildflowers. There were exclamations of delight when I announced that we would camp in this exquisite setting at nine thousand seven hundred feet elevation. A half-mile down stream we came to the camp site spangled with teepee tents for two, and saw activity at the kitchen. We tethered our horses to the hitching line (a long rope stretched between two trees) and I called out, "Coffee is ready at the cook-tent," for I knew it would be.

Wranglers came and unsaddled the horses, hobbled some, belled a few and turned them out to graze in the bunch grass park.

Some Riders went with me to the kitchen for coffee, while others, anxious to get ready for the night, dug out their duffel bags and bedrolls from the pile where they had been unpacked, and with a chosen tent mate of the same sex, picked out their tents and arranged duffel and beds.

I was happy to see my friend, Dave Wilson, who for the fifth time, had come from Upper Marlboro, Maryland to cook for us. "Now," I assured everyone, "I know we'll be well fed."

With a packer and a couple of Riders helping, I arranged the sitting logs in a "square circle" around the evening bonfire site, and soon had a big fire blazing. Rain or shine, nothing in the woods cheers one up like a cup of hot coffee and a good camp fire! Some of the Riders delayed readying their tents a bit too long enjoying it.

At sundown I saw Dave's familiar wave from the kitchen and I startled the Riders by suddenly calling out

297

in a stentorian voice, "COME NOW AND GET IT OR YOU'LL REGRET IT!" No one needed a second call.

Dave had broiled fine steaks on a long griddle over the camp fire which, with all the fixin's, would satisfy the most discriminating gourmet. All meals are served cafeteria style. Some Riders chose to eat near the kitchen but most of them went back to the square circle at the fire seventy yards away.

After dinner there was a period of conversation around the fire, before I began my usual informational evening program. As a starter I told the details of how Horse Thief Meadows got the name. It was the result of the Silva gang of thieves in the 1870's hiding stolen horses here until the changed brands haired over, when they would move them farther west and sell them.

Then I related the history of the Wilderness System. In 1924, it was begun when the Gila Wilderness Area, consisting of nearly a half million acres was established by executive order of the Secretary of Agriculture. The system grew until by 1964 there were 84 Wilderness, Primitive and Wild areas in the National Forests, mainly in the west. To obtain greater stability and have wilderness preservation recognized as a national policy, Senator Hubert Humphrey introduced a bill in 1958. Many other Wilderness Preservation Bills were introduced in Congress during the next six years and many hearings held.

But until 1964 all were defeated through the influence of selfish interests. Then a Bill was passed declaring wilderness preservation to be a national policy, and setting aside some nine million acres to be preserved perpetually as wilderness with no roads, no commercialization and no habitation. While Primitive areas were not included, and the number and acreage thus reduced, provision was made for their possible future designation as Wilderness along with additional areas suitable for the purpose. Gradually the number and acreage is being increased. Wilderness Areas are now established by law instead of administrative order.

The program was ended with a question and answer period. Bed time came all too soon, and the evening ended with singing of a few old songs.

When a few horses came in before sunrise for their morning ration of grain, the jingling of multi-toned bells awakened some of the Riders. By the time I got a fire started at the square circle the early risers began gathering around, for the mornings are chilly at this elevation. When the first rays of sun flooded the scene it was time everybody was up. As is my custom to get late sleepers up, I gave out with a loud, raucous call, "EVERYBODY UP — CRAWL OUT OF THAT SACK," and repeated it at intervals until it appeared everyone was stirring. Hot water and wash pans were available at the kitchen, but some went to the creek for their ablutions.

By now the wranglers were bringing the other horses in, haltering and tethering them to the hitching line, and hanging the grain-filled morrals (nose bags) on. Then they began saddling them preparatory for the day's ride. These procedures would be followed each morning except an hour earlier on camp-moving days.

Breakfast had been scheduled for 7:30 and on the minute Dave sent his helper to ask me to give my 'COME GET IT' call. Breakfast consisted of fruit juice, oatmeal, sausage, scrambled eggs, toast, jam, coffee and hot chocolate. The "makin's" for noon lunch were spread out on the long, waist-high table made of poles covered with heavy, half-inch mesh wire netting. Everyone made his own lunch, thus choosing how much and, within limits, what he wanted. Lunch carrying bags were hung over the saddle horn. Cameras and other small articles could be carried in the bag also.

By eight-thirty we were lined up on the trail, noses counted, ready for the day's seven-mile ride to Johnson Lake. We back tracked to Cave Creek, then climbed through aspens, past beaver dams and through a heavy spruce and fir forest to a lush mountain meadow where I called a rest stop. It was my job to decide when and where to stop, and when we stop to call out so all can hear, "Ladies to the front, Gentlemen to the rear." Nature cannot be ignored.

We continued up and up through an alpine forest to the placid, four-acre lake at 11,100 feet nestling against high ridges to south and west. Horses were tied to small trees at a height of four feet and four feet from tree to halter, and saddle cinches were loosened.

A half dozen fishermen readied tackle and began casting for cutthroat trout. I built a fire to heat water in the two gallon coffeepot which Margie, the outfitter's charming wife, had brought along for hot drinks at lunch. Riders asked me to catch a limit of trout. I tried my luck, but it soon became windy and cloudy and I had to settle for three ten-inchers. The others likewise took only a few.

After lunch Riders sat around the fire, took short hikes and took pictures until two o'clock when saddle cinches were tightened and we headed for camp. On the way it showered and we put on raincoats, but by the time we got to camp the sun was again shining. When we dismounted, a man, standing stiff-kneed by his horse, said, "Barker, is there a psychiatrist in the party?"

"We've a doctor, but no psychiatrist," I replied.

"I need a psychiatrist," he insisted.

"Why a psychiatrist?" I asked.

"Because," he said, "I feel I've a split personality."

Coffee at the kitchen, a nip at some tents, washing up, gathering around the bonfire, a fried chicken dinner and we were ready for the evening program. A Forest Ranger had joined us and I turned the program over to him. He spoke of his work, his problems and how he solved them, the policies and objectives of the Forest Service and ended with a question and answer period.

I was asked to read some of my Wilderness poems, then there was singing of old songs until Morpheus beckoned Riders to their tents.

It was EVERY BODY UP at six, duffel readied, breakfast, lunches made, and then I demonstrated how to take down tents and fold them for packing. Tent poles were stood up under trees so they would be dry and ready next year. Riders brought everything to a central location for the packers. By 8:30 we started on the eighteen-mile trip to Pecos Baldy Lake camp. The pack string would be taken over a short cut, and camp would be set up when we arrived.

There were thirty-two of us, including the Ranger and Margie. We passed the meadows split by a meandering trout stream and headed up Horse Thief Creek. Here was an example of how a river is born by tiny springs making their contributions, and at the head only a trickle coming from under a moss-covered rock.

We rested on the divide which separates the waters of the Rio Grande and Pecos River. From there we meandered around seventeen switch-backs down into a canyon, thence down it to Rio Medio and up Rio Medio to

301

Brazos Fork where we made coffee and had lunch in the scenic canyon.

After lunch we rode up the spectacular canyon along side a beautiful, wildly rushing stream. We passed wonderful red granite cliffs, rode through aspen and spruce woods and finally topped out on a massive 12,000-foot, open divide running betwen Pecos Baldy and Truchas Peaks towering away above timberline.

From an escarpment called Trail Riders' Wall, the Riders got a magnificent view of the fabulous upper Pecos Watershed. There were exclamations of wonder as shutters clicked all over the place. A New Yorker said, "I never dreamed I'd live to see such a wondrous wilderness scene."

Interest and enjoyment was intense as I pointed out landmarks and sites of future camps. At last I had to call boots and saddles. We headed down the divide then dropped off it to Pecos Baldy Lake and on to camp at 11,300 feet beside a spring in a beautiful glade in the alpine forest.

It had been a wonderful day, but a long one. Riders set up their tents, made beds and arranged duffel, then were ready for the boiled ham and pinto bean (*frijole*) dinner. The bonfire session was brief, and everyone retired early. Next morning we slept late, then rode for an hour and a half to the summit of Pecos Baldy where this story began.

After returning from Pecos Baldy and lunch, the Riders rested, washed some clothes, took short hikes and took pictures. I fished to supplement the nice catches already made. The fish fry that evening with plenty of trout for all was a memorable feast. The Forest Ranger had left, and that evening I told the story of New Mexico's wildlife — extermination of some species, their restoration, protection, management and harvesting. Then they wanted more of my wilderness poems, and after that it was singing old songs and to bed.

We got an early start the fifth day and rode out to the trail where we got a last close-up look at rugged, granite-faced Pecos Baldy. Then we rode down through a dense forest for three miles to Jack's Creek Meadows, where we turned northeast to Noisy Brook Parks and on to Terrace Parks for a rest stop. Proceeding on down through Beatty's Parks we saw some deer and a covey of blue grouse, then had lunch on the Pecos River at its junction with Rito del Padre. This was the site of Beatty's cabin built by an old prospector in 1870.

From there we rode through very fine aspen woods on bench lands to Jarosa Creek. Enroute we passed the world record aspen, 11 feet, 6 inches in circumference breast high, and one 9 feet, 9 inches. A nasty little tornado has since thrown the big aspen. Near Beatty's Cabin there was the world record cork bark fir, 10 feet in circumference and 117 feet tall. A larger one has since been found.

Camp was in an opening in the spruce timber, a pleasant site with a large meadow above and steep, grassy hillside beyond. Horses and mules would fare well and be far enough away so that bells wouldn't keep Riders awake. Dave had hamburger steaks for dinner and Wes made two 16-inch Dutch ovens of sourdough biscuits, a novelty and a real treat.

That evening I told how Rito del Padre (Priest's Creek) got its name, and the story of George Beatty who built the cabin nearly a hundred years ago. I read my poem entitled *Beatty's Cabin*, and outdoor poems.

There had been quite a few cattle around and a shovel had to be used to prevent feet getting cut on a "broad ax." Why cattle in the Wilderness Area? Riders wanted to know. I explained that the many settlers around the perimeter of the forest had long used the range in summer to supplement their meagre farm revenue, and the privilege could not be denied without inflicting hardships.

That evening I noticed a young lady fumbling about the pile of saddles. I went over with flashlight and asked if she had lost something. She said, no, but continued examing her saddle. I said if anything was wrong we'd fix it. "Nothing's wrong, I guess," she said. "I was just wondering why the soft wool side goes next to the horse!"

Next morning we rode over a ridge where we got an unsurpassed view of the Truchas Peaks towering over vast green alpine forests below. The trail led into Rito del Padre, then up it and around the base of big 12,841-foot Cerro Chimayosis where we got a magnificent close-up photogenic view of the peaks. Contouring through rugged terrain we suddenly came to Truchas Lake at 12,000 feet lying placidly between the bases of Middle and North Truchas Peaks.

There we had lunch and fishermen tried their luck but it was not good. Two of the gals had brought bathing suits and took a dip in the lake but scrambled out in a hurry for 50-degree water is too cold for swimming.

It was such an attractive spot that we stayed for three hours, and some of the Riders hiked up half sides of the rugged peaks. They got some interesting geological specimens, and I told them of some fossil beds at the base of Cerro Chimayosis, though we wouldn't be going by there.

On the way back to camp we saw a bunch of elk, and one huge bull provided a thrill when he ran parallel back past the cavalcade at no more than a hundred yards away. At camp, Riders could hardly wait for the steak and sourdough biscuits Wes had promised for dinner. A packer coming every third day from the ranch makes fresh meat possible.

Now we had a Forest Officer with us who had a guitar and a good voice, so he not only led the evening singsong but regaled us with some salty cowboy ballads. For me it was more ancedotes, poems and the dramatic adventure story of a horse-loving rancher's perilous, midwinter rescue of a bunch of snow bound horses from Beatty's Parks.

It was camp moving day again. After the usual hustle and bustle of taking tents down and getting bedrolls and duffel ready, we got off to a good start for the day's long ride. The pack string's would be a short one. We took the Santa Barbara trail to a saddle in the Santa Barbara Divide where we rested and hunted arrow heads. Before white men came, Indians staged game drives through this and other gaps from one watershed to another and archers were stationed in the gaps to bag deer, elk and mountain sheep as they came by. One nice arrowhead was found and lots of chips and pieces.

The wind had come up and I knew it would be stronger and cold on top of Santa Barbara Baldy at 12,626 feet, over which we would go. So I had everyone put on raincoats to break the wind and help keep warm. On top we found that was a wise move.

The view was one of our best. To the north lay the beautiful Santa Barbara watershed with the Taos Mountains beyond, and still farther on some in Colorado. To the east lay the charming tributaries of the Canadian River and the horizon a hundred or more miles away. To the south we had a magnificent view of the upper Pecos basin. Regrettably, the cold wind drove us off of the mountain too soon.

A very steep, rocky trail took us down into Rincon Bonito (Pretty Cove) and around a point to Middle Fork Lake. We lunched there in a pleasant sheltered spot with no wind at all. But it was too windy on the beautiful, ten-acre lake for fishing. Below a rim above the lake were some snow banks from last winter's drifting snow. Three Riders climbed the precipitous, half-mile slope and found blue columbines blooming at the snow's edge.

As we were coming off of Santa Barbara Baldy I waited for some who had fallen behind. There were no boulders or cliffs, but the trail and mountain-side were covered with small rocks. A gray-haired lady rode up to me and said, "I don't like this at all." I assured her we would soon be off the mountain and have lunch in a sheltered place, but she was not pacified. "I don't like it," she said. "I came here to see the Rocky Mountains, but not rock by rock."

The hour-and-a-half ride back through Rincon Bonito to camp was an attractive one with gentians and other wildflowers all over. We saw two covies of blue grouse, some deer and an elk. We found camp at the headwater spring of Rio Valdez in a protected glade in heavy timber with a long meadow for the horses a hundred yards west. At 11,500 feet it was our highest but, in many respects, the best — wood, water, smooth tent sites, abundant forage and well protected. But here the Medical Officer had his first injured patient. A Rider had got her knee bumped against a tree, but it was not serious.

At the square circle there are always lively discussions on current events and controversial subjects. Also, they tell many jokes and stories trying to outdo each other. Oftentimes I found it difficult to keep up. On this occasion they were telling personal experiences that had put them in very embarrassing positions. When my turn came, at the risk of offending someone's sense of propriety I told this incident: — You have observed that of a morning, starting out full of green grass the horses, particularly going up hill, may raise their tails and break wind with some more or less musical tootie, toot, toots. A beautiful young lady was riding close behind me when my horse did that. Turning in the saddle I said, "I'm sorry, but that just can't be helped."

"Think nothing of it," she said, "until you apologized I just thought it was your horse."

With that they gave up and asked me to tell the story of a nearby outlaw cabin, and how Lost Bear Lake got its name. They are both too long to relate here. But outlaws did build and use the cabin and I helped apprehend them. Sixty years ago I had followed a grizzly bear past the unnamed lake and lay out on his track that night.

The layover day's ride was eastward across broad open country for views from the escarpment of the east fork of the Sangre de Cristo Range. We visited several view spots, but the best was Penasco Grande. In three miles, the mountain drops off from 12,000 to 7,500 feet where settlements and farms begin with the vista extending out over foothills and ranch country as far as the eye can reach. Here we see wilderness merge into civilization.

We were back a bit after noon for lunch — hot soup,

307

sandwiches, coffee and tea. Later some of us rode down stream to fish, while others hunted Indian arrow points and fossils on a nearby ridge. A great many have been found there but hunted annually they are now scarce. Dinner was pork chops, vegetables, muffins and peach cobbler which Wes made in a Dutch oven.

I turned the evening programs over to the Ranger with the guitar, and before the singing began he gave an informative talk on various phases of the Forest Service's work. The question and answer session following his talk was lively and provoked some good discussions.

Tomorrow we'd move from our highest to our lowest camp at Mora Flats, 2,300 feet lower. There we would not be quite as short of breath as up here.

I was dismayed to find a dense fog enshrouding the area when I got up before six to start the fire. When I yelled, "CRAWL OUT OF THAT SACK," a lady in one of the tents yelled, "Go back to bed, Elliott, it's still dark." So I had to shake tents and explain the darkness. We'd been fortunate so far, but this looked like a bad day ahead. Riders and crew were about as gloomy as the weather through breakfast and while breaking camp. Moving camp in the rain is tough.

Right after I called boots and saddles, the fog thinned, the sun came out and the Riders cheered. I think the outfitters cheered too.

Our first stop was at spectacular Pecos Falls where the river plunges down over a hundred-foot cliff. Riders climbed down and back up beside the falls seeking vantage points for pictures, and were reluctant to leave the charming scene.

The next stop was on the highest point of Hamilton Mesa in the center of the upper Pecos watershed bounded by the horseshoe divide, dotted with timberline peaks, that forms the two branches of the Sangre de Cristo Range. From there the view was exquisite in all directions — a superlative spot for pictures.

We dropped off of the Mesa to Rio Valdez, which had grown from the spring at camp into a nice trout stream. While we lunched there the outfitter with his 25-mule pack string came by, crew members each leading several mules. The Riders took advantage of this opportunity for pack string pictures.

About half the party followed the pack outfit down stream to camp, while I piloted the others over Bordo Medio to the Mora River and down it past beaver dams and a tornado-hit area to camp at Mora Flats. It is a pleasant and suitable spot. I'd packed in to here with adults in 1896 when I was a ten-year old kid. Some fished a bit before dinner.

For dinner Dave again served steaks broiled over the camp fire, and Wes made two Dutch ovens of sourdough biscuits. The bonfire session was devoted to discussion of the trip, the wilderness country, and Rider reactions, which were varied, but no dissatisfaction nor disappointment was expressed. One thing upon which all agreed was that as a place to relax and a means of escaping modern life's tensions it would be impossible to find anything to equal a Wilderness Trail Ride such as this one had been.

Our last layover day's ride was to Spring Mountain for an unrivaled sighting of the east side of the Range, of famous Hermit's Peak and of the upper Pecos from a new angle. We rode down the Mora Flats for a mile before taking to the timbered mountain. I noted how very much better the group was riding than during the first few

309

days. They were relaxed in saddles, kept their horses stepping along and maintained close ranks — no stragglers now. It was a beautiful and colorful cavalcade following me.

Leaving the Flats we climbed up a very steep trail through a composite forest of aspen, spruce and fir. Fortunately Wes was along, for we had to clear logs out of the trail in several places to get through. As the terrain flattened out we rode through the finest aspens imaginable. Trees 12 to 20 inches in diameter were over a hundred feet tall and devoid of limbs, like palm trees, except at the very top. Beyond that there were dense stands of smaller aspens, then we broke out into the Rito de las Trampas parks where stirrups dragged the bunch-grass heads.

Next we passed through a dark alpine forest and emerged into a hundred-year old burn, logs now mostly rotted down and reproduction coming in — natural reforestation. Two miles farther on we stopped briefly at a little spring from which the Mountain gets its name. Wes filled the big coffeepot for we would lunch a short distance beyond, just back from the crest of Spring Mountain.

We tethered the horses at the lunch site and walked out to the view point. Below in the midst of several spectacular canyons running eastward from the Range I pointed out Sapello Canyon where I was raised, and Lone Tree Mesa where we grazed our cattle. To the north of Sapello Canyon lay broad Rociada Valley with its fascinating mosaic pattern of farm crops and pastures.

To the southeast, Hermit's Peak bulged up, a huge, double humped, 10,100 foot mountain turned crossways of the ridge that divides the Rio Grande and Mississippi watersheds. An historic landmark, northwest of Las Vegas, the peak's sheer cliffs on three sides drop off almost perpendicular from one to two thousand feet. This scene, my Riders agreed, was one of the most fascinating vistas of the ride, and they were intrigued by my assurance that a hermit really had lived there. I promised to tell them the hermit's story that evening.

Now I related how, in 1907 and 1908, this had been my favorite bear hunting camp where I had taken both grizzlies and black bears. While wrangling my horses I had lost a silver dollar here and while hunting Indian arrow heads with trail riders just fifty years later I found it. Grouse formerly were very abundant and we hunted them here.

We hunted arrow points for a half hour and found some pieces, then headed back to Mora Flats by way of the old Sapello trail which my father had blazed out in 1892. The Riders were unusually quiet on the trail and at the rest stop. Perhaps, I thought, it was due to a touch of nostalgic brooding because only the half day trip to the Ranch was all that was left.

This evening Margie made a delicious peach cobbler for dessert at dinner, and Dave, as usual, did his thing. At the square circle fire I told the hour-long story of the Hermit of El Cerro del Tecolote, as Hermit's Peak originally was known. Juan Maria Agostini Ana, son of an Italian Nobleman, lived in a crude cave there from 1862 to 1868, and died with an Indian arrow in his back in the Organ Mountains near Las Cruces, New Mexico.

After my story there was a brief period of singing which, appropriately, ended with Auld Lang Syne, and the Lord's Prayer.

Breaking camp for the last time was unhurried for

we had only a seven-mile ride to the Ranch to make by noon. After a sumptuous breakfast of orange juice, bacon, eggs, griddle cakes with maple syrup, coffee and chocolate, there was a half hour of picture taking. Everybody wanted a picture of everybody else, and especially of Wes and Margie and the service crew who had taken such wonderful care of us. The Medical Officer had to pose with them too.

For the last time I called 'boots and saddles'. The seven-mile trip was through nice country but nothing spectacular. The rest stop was in a shady glade in white and Douglas fir, spruce and pine timber characteristic of of the lower elevation. It had been a wonderful, tension-relaxing vacation in a fabulous Wilderness Area remote from the works of man.

At the Wilderness boundary, where the trail ends and the road begins, a young lady who was leading the cavalcade suddenly pointed ahead and exclaimed, "What's that?" A car was approaching.

Another wonderful Trail Ride in a majestic wilderness was over—an experience which none of the participants would ever regret or forget. It was a consoling thought that should they, or their descendents return, the wilderness would be there waiting to enfold them and soothe raw nerves and relax life's tensions.

Sportsmen would soon come to harvest the annual crop of elk and deer. Then, with the approach of winter, game herds would drift down to lower ranges. Snows would spread blanket after white blanket over the landscape and tuck the wilderness in to sleep in solitude. Grouse live in spruce trees feeding on the needles. Chickaree squirrels garner food from hoarded caches of cones, and sleep in their warm tree nests. Beavers take to the security of their lodges, while bears and marmots hibernate in their dens.

With the coming of spring, snow melts but deep drifts beneath windswept ridges linger on to feed brooks and streams. Gray aspens again are verdant with quaking leaves. Meadows and parks become lush with fresh grass and forbs and, with the coming of summer, become spangled with gorgeous wildflowers. Birds return to nest and sing, and elk and deer to raise their young.

The majestic wilderness will still be there, unspoiled, with its latchstring out for all those who come with respect and reverence to partake of the soul-satisfying solace and thrills that it freely offers.